Richard Heber Wrightson

The Sancta Respublica Roma

A Handbook to the History of Rome and Italy from the Division of the...

Richard Heber Wrightson

The Sancta Respublica Roma
A Handbook to the History of Rome and Italy from the Division of the...

ISBN/EAN: 9783337042837

Printed in Europe, USA, Canada, Australia, Japan

Cover: Foto ©ninafisch / pixelio.de

More available books at **www.hansebooks.com**

THE SANCTA RESPUBLICA ROMANA

A HANDBOOK

TO THE

HISTORY OF ROME AND ITALY

From the Division of the Roman World to the Breaking-up of Charlemagne's Empire

A.D. 395-888

BY

RICHARD HEBER WRIGHTSON, M.A.

SECOND EDITION

London
HENRY FROWDE
OXFORD UNIVERSITY PRESS WAREHOUSE
AMEN CORNER E.C.

1891

PREFACE.

THE materials for the composition of this little book were collected and arranged from contemporary authorities, and such ancient records as have come down to us, some years ago; when, during a residence in Italy, I had felt the want of such information as it is intended to furnish.

Since those days increased attention has been directed to mediaeval history; and especially to that of Rome and Italy. The subject has been taken up by writers whose researches have thrown new light on the subject, and made it most attractive. Yet the study of complicated and necessarily voluminous details can only be carried out by those who have leisure hours at their disposal.

Under these circumstances, I hope to be acquitted of presumption if I endeavour to supply a want which still exists—That of a continuous account of the changes and calamities which befell the ancient centre of Roman power during five eventful centuries—From the division of the Roman world between the sons of Theodosius to the breaking-up of Charlemagne's empire of the West. I have been at pains to do this as briefly as possible. Yet not with such brevity as would render the narrative obscure and devoid of interest.

CUSWORTH, *Jan.* 16, 1890.

CONTENTS.

CHAP.		PAGE
I.	From the Division of the Empire by Theodosius the Great to the Second Visigothic Invasion of Italy. A.D. 394–408	1
II.	From the Second Visigothic Invasion of Italy to the Death of Honorius. A.D. 408–423	25
III.	From the Death of Honorius to the Extinction of the Theodosian Dynasty in the West. A.D. 423–455	42
IV.	From the Death of the last Theodosian Emperor to the Extinction of the Western Empire. A.D. 455–476	62
V.	Protectorate of Odoacer, 476–492. Reign of Theodoric the Great, 493-525. Regency of his daughter Amalasunta, 525-534. Suppression of the Nika tumult, and re-conquest of Africa, by Belisarius. Death of Theodoric's only male descendant, and Murder of Amalasunta. A.D. 476–534	84
VI.	The first six years of the Gothic war: From the landing of Belisarius in Italy to his return to Constantinople bringing with him King Vitiges. A.D. 535–541	115
VII.	The recommencement and continuance of the Gothic war, until its final termination by Narses. A.D. 541-567	143
VIII.	Italy under the Lombard Kings. Alboin to Agilulph. A.D. 568–605	168
IX.	Maintenance of the Lombard Kingdom. Conquest of Persia by Heraclius. The successful defence of Constantinople, relieves Italy from the fear of a Moslem invasion. Venice elects her first Doge. Prosperity of Italy under the restored Lombard King, Bertharis. A.D. 605–717	187

Theodosius, when he had put down the rebellion of Eugenius, and with it the last serious attempt to re-establish the Pagan worship, proclaimed the division of the empire. To Arcadius, the elder of his two sons, was allotted the new capital, with the Eastern provinces, from the Ionian Sea to the Tigris; Honorius, the younger of them, had Rome, with the whole of Italy, Sicily, Sardinia and Corsica, Spain with the Balearic Islands, Gaul, Britain, one half of the great Illyrian prefecture, and the African provinces with Carthage.

This decree for a partition, published by Theodosius shortly before his death, appears to have been generally expected and approved. The incapacity of Arcadius and Honorius, of whom the former had only attained his eighteenth and the latter his eleventh year, had not then been discovered. These princes showed more and more clearly, as time went on, that they inherited no share of their father's abilities, their weakness being such as to render their sovereignty little more than nominal.

A. D. 395. Experience had led to the conclusion that, with a view to facilitate the defence of so vast an empire, the establishment of a Western as well as Eastern centre of executive power had become desirable. Yet it was never intended that the two jurisdictions should be independent of each other, but rather that the Emperors should be colleagues and coadjutors, the defenders of one commonwealth. Consanguinity, community of interests, and the pressure of dangers from without, might well appear to render dissensions between the brothers improbable.

At the time of the decree, belief in the unity and immortality of the *Sancta Respublica Romana* was universal. The relative position of Arcadius and Honorius is explained by Paul Warnefrid, when he says 'Commune Imperium, diversis tantum sedibus, tenere cæperunt[1]'—an account of the constitution of the dual empire confirmed by acts and usages which, for eighty years, were religiously kept up. Enactments were invariably made in the names of both Emperors; and, so often as a vacancy of either throne occurred, the title of the Caesar elect remained incomplete until his elevation had been approved and confirmed by the occupant of the other. It was only after such approval that his effigy was admitted into Rome or Constantinople, as the case might be, to receive the veneration of the multitude, and to be placed beside that of his brother Augustus.

Rome, once more the capital of a vast empire, became re-invested with a primacy that had never been entirely lost. Augustus Caesar conferred the right of citizenship on all the free men of the peninsula. Between them and the provincials there existed, for about two centuries, a palpable distinction; and although Caracalla extended citizenship to the free inhabitants of the provinces, those of Italy were still regarded as more essentially Roman.

Augustus, when possessed of absolute power, abstained from interference with the forms and

[1] Historia Miscella, L. xiii.

prescriptions under which liberty had been enjoyed. The frame-work of the Republic was respected; the Senate retained its venerable aspect; and the consular office, though divested of all power, and involving the cost of a ruinous pageant, did not cease to be coveted, for it immortalized the possessor by giving his name to the year. Augustus himself, as civil head of the state, had no higher title than 'Princeps Senatus,' for that of 'Imperator' was still, as in its origin, purely military, awarded to a successful leader by the shouts of his victorious legions.

This retention of time-honoured forms was of more importance than it may have appeared to be. During the Middle Ages, in times of disaster and confusion, when all other authority had failed, that of the Senate was, as it were, resuscitated, and exercised a beneficial influence in preventing the miseries of anarchy.

Theodosius left the Roman world in peace, and provided with a disciplined army sufficient, if rightly directed, for its defence; but his choice of the men to whom he confided the guidance of his sons was unfortunate. Rufinus, to whom the guardianship of Arcadius was entrusted, by birth a Gascon, owed his advancement to his eloquence as an advocate, and his plausible duplicity had so far imposed on the confiding nature of Theodosius as to obtain for him the prefecture of the East. Stilicho, the guardian of Honorius, was by descent a Vandal, and is styled by St. Jerome a semi-barbarian. Yet his father had served in the army of Valens, and he had himself accompanied Theodosius in **most of his wars.** His military abilities, combined with a **prepossessing** exterior, induced Theodosius to confer upon him the **chief** command of the imperial forces, and the hand of his niece, Serena.

Of these two occupants of irresponsible power the most trustworthy account is that of the impartial heathen Zosimus, from whom we learn that Stilicho, no less than Rufinus, amassed enormous wealth by the acceptance of bribes, the perversion of justice, **and the ruin of innocent** families.

When **the** division of the empire rendered a division of its forces requisite, Stilicho, who had the whole of them under his command, **selected for** Honorius, or rather for himself, the strongest **and** best disciplined legions, leaving the weaker and **less** efficient for Arcadius. On the plea that **Theodosius** had entrusted him with the care of both his sons, he resolved to visit Constantinople in order that he might acquire over Arcadius an ascendancy equal to that which he already possessed over Honorius. Rufinus, **aware of his danger,** would fain have strengthened his position **by a connection with the** imperial family. Accounting the acquiescence of his submissive ward as certain, he began to speak of the marriage of Arcadius to one of **his own** daughters as a settled affair; a presumption which caused disgust and added to an unpopularity already great. During his temporary absence at Antioch, where he perpetrated the judicial murder of the guiltless and meritorious governor, a court intrigue put an end to his aspirations. In Eudoxia, the daughter of a general in the imperial service, a consort of superior charms and endowments was found for the young Emperor by the favourite eunuch, Eutropius.

Conscious of having incurred the hatred of the Senate and people of Constantinople, and undermined by the arts of the new favourite, Rufinus resolved, as his only remaining resource, to court the favour of the Visigoths who, as confederates, had recently fought under the imperial banner, but who were then in open revolt.

Theodosius the Great had found in the Visigoths useful auxiliaries. Thinking to make them permanently available for the defence of the empire, he had granted them settlements in Thrace combined with Roman citizenship. Under Alaric, a scion of the great Gothic family of Balti, they had done good service by checking the incursions of their old enemies the Huns, and Alaric, with his Romanized countrymen, had afterwards afforded to his benefactor material aid during the rebellion of Eugenius. Regarding himself entitled to entire confidence, he had asked to be entrusted with the command of the Eastern forces, and had been refused; and the annual subsidy allowed by Theodosius to his

A.D. 395. followers had been discontinued. Under a sense of wrongs, real or imaginary, he commenced a predatory invasion of the Eastern provinces. His fame as a skilful and fortunate leader, attracted numerous adherents, and when Macedonia and Thessaly were exhausted he entered Greece. In accordance with secret orders from **Rufinus** the straits of Thermopylae were left without defenders, and the people, down-trodden, and debased by their Roman masters, made no attempt at resistance.

Meanwhile, the assumption by Rufinus of the dress and manners of the Goths alarmed and disgusted the citizens. And when in that array, on the plea of negotiations for peace, he visited Alaric's head-quarters, the friendly terms on which he appeared to be with the Gothic leaders confirmed the suspicion of treason.

Alaric's invasion of Greece provided Stilicho with an ostensible plea for unasked intervention. With forces sufficient to overcome all opposition and to establish his predominance at Constantinople, he made good his march to Thessalonica. On arriving there he received a peremptory order, dictated by Rufinus and signed by Arcadius, to proceed no further, but to send forward to Constantinople the troops allotted to the Eastern empire. Disobedience to the imperial mandate would have been tantamount to a declaration of war. Stilicho at once complied, but he despatched the troops, under the command of Gainas, an officer on whose punctuality in the execution of his orders he could rely. Arcadius, with his officers of state, on the approach of his father's legions, rode forth to bid them welcome and to receive their homage. The meeting took place in a 'Campus Martius' adjacent to the Palace of Hebdomon, seven miles from the city, and while all eyes were intent on the spectacle, a signal was given, and in a moment Rufinus was cut to pieces[1]. In vain did the Emperor, in whose immediate presence the deed was perpetrated, utter a cry of terror; the head and hands of the victim were carried on a pike through the city, where the grasping prefect had no friends, and the ghastly exhibition was greeted by the multitude with exclamations of joy.

A.D. 396. The following year, a repetition of the Visigoths' invasion of Greece afforded Stilicho a fresh pretext for intervention. With superior forces he landed in the Peloponnesus, defeated Alaric in several encounters, and, having surrounded his camp with fortified posts, left famine and pestilence to do the rest. In the meantime the rapacity of his soldiers inflicted on the unfortunate Greeks miseries quite as severe as those to which they had been subjected by the Visigoths; but a deliverance from this two-fold misery was at hand. While Stilicho allowed himself to be engrossed by ignoble pleasures, Alaric, having evaded the toils, reached in safety the isthmus of Corinth, and found sustenance for his people in the fertile province of Epirus[2].

After this, the devastations inflicted by the Goths came to an end. Alaric, as the price and pledge of peace, obtained from the Eastern government the command of its forces, a proof of confidence which

---

[1] Chronicon Paschale, often quoted under the title of Chronicon Alexandrinum. Historiae Byzantinae. Niebuhr.

[2] According to Zosimus this escape could not have been effected without gross neglect on the part of Stilicho: ' Nisi deliciis et mimis ridiculorum, et parum verecundis mulierculis se dedisset.'

he had previously solicited, and the refusal of which he had regarded as a wrong.

The news of his escape, so humiliating to a leader of Stilicho's experience, was followed by an intimation that the Senate of Constantinople had declared him a public enemy, and that a decree had been signed for the confiscation of his palace with whatever he possessed in the Eastern empire. He then returned to Italy, where his presence and counsels were urgently required.

Count Gildon, the Governor of Africa, whose ultimate aim it was to make himself independent of both Emperors, had offered to transfer his allegiance from the Western jurisdiction to that of the more distant East, and when Eutropius who now ruled the Eastern counsels accepted his proposal, the Senate of Rome, dreading the loss of a region on which the city depended for bread, despatched an embassy to remonstrate, and also to deprecate imperial jealousies which could not fail to prove ruinous.

A.D. 397.

Stilicho, being aware that between Gildon and his brother Masceldelus there was an open feud, by a dexterous stroke of policy conferred on the latter the command of an African expedition. Masceldelus, exasperated at the loss of his children whom Gildon had murdered, accepted the charge, and by one decisive victory terminated the contest. Gildon, being taken prisoner, ended a career of perfidy and crime by hanging himself. Masceldelus returned triumphant, but the magnitude of his services and of his expectations, rendered his presence inconvenient, until Stilicho got rid of his importunities by causing him to be drowned. The particulars of this murder, of which Gibbon ingeniously attempts to palliate the atrocity, are related with sufficient clearness by the less partial Zosimus [1].

A.D. 398. Stilicho, after the successful result of his policy in Africa, drew closer his connection with the imperial family by giving his infant daughter Maria to her cousin the boy-Emperor, a marriage celebrated by Claudian as one that might be expected to supply the Romans with a progeny of illustrious rulers. After this marriage, the power of Stilicho over his son-in-law became, we are informed by Zosimus, absolute, while in the East Eutropius 'led Arcadius like a sheep;' and the unscrupulous hostility of these rival dictators was a matter of public scandal, inasmuch as they each of them retained a staff of false witnesses, on whose evidence they did not scruple to deprive each other's dependents of their property, enriching themselves with the spoil [2]. This miserable condition of affairs is declared by the same author to have been regarded by the senators and principal citizens of both capitals with bitter indignation; and yet Stilicho, during the last year of the century, was honoured with the consulate.

At Constantinople, Gainas, though rewarded for

---

[1] 'Satellites ab eo dato signo hominem in flumen detrudunt. Ibi Stilicho ridere, Masceldelus fluminis abreptus impetu suffocari' (Zosimus, L. v. c. 2).

[2] Zosimus, L. v. c. 12.

the destruction of Rufinus with the chief command of the forces, became envious of the prime minister's ill-gotten wealth. The intrigues of Gainas were not altogether successful until he obtained the support of the Empress; but the influence of the beautiful Eudoxia, now the mother of a family, prevailed, and she obtained from her imbecile husband, first the banishment and afterwards the decapitation of Eu-tropius. Gainas had then an interval of power A.D. 399. which he grossly misused. Having failed in an attempt to make himself absolute, he incurred universal hatred, and was driven by the indignant citizens from the capital. For a time, having troops of mercenaries at his command, he preyed upon the adjacent country; but the following year he was defeated and slain, a result which relieved the Eastern jurisdiction from a semi-barbarian and anti-Roman dictator.

After an interval, the Visigoths became weary of inaction. Full of confidence in their own energies and in the fortune of their leader they declared him their king, under whose guidance they might attain a less dependent existence and acquire some territory which they might call their own. Alaric, by a recent and advantageous compact, was debarred from a renewal of hostilities with the Eastern government, but the West lay open to his ambition; and Italy, with her fabled wealth, presented to him and to his people a tempting field.

It appears, on the reliable authority of St. Prosper A.D. 400. and Jornandes, that during the consulate of Stilicho

(A. D. 400) Alaric, together with the barbarian king Radagaisus, made an irruption into Venétia and wasted the territory of Aquileja; but this would seem to have been no more than a tentative incursion and without permanent result. It was not until the second year of the fifth century that the centre of the Western empire became subjected to its first serious attack. In the course of that year, Alaric, with his Visigoths and a multitude of adherents, effected an unopposed descent into Lombardy, and sacked several of the cities. During the panic caused by this irruption the wealthy fled with their moveables, some to Corsica, others to Sardinia. Stilicho, though he had left unguarded the passes to the Alps, displayed, at the eleventh hour, an energy that contrasted strangely with his previous neglect of precautions; but it was only by a hasty withdrawal of garrisons needful for the security of Gaul, and by forced marches in mid-winter, that he was able to assemble an army. Honorius, with his affrighted court, betook himself to Ravenna, and his ministers commenced negotiations.

At the time when the battle of Pollentia [1] took place, it appears from the clear and trustworthy narrative of Jornandes that a treaty had been actually concluded; that Alaric, having accepted for his people certain territories in France and Spain, had agreed to leave Italy; and that, in accordance with this engagement, he had already commenced his retrograde march when subjected to an unprovoked attack.

---
[1] A city of Liguria, which no longer exists.

This account derives confirmation from the statements of Orosius, who wrote at the beginning of the fifth century. Orosius, declares that Alaric only wanted a settlement for his people, and that he desired to live in peace and harmony with the Romans; but that Stilicho wished to enchance the value of his services and to create a belief that his dictatorship was a necessity[1].

Of the conflict which took place the accounts are contradictory. St. Prosper, a contemporary, describes it as sanguinary and protracted: 'Pollentiâ, adversus Gothos, vehementer utriusque partis clade, pugnatum est.' The idea of a drawn battle may seem inconsistent with the fact that the family of Alaric was taken; yet such a capture may have taken place during the first surprise, and before the Visigothic leaders had time to deploy their forces. Jornandes and Cassiodorus claim for the Visigoths the ultimate victory; whilst Claudian describes their defeat as a rout; and Prudentius attributes the victory to the Romans, but in verses, it must be borne in mind, which, as a courtier, he addressed to the Emperor.

29 March, Easter-day, A.D. 402.

The results which followed were certainly unlike those which attend on decisive success. Alaric, whatever may have been his losses, had still a formidable army, and does not appear to have relinquished his expectation of reaching Rome. 'The capital,' to use the words of Gibbon, had still to be 'saved by the active and incessant vigilance of Stilicho; but he respected the despair of his enemy; and, instead of

---

[1] Orosius, L. vii. c. 37.

committing the fate of the republic to the chance of another battle, he proposed to *purchase* the absence of the barbarians.'

Stilicho had the children of Alaric in his power, an advantage which fully compensated for any incompleteness of his victory. By offering to restore these precious hostages, he induced his opponent to relinquish for himself and his followers a raid on Tuscany, and to re-cross the Po. But no sooner had the Visigoths reached the left bank than discontent broke out. The chieftains, disappointed of their expected booty, became amenable to corruption, and withdrew. Alaric, weakened by desertion and by pestilence, sustained soon afterwards, at Verona, such a defeat as compelled him to relinquish for a time the prosecution of his enterprise. Meanwhile the Romans used the interval in strengthening their walls, of which a portion that still exists is attributed by antiquaries to this period.

A.D. 404. The following year Honorius, on the invitation of the Senate and accompanied by Stilicho, celebrated at Rome the deliverance of Italy; and it was on this occasion that the combats of gladiators were witnessed for the last time. The exhibition of death-struggles on the stage had been forbidden by Constantine; but custom, and the popular craving for excitement, prevailed over edicts, and Christian writers remonstrated in vain, until an act of self-sacrifice produced a revulsion of feeling. Telemachus, an Asiatic monk, descending into the arena, rushed between the combatants, and the spectators,

enraged at his interference, stoned him to death.
But the martyr won his converts, and a decree of
Honorius for the abolition of these barbarous shows
was submitted to without open expressions of discontent. About this time Claudian ceased to sing
the praises of his patron, his patron's consort,
Serena, having found for him an African heiress, the
management of whose estates after his marriage
appears to have engrossed his attention.

Ere Honorius had completed a year's residence at   A.D. 405.
Rome a new alarm drove him back to Ravenna.
The barbarian king Radagaisus, to whose standard
promises of pay and expectations of plunder had
attracted hosts of adventurers, was crossing the
Alps. The Roman magnates, of whom a majority
secretly adhered to Paganism, when they found
themselves deserted, protested against the laws which
prohibited sacrifices, and demanded permission to
propitiate the deities under whose protection Rome
had attained her greatness. Meanwhile the torrent
swept over Lombardy. Stilicho, for the second time
consul, unable to stem its violence, remained on the
watch at Pavia. While the neighbouring cities
succumbed, Florence acquired her first renown.
The citizens defended their gates and endured
severe privations until the besiegers were compelled
by want of food to divide their forces [1]. When two-
thirds of the barbarians had taken their departure,
Stilicho was able to inflict on the remainder a
sanguinary defeat; and the survivors, when they

[1] Paulinus, quoted by Muratori.

reached their fortified but provisionless camp, had no alternative but an unconditional surrender, and were sold for slaves, while Radagaisus, who had sworn to appease the gods of his country with a holocaust of Roman senators, was overtaken in his flight and beheaded.

From this ill-starred enterprise Alaric stood aloof; for Stilicho, when he found the court of Constantinople unwilling to submit to dictation [1], had engaged him to assist in conquering from Arcadius Eastern Illyricum; an expression used to designate the all-important territories of Dacia, Macedonia, Epirus, Thessaly, Achaia and Crete. Alaric only awaited orders to join his forces with those of the Western empire, and the threat of dismemberment kept the Eastern government in a constant state of alarm.

The allies of Radagaisus, warned by his fate, withdrew from Italy, but only to assist in the ruin of Gaul. Had the youth of the seventeen provinces been trained to defensive warfare, the ruin of many noble cities, enriched and embellished during centuries of peace and security, might have been averted. But by the guardian of the child-like Honorius, though he had now for twelve years wielded at will the resources of the West, no defensive means had been provided. The colonists, if they escaped a captivity worse than death, were compelled to abandon their paternal hearths and to exchange a life of ease for beggary and exile.

A.D. 408. Rome, notwithstanding the loss of Gaul, was

---

[1] Zosimus, L. v. c. 26.

called upon to celebrate for a second time her deliverance from the Goths, a 'nomen generale' applied indiscriminately to distinct races of barbarians. A statue composed of silver and brass was raised in honour of Stilicho, who, according to Zosimus, was 'propemodum coronatus.' Yet on the triumphal arch were seen effigies of the three existing Emperors, Arcadius, Honorius, and Theodosius II (the infant son of Arcadius, already declared his associate),—a proof that the Romans, notwithstanding the unnatural estrangement of the two empires, had not ceased to regard themselves, at least in theory, as members of one commonwealth [1].

After the collapse of Roman authority in Gaul, the legions stationed in Britain, finding themselves cut off from all communication with Ravenna, became weary of a government that had ceased to exhibit in their behalf any sign of vitality, and their resolution to proclaim an emperor of their own choice, however bold, was not altogether without precedent, since Constantine the Great owed his elevation to the legions assembled at York. After an interval of violence and confusion, the choice fell on a private soldier named Constantine, who, but for that name, might have lived and died in obscurity; yet a successful career of about three years seems to show that the usurper Constantine was not altogether deficient in

A.D. 407.

[1] The Byzantine historians designate the citizens of both jurisdictions as 'Ρωμαῖοι. Where distinction is required the inhabitants of Italy and the Western provinces are entitled οἱ ἑσπέριοι 'Ρωμαῖοι, and those of the Eastern jurisdiction as οἱ 'Ρωμαῖοι τῆς ἕω (Priscus, Hist. Byzant. Niebuhr).

the tact and ability requisite for a commander. When Constantine, soon after his election, crossed the Channel, the scattered and isolated legions that remained in Gaul, glad to rally around any Roman standard, acknowledged him. He was then able, though with comparatively small forces, to make head against the barbarians, and to restore order; a proof that, but for the neglect of the central government, the noblest provinces of the Western empire might have been saved from ruin.

Stilicho, still occupied with the intended hostilities against Arcadius, deputed Sarus the Goth, a partisan leader in the imperial pay, to act against Constantine. Sarus entered Dauphiny, and commenced the siege of Vienne, but, on finding himself overmatched by the forces brought against him, was fain to negotiate for an unmolested retreat.

Constantine, whose rule had by this time extended itself from the Channel to the Gulf of Lyons, established his court at Arles; conferred on his son Constans, who had previously been a monk, the title of Augustus; and sent him to Spain, where he was able to effect the capture of the Emperor's Spanish kinsmen, of whose murder he, in conjunction with his father, afterwards incurred the infamy.

A.D. 408. On the death of Maria, the virgin consort of Honorius, she was promptly replaced by her sister Thermanzia, a child of tender years. This strange and suspicious family arrangement led to a belief that her mother Serena was acting an odious part in sacrificing a second daughter, to secure for her son

Eucherius the imperial succession [1]; a belief which, whether well or ill founded, aggravated the unpopularity of her husband.

Stilicho, though twice invested with the consulate, had failed to exhibit any sympathy with public feeling, and his selfish policy had reduced the Roman world to the perilous condition of a house divided against itself.

The compact whereby Alaric stood engaged to assist him in the conquest of Eastern Illyricum, had now remained for more than two years in abeyance; its execution having been deferred, first on account of the invasion of Radagaisus, and secondly, by the rebellion of Constantine. Impatient of repeated delays and contradictory orders, Alaric, during the summer of A. D. 408, took up a menacing position on the Venetian confines, and demanded the arrears of the stipulated subsidies together with an idemnity for the cost of his march.

On the arrival of the Visigothic envoys, Stilicho hastened to Rome and convoked the Senate. When the majority hesitated to comply with these demands, he spoke of the dangers that would result from their refusal, and produced letters to show that Alaric had acted in obedience to orders signed by the Emperor Honorius. Whether influenced by these documents or by the fear of giving offence, the senators ultimately consented to the payment of four thousand pounds weight of gold: but not without a protest; for Lampadius, one of the most distinguished of their

[1] Zosimus, L. v. c. 29.

body, ventured to exclaim, 'This is no peace, but an acknowledgment of our slavery,' and, hastening from the palace of the Caesars, took refuge in a neighbouring church.

This utterance of a man whose name and character were widely known, for Lampadius had served as consul, found an echo in every bosom that retained a vestige of Roman feeling; yet it was evidently made in fear[1]; and that such fear should have existed shows but too plainly that, under the dictatorship of Stilicho, time-honoured customs and immunities had ceased to afford security.

But the immediate cause of the dictator's ruin was the defection of the army. A camp had been formed at Pavia where the forces intended to act against Constantine were assembled, and where they awaited a formal inspection by the Emperor. Of these the greater part consisted of legionaries, who still prided themselves in the Roman name, and of whom Stilicho had incurred the hatred. But he had also given offence to a portion of the barbarian troops by his marked preference for the Huns.

At Ravenna he retained in an advocate named Justinian, an astute observer of the signs of the time, and a confidential informant. This man, who in the hour of danger took part with his patron's enemies,

---

[1] Rutilius complains that by the introduction of his fur-clad satellites, meaning the Huns, Stilicho destroyed the freedom of Rome.
'Ipsa Satellitibus pellitis Roma patebat,
Et captiva prius quam caperetur erat.'
Itinerar., L. 1.

warned him of the approaching crisis and urged upon him the necessity of preventing the Emperor's intended visit to the camp. In accordance with this advice Stilicho employed every art to detain Honorius at Rome, and when he failed to do so, accompanied him as far as Bologna. When mutinous proceedings were detected amongst a portion of the troops, he made a disloyal attempt to regain the good opinion of the soldiers by telling them that the Emperor had ordered them to be decimated, and that he, by tears and entreaties, had obtained their pardon.

A.D. 408.

When the decease of the Emperor Arcadius became known, Honorius expressed his desire to visit Constantinople, and to watch over the interests of his infant nephew, Theodosius II, of whom he had become the legitimate guardian. Stilicho objected that the doubtful attitude of Alaric and the rebellion of Constantine, required that the head of the state should remain in Italy, and offered to go himself,—a proposal to which he did not adhere, but one which subjected him to increased suspicion and obloquy.

Honorius had now attained his twenty-fourth year, and his mind, however feeble, may well have become occupied with longings for a less dependent existence. The courtiers would naturally commend and encourage such aspirations, and the occasion was one on which the least scrupulous and the most artful counsellors had the advantage. Olympius, who owed his advancement to Stilicho, proved himself a successful intriguer, and succeeded in obtaining for himself a confidence that knew no limits. When Honorius left Bologna, Olympius accompanied him, and had thus an opportunity of re-iterating accusations against his former patron.

The troops assembled at Pavia, whose discontent had thus far been concealed, greeted the Emperor and his new minister with acclamations; and after three days had been spent in underhand plotting, a sanguinary outbreak at Pavia and also at Ravenna was the result. The functionaries, whether civil or military, who remained faithful to Stilicho became the victims of blind and reckless fury; and amongst the slain were the pretorian prefects of Gaul and Italy. Honorius, in an attempt to restrain the madness of the soldiery, imperilled his own life: yet he afterwards consented to overlook, and eventually to justify, crimes of which he had been the reluctant and appalled spectator.

Stilicho, when apprised of these horrors, seems to have lost all power of decision. He lingered on at Bologna, until Sarus, who had lately returned from Gaul, and who retained the command of the barbarian forces, surprised and put to the sword the Huns who formed his body-guard; and from this attack, made in the dead of night, Stilicho himself escaped with difficulty to Ravenna.

Perceiving that his cause had become desperate, he forbade his adherents to embark in a hopeless struggle, and when informed that his arrest had been ordered, he betook himself to the sanctuary of a church. The following day the officials charged with his destruction swore in the presence of the bishop that they only came to secure his person: but after he was led away the death-warrant was produced, and Count Heraclian acted the part of the executioner.

The man who had twice been greeted with ovations as the deliverer of Italy, and in whose honour a statue had been erected, was now declared a public enemy; his vast estates were confiscated; and his son was sent with an escort to Rome, but only to be deprived of his life. His daughter, the infant Empress, was returned to her mother Serena; and, so rancorous was the popular animosity against the Huns, that in several of the towns their wives and children were massacred.

The hatred of Stilicho and the sanguinary revolution that hastened his downfall derived their strength from an almost universal conviction that, while seeking to prolong his power and to secure the aggrandizement of his family, he had sacrificed Roman interests. The crimes by which that revolution was disgraced were mainly attributable to the worthless minister into whose hands Honorius had fallen, and whose incapacity was only surpassed by his cruelty.

The existing records of these occurrences are scanty and often contradictory, and of the delinquencies with which the memory of Stilicho is charged, some appear to be incredible; but that, from the commencement to the close of his career, the use that he made of his overwhelming influence created and kept up a ruinous hostility between the Eastern and Western sections of the Roman world, there is sufficient evidence. By a tyrannical edict he had suspended all commercial intercourse between the two empires, and one of the first consequences of his fall was the removal of this odious embargo and the restoration of friendly intercourse.

CHAPTER II.

FROM THE SECOND VISIGOTHIC INVASION OF ITALY TO THE
DEATH OF HONORIUS.

A.D. 408-423.

Rejection of Alaric's offers. Terms on which a truce is obtained. Indecision of the government. Nomination, acceptance, and deposition of the puppet emperor, Priscus Attalus. Rome after an obstinate defence is sacked. Departure and death of Alaric. Succession of his brother-in-law Ataulphus. Ataulphus aspires to the hand of his prisoner, the Roman princess, Placidia. Constantius, an experienced Roman general, having obtained the command of the army, subdues Constantine. Rivalry between Constantius and Ataulphus for Placidia, who marries Ataulphus. Assassination of Ataulphus. Trials of Placidia. Honorius having obtained her liberation compels her to marry Constantius, whom he declares his colleague. Refusal of the Eastern court to acknowledge Constantius as Cæsar. Placidia after the death of Constantius becomes all powerful at Ravenna. The jealousy of Honorius compels her to seek refuge at Constantinople. Death of Honorius. Retrospect as to the progress of affairs in the East.

ALARIC, though his ranks were swelled by Stilicho's Huns, who after the fall of their patron became subject to a cruel persecution, seemed loth to commence hostilities; but, together with a large indemnity, he required the cession of some territory for the permanent settlement of his people; and, on this basis, proposed to give and receive hostages for the maintenance of peace.

A.D. 408.

The counsellors of Honorius seemed incapable of decision: they would neither purchase peace by concession, nor employ their defensive resources to the best advantage. In Sarus they had a general whose experience in desultory warfare might, had he been entrusted with the command, have rendered Alaric's progress through an exhausted country difficult; and in Ravenna they had an unassailable position where resistance might have been indefinitely prolonged, and where supplies and reinforcements could have been landed. Harmony between the East and West being restored, time only was required to bring succours from Constantinople; and Anthemius, the guardian of the infant Emperor, was actually preparing an expedition for the relief of Italy. The general feeling was for resistance; but the known incapacity of the generals nominated by Olympius destroyed all confidence.

Alaric, on finding his overtures rejected, ordered his brother-in-law Ataulphus to follow him with additional forces, and commenced the invasion. His march of destruction was unopposed. Having crossed the Po at Cremona, he made his way by Bologna to Rimini, and from thence to Rome, where he established a strict blockade.

Meanwhile, within the walls, a suspicion became rife that the widow of Stilicho had called in the barbarians to avenge the death of her husband, and on this improbable charge Serena was condemned to die; but the heathen, Zosimus, regards her fate as merited, inasmuch as she had appropriated to her own use a necklace dedicated to the goddess Rhea.

When famine left the Senate no alternative but to sue for peace, its envoys spoke to Alaric of the consequences that might be expected if a vast and armed population were driven to despair; a suggestion which only drew from him the well-known answer, 'The thicker the grass, the more easily it is mown.' He then declared that nothing less than the total amount of gold and silver possessed by the citizens would induce him to withdraw, and that every barbarian slave must be liberated; and on being asked 'What then will you leave us?' he replied, 'Your lives.'

Alaric, nevertheless, appears to have been aware that time, as well as money, has its value, and he finally consented to accept as a ransom five thousand pounds weight of gold, thirty thousand pounds weight of silver, four thousand silken tunics, three thousand pieces of fur, and three thousand pounds of pepper, together with a promise that the Senate would urge upon the Emperor the necessity of peace. On these terms a truce was obtained.

In the beginning of 409 a deputation in favour of peace reached Ravenna; but the government still clung to the hope of successful resistance, and having engaged six thousand Dalmatians, sent them to assist in the defence of Rome. The commander of this reinforcement marched without due precaution, and his Dalmatians, on finding themselves

A.D. 409.

surrounded, laid down their arms. The Senate, when informed of this misfortune, sent a second deputation headed by the good Pontiff, Innocent, but without any different result, and in the mean time the forces employed by the government, though unequal to a pitched battle, continued to harass the invaders and inflicted on the army of Ataulphus considerable losses before he was able to effect his junction with Alaric.

About this time Olympius, to whose incompetency the perilous state of affairs was attributed, fell from power, and Jovius, who had recently been appointed pretorian prefect, undertook the direction of affairs. Jovius, during the dictatorship of Stilicho, had been in frequent communication with Alaric, and had become acquainted with his disposition; an advantage which had its counterpoise, for he was obliged to guard himself against suspicions of connivance with the enemy. During his brief administration, the rigid exclusion of officers who adhered to the Pagan worship was no longer enforced, and Gennerid, a leader of known ability, was allowed to take the command in Dalmatia, where he equipped a contingent of ten thousand men to aid in the defence of Italy.

When the second Roman deputation reached Ravenna, Alaric, on the invitation of Jovius, or, according to Sozomen, on that of Pope Innocent, consented to open negotiations at Rimini: but, in addition to settlements for his people in Venetia, he now demanded for himself the command of the imperial forces. In reply, the advisers of **Honorius** expressed the Emperor's willingness to comply with demands for money, but refused either to tolerate the location of the barbarians on the soil of Italy, or to confer on Alaric any command whatever. When these instructions reached Rimini, Jovius, instead of making a private communication as to their import, had the imprudence to read them aloud; and Alaric, incensed at the expressions employed, departed in anger: yet, on reflection, he offered to accept a settlement for his people in Noricum, with a reasonable subsidy, and supplies of grain.

This last opportunity was lost. Jovius, to guard himself against suspicions, had bound himself by a promise that he would never make peace with Alaric; a declaration fatal to the hopes of peace. The cessation of the truce was declared, and the Romans, again beleaguered, made a good defence, until the capture of Ostia rendered perseverance hopeless. Alaric was then able to convince the ruling powers that they and their famishing people had already done and suffered enough for Honorius who had shown so little anxiety as to their fate; and persuaded them to elect another Emperor with whom he might treat for peace.

The suggestion seems to have been grasped as a *tabula in naufragio*; and the choice fell on the prefect of the city, Priscus Attalus, who, though indebted to Honorius for his promotion, consented without compunction to his patron's deposition. In an address to the Senate, he prophesied that, under his auspices, Rome would become once more mistress of the world : but, before she could do so, bread was a primary necessity, and an answer to his demand for recognition and for a supply of corn had not yet been obtained from Heraclian the Governor of Africa. Meanwhile with such forces as he could muster, he accompanied Alaric to Rimini, where Jovius met them with an offer from the terrified Honorius to accept him for a colleague, and the only reply that he vouchsafed to his former patron, was an offer of some island where he might spend the residue of his days in obscurity.

Jovius, after a fruitless attempt to bring about some compromise, deserted the cause of Honorius, —an example which was followed by other officials ; and cities of the Emilia, with the exception of Bologna, acknowledged Attalus. Honorius was meditating an escape to Constantinople, when the landing of four thousand men, sent to his aid by Anthemius the patriotic regent, encouraged him to wait.

Meanwhile, when it became certain that Heraclian had refused supplies from Africa, and had treated the demands of Attalus with contempt, Alaric, finding that his puppet had failed to accomplish the one thing needful and that he was only an impediment to peace, divested him of the purple.

Negotiations were then resumed with better prospect of success, but were only in their commencement when frustrated by an unforeseen collision. The bewildered adherents of Honorius retained no longer any sufficient control over the military, and Sarus, by birth a Goth, was an hereditary enemy of Alaric's family. Sarus, acting on his own inspiration, when he had surprised and cut to pieces the body-guard of Ataulphus, sent out a herald to proclaim his victory and publicly to denounce Alaric as unworthy of the Emperor's regard! An affair like this might well inspire Alaric with grave suspicions: he put a stop to the conference and prepared to wreak his vengeance on Rome.

For the third time within the space of little more than a year, the Romans found themselves hemmed in. Aware that no terms would be accepted, they persevered in a hopeless resistance and endured the extremities of famine; until, on the night of the 20th of August, by an act of treachery, the Salarian gate was left open. Alaric, before he permitted his troops to enter, gave orders that the churches should be respected; a command which his Visigoths, being for the most part Arian converts, religiously obeyed: but, with this exception, havoc and rapine had free scope.

Since Constantine the Great transformed Byzantium into a new Rome, and removed the seat of empire to the shore of the Bosphorus, nearly eighty years had elapsed: yet, until this, the day of her utter humiliation, the splendour of the ancient capital had scarcely diminished. According to the most moderate estimate, her population amounted to one million two hundred thousand; the fortunes of her wealthier citizens, even compared with those of our modern millionaires, were enormous; the palaces, in their extent, were like towns; the aqueducts, baths, and fountains, had undergone, as time went on, a constant increase in magnificence; and the city itself might fitly be compared to an amalgamation of many cities [1].

During three days the palaces and houses were ransacked; the spoils of vanquished nations and oppressed provinces changed hands; sideboards of massive plate, collections of precious stones, and, what was worse, inestimable treasures of art, fell into the hands of indiscriminating pillagers.

The needful supplies from Africa being withheld, the impossibility of sustaining his army in the midst of a dense and starving population may well account for the hasty departure of Alaric to the less exhausted region of Campania. He appears moreover to have contemplated the conquest of Sicily, and a descent from thence on Africa with a view to the punishment of Heraclian, who, by his refusal to acknowledge Attalus, had been a principal obstacle to peace; but when, with these intentions, he approached the southern shore, the resistance of Reggio caused a delay of several days, and when at length the embarkation of a portion of his army was effected, a hurricane swept the straits and wrecked the crowded galleys. After this misfortune, which took place under his eyes, Alaric sickened and died.

[1] 'Est urbs una domus: mille oppida continet una urbs.' Fragment of Olympiodorus, preserved by Photius, quoted by Muratori.)

The coffin containing his body, and the regalia wherewith it was the custom of the Goths to bury their princes, were deposited in a grave dug in the bed of a river, the waters of which, after they had been diverted, were restored to their channel, and the slaves employed in the work were put to death, lest they should reveal the secret of the locality.

The Visigothic warriors chose for their second king, Alaric's brother-in-law, Ataulphus. Of the proceedings of Ataulphus during his stay in Italy there is no record, but it may well be conjectured that he already contemplated a marriage with his imperial captive, Galla Placidia.

Placidia, the daughter of Theodosius the Great by a second marriage, when carried off from Rome had been treated by Alaric with the respect due to a Roman princess; and it seems probable that Ataulphus, by a dilatory and forbearing policy, already desired to cultivate the goodwill of her family.

When the Western empire obtained a respite from impending ruin, the most urgent want was that of an experienced commander capable of re-organising its military resources, and animated by zeal for Roman interests. In Count Constantius, an officer who had served under Theodosius the Great, and whose presence has been described as that of a man born for command, these requisites were combined.

Though between Ravenna and Constantinople A.D. 410 harmony was restored, the West was still distracted by the usurpation of Constantine; and while Honorius reigned at Ravenna, he had a dangerous rival at Arles. During the siege of Rome, Constantine sent an embassy to Ravenna with assurances that his acceptance of the purple had been made under constraint; and Honorius, being at that time ignorant of the fate of his kinsmen, and hoping to obtain their liberation, consented to accept him as a colleague. In 410, Constantine embarked in a conspiracy for the dethronement of Honorius, and having first corrupted a portion of the imperial forces, he crossed the Alps with an army; but, finding that his accomplices had been detected and punished, he hastened back to Provence.

The fortunes of this adventurer, which for three years had been prosperous, had now reached their turning-point. His son, Constans, had failed to acquire the confidence of the Spanish legionaries, whose general, Gerontius, persuaded them to elect a phantom Emperor of his own nomination; and when Constans fled, Gerontius pursued him into Gaul, and, having circumvented him at Vienne, put him to death. Gerontius then turned his arms against Constantine, and compelled him to shut himself up in Arles.

A.D. 411. When Constantius, with a re-organised army, entered Gaul, he found the provincials suffering from a renewal of barbarian inroads, and Constantine closely beleaguered by Gerontius. With the latter he had no difficulties; for his own officers, being sick of his tyranny, betook themselves to the standard of their legitimate sovereign.

For a while Constantine held out in the expectation of being relieved by forces which he had caused to be assembled on the right bank of the Rhone; but Constantius, with the decision of an **able** leader, at once crossed the river, routed those forces and, having done so, resumed the siege. Constantine then surrendered, **on the assurance** that his life would be spared; but Honorius, unable to forgive the murderer of his relatives, signed his death-warrant.

The re-organisation of the Roman forces by Constantius made it unsafe for Ataulphus to retain any longer an undecided attitude in Italy: he therefore crossed the Alps under an engagement that he would assist the Romans in the deliverance of the Gallic provinces from the barbarians; and while engaged in the fulfilment of this promise, he found an opportunity for wreaking his vengeance on his old enemy, Sarus.

Cordiality between the Roman general and the Visigothic king soon came to an end, for they both aspired to the hand of Placidia; and when Honorius, who favoured the suit of Constantius, demanded the liberation of his sister, Ataulphus interposed such delays as were tantamount to a refusal, and showed an intention of retaining for himself Narbonne and the other cities of which he obtained possession. Such was the commencement of the Visigothic dominion in Gaul. [A.D. 412.]

While these events were in progress, an attempt to dethrone Honorius was made by Count Heraclian, the executioner of Stilicho, and the actual Governor of Africa, who, though described by St. Jerome as a [A.D. 413.]

monster of vice, had been honoured with the consulate, **as a reward** for his refusal to acknowledge Attalus; but although, with a considerable army, he made good his landing, he encountered a signal overthrow, a result which implies that the imperial government was no longer deficient in energy. Heraclian then returned, a discredited fugitive, to Africa, where he was taken and put to death.

A.D. 414. In the beginning of the next year, the marriage of Ataulphus with Placidia took place at Narbonne. The ceremony is described by Olympiodorus. Fifty pages, with basins full of gold and precious stones, presented to the Roman princess a portion of the spoils which Alaric had carried off from Rome; while Attalus, the puppet Emperor, appeared on the occasion as leader of the choir that sang the epithalamium [1].

As the consent of Honorius had not been obtained, there was no immediate recognition; and Constantius, whom he would have preferred for a brother-in-law, continued to watch and to restrict, as far as he was able, the successful progress of his more fortunate rival in Southern France.

But a change had come over the spirit of Ataulphus: his prolonged sojourn in Italy had enlarged his views and elevated his ambition. Aware of the unfitness of his countrymen to be the guardians of civilisation, he ceased to desire the establishment of a Gothic ascendancy, and looked to the peaceful fusion of the two races, as a means of imparting new

[1] Olympiodorus apud Photium, p. 187.

life and vigour to the time-honoured supremacy of the 'Sancta Respublica.'

With these feelings, he left Constantius to deal with the barbarian invaders of Gaul, and undertook the expulsion of the Vandals from Spain. At Barcelona, where he established his head-quarters, Placidia gave birth to a son who received the name of his grandfather, Theodosius the Great, and might, had he lived, have been the successor of Honorius. But the bright anticipations of Ataulphus and his consort were overclouded by the untimely death of their child, who was buried, in a silver coffin, in one of the churches of Barcelona; a sorrow which Ataulphus himself did not long survive. When, stricken by the dagger of an obscure assassin, he directed that Placidia should be restored to her brother, and with his latest breath enjoined the maintenance of harmony between his countrymen and the Romans.

A.D. 415

The confusion that prevailed after this unforeseen casualty enabled Singeric, a brother of Sarus, to grasp for a few days the reins of power. Singeric gratified his revenge by a cowardly persecution of the widowed queen. Placidia, linked with a gang of prisoners, was driven before him for the distance of twelve miles; but, ere a week elapsed, the downfall of this usurper saved her from further indignities; and by Wallia, her husband's brother-in-law and elected successor, she was treated with becoming respect.

The war-loving Visigoths urged their new king to

undertake the conquest of Roman Africa, and it was not until a fleet collected for that purpose had been wrecked by a tempest, that Wallia was able to avoid hostilities with the empire, and to follow, with cautious steps, the policy indicated and enjoined by Ataulphus.

A.D. 416. About a year after the assassination of her husband, Placidia was given up to Honorius, in consideration of six hundred thousand bushels of wheat!—the ransom long previously stipulated for, in a time of scarcity. Friendly relations being thus confirmed, Wallia engaged to re-conquer for the empire the Spanish provinces occupied by the Vandals and other barbarian settlers—an undertaking which he loyally accomplished; but though Seville was amongst the recovered cities, the Vandals, it seems, were able to keep a footing on the Southern coast of the beautiful region which still bears their name[1].

A.D. 418. As a reward for these services, Wallia obtained from Honorius the second Aquitania, a grant which extended the Visigothic possessions in Gaul from Toulouse to the Atlantic, and included Bordeaux. On the death of Wallia, which took place the same year, the Visigoths chose for their fourth king, Theodoric, a son of their great founder, Alaric.

Theodoric, during a reign of two and thirty years, maintained and strengthened his position. His transactions and acquaintance with the prefects of Gaul confirmed certain Roman leanings, which

[1] Olympiodorus apud Photium.

in the end prevailed; and that at a time when the very existence of the Western empire depended on the Visigothic alliance.

The life of Placidia, while the dew of her youth was still fresh upon her, had been one of strange vicissitudes: yet changes, equally unforeseen, awaited her: and after her return to Ravenna, she was induced, if not compelled, by her brother to marry Constantius.

In 421, after she had given birth to a son, who was named Valentinian, she prevailed with Honorius to declare her husband his colleague, an act which the court of Constantinople refused to ratify, hopes being entertained that on the death of Honorius the Roman world might be re-united under Theodosius; and when the effigy of the Caesar elect was sent, according to custom, to receive the homage of the East Romans, its admission into the city was forbidden; an insult which Constantius was preparing to repay when he died. After this Placidia became virtually Regent of the West, until the jealousy of Honorius compelled her, during the few remaining months of his life, to accept for herself and for her children from her nephew, Theodosius, a temporary home at Constantinople. Honorius, like his brother, was short-lived, having only attained his thirty-eighth year, when he died of dropsy. A.D. 423.

It now becomes necessary to take a cursory retrospect of the progress of affairs in the East. Arcadius, during the fourteen years of his nominal reign, left the powers of the executive to be wielded by others; first, but only for a few months, by Rufinus, whose destruction by Stilicho has been described; and, after that, for about four years, by Eutropius. But when the dignities of patrician and consul were heaped on that unworthy subject, Gainas, who since the fall of Rufinus had commanded the Eastern legions, became indignant; and his enmity, combined with that of the Empress Eudoxia, proved fatal to a minister who had long been an object of contempt. Eudoxia, who acquired an evil celebrity by her persecution of St. Chrysostom, then reigned supreme until her death (A. D. 409).

A.D. 399.

Arcadius, during his latter years, was kept in suspense and terror by the machinations of Stilicho. On his death, which took place in his thirty-first year, he left an only son, Theodosius II, and three daughters. Had he lived a few months longer, his fears would have been at an end, by the fall and assassination of Stilicho.

A.D. 408.

Happily for the East Romans, the infant Emperor had the good fortune to obtain for his guardian the pretorian prefect Anthemius, a man of ability and worth, who, as ambassador to Persia and in the discharge of various public employments, had done good service. During an administration of five years, Anthemius succeeded in extricating the Eastern empire from besetting dangers; in restoring those bonds of Roman unity that ought never to have been broken; and in affording aid to the Western government against Alaric.

The East and West no longer at variance. 41

On the death or resignation of Anthemius (A. D. 414) Pulcheria, the eldest of the feeble-minded Emperor's three sisters, was chosen for regent; and by her virtues, combined with intelligence of no common order, made up for her brother's weakness. A.D. 414.

Even in the selection of his consort for life, Theodosius relied on his sister's judgment; and in Athenais, the daughter of a Greek sophist, Pulcheria found for him a wife in whom the gifts of beauty and of genius were united. Athenais, on her conversion to Christianity, received the name of Eudocia (A. D. 420). A.D. 420.

Soon after the arrival of Placidia with her infant children at Constantinople, the eldest of them, Valentinian, whom she regarded as rightful heir to the throne of the Western empire, was affianced to the infant daughter of Theodosius and Eudocia. An engagement, which removed any further jealousy between the two branches of the Theodosian family, gave rise to a feeling of a common interest.

CHAPTER III.

FROM THE DEATH OF HONORIUS TO THE EXTINCTION OF THE THEODOSIAN DYNASTY IN THE WEST.

A.D. 423-455.

Revolt of the Italians against the Theodosian dynasty. They proclaim the Primicerius Johannes, and obtain for him the support of Aetius, with an army of Huns. Suppression of the revolt, re-establishment of Placidia at Ravenna and her condonation of Aetius. The circumstances that led to the loss of Africa. Jealousies between Aetius and the Roman governor Bonifacius. Aetius, having slain his rival, becomes absolute at Ravenna. Attila the Hun overawes and insults both empires. Disgrace and death of Theodosius II. The East Romans invest his sister Pulcheria with power. Her marriage with Marcian, who, when named Emperor, defies Attila. Attila directs his attack against the Visigoths and the Western empire. Theodoric, king of the Visigoths, makes common cause with the Romans. Battle of Chalons. King Thorismond, whose father Theodoric is slain, restores the battle. Attila, though repulsed, is allowed an unmolested retreat. The following year he lays waste Northern Italy, and the refugees from the ruined cities become the founders of Venice.

A.D. 423. TO Placidia the decease of Honorius brought no cessation of troubles, nor any immediate prospect of a return to Italy. The inhabitants of Ravenna and the principal cities, after their experience of the Theodosian family, desired an Emperor of their own selection, and their choice fell on the Primicerius Johannes, from whose ministerial intelligence and labours they had experienced substantial advantages.

Johannes, in compliance with the general wish, assumed the purple and sent his envoys to Constantinople to ask for recognition; but the demand was haughtily rejected. Johannes, nevertheless, with the acquiescence of the Western consul, continued, for two years, to exercise supreme authority; but while throughout Italy his power seemed established, in the provinces it was otherwise; Bonifacius, the proconsul of Africa, defeated the forces sent against him, and in him Placidia and her infant son, Valentinian III, had a zealous supporter.

Meanwhile, at Constantinople, the betrothal of Valentinian to the infant daughter of Theodosius II extinguished jealousies, promoted a stricter family agreement, and was followed by active preparations for an attack on Johannes. Ardaburius and his son Aspar, leaders, of barbarian lineage, who had shown their military worth in warfare with the Persians, were ordered to levy forces and to uphold the cause of Placidia and her son. The military resources of the East ultimately turned the scale: Ravenna was sacked, and Johannes, whose virtues deserved a better fate, became the victim of a cruel sentence. A.D. 425.

When called upon to make good his pretensions by force of arms, Johannes had placed his main reliance on the abilities of his major-domo, Aetius. The father of Aetius, by birth a Scythian, having attained the rank of general in the Roman service, married an Italian lady of wealth and position.

Aetius, as he grew up, became remarkable for manly beauty, and for his skill in martial exercises; and during a residence of three years at the court of Attila, where he had been sent as a hostage, he acquired the friendship of the barbarian chieftains amongst whom he lived on terms of intimacy.

When, as the envoy of Johannes and furnished with a supply of Roman gold, he re-visited his old associates, he found no difficulty in engaging them to assemble their forces for a descent into Italy; but as he approached Aquileja with an army of sixty thousand Huns, he received intelligence of his patron's destruction. Yet he was able to make good terms for himself; for he, and he alone, could induce his barbarian following to relinquish their hopes of plunder and to retrace their steps; a service which he promptly effected, and one which caused his treason to be condoned [1].

A.D. 426. During the confusion caused by the usurpation of Johannes, the Visigothic king Theodoric, hoping to obtain an extension of his boundaries, commenced hostilities. Bonifacius, the most able of the Roman generals, was engaged in Africa, and, in this emergency, Placidia was fain to rely on the services of the gifted semi-barbarian, Aetius. The success of Aetius was complete; and, having compelled Theodoric to sue for peace, he returned triumphant to Ravenna. But when he found that Bonifacius was in all important affairs the trusted adviser of Placidia,

---

[1] Philostorgius. After this we lose the guidance of this contemporary writer.

his jealousy led him to embark in an intrigue which must for ever blight his memory.

By artful whisperings he contrived to disseminate a suspicion that Bonifacius was taking steps to render his African government independent. Placidia, though incredulous, was at last persuaded, as a test of his fidelity, to decree his recall; but Aetius took care that the order should be accompanied by a private letter from himself, in which, with protestations of friendship, he warned Bonifacius that his ruin was resolved upon, and advised him to interpose delays [1].

Bonifacius fell into the snare: his excuses and postponements were regarded as a proof of criminality, and he was denounced as a public enemy. In his despair he adopted a course fatal alike to himself and the empire; for, thinking to secure the support of the Vandals who had lately established themselves on the opposite coast, he allowed their astute and powerful ruler, Genseric, to obtain a footing on the hitherto intact soil of Roman Africa [2].

Meanwhile, his friends, convinced of his rectitude, with the consent of Placidia, sent a commission to Carthage for the purpose of ascertaining the truth. On reference to the letters, the double dealing of Aetius became evident; but the discovery came too late, for Bonifacius had opened a floodgate that he could not close. Neither his gold nor his remonstrances were of any avail: his forces were insuffi-

---

[1] Procopius de bello Vandalico.
[2] The fraud ascribed to Aetius is fully believed in by Gibbon, ch. xxxiii; but has been called in question by recent enquirers.

cient to cope with those of Genseric, and he was obliged to shut himself up, with his friend St. Augustine, in Hippo.

A.D. 430. Hippo then became a city of refuge for the Catholic clergy who escaped the persecution of the Arian Vandals, and resisted, for fourteen months, the attacks of Genseric. During that season of distress and terror, the great luminary of the African churches died; and though famine finally compelled Genseric to abandon the siege, the surviving clergy, dreading its renewal, and precluded from a resumption of their duties, became homeless exiles.

To the Roman world the preservation of Africa became an object of primary importance; and the ministers of Theodosius II and of his sister Pulcheria resolved to send an armament to Carthage under the command of Count Aspar, who, since his successful vindication of the rights of Placidia and her son, had enjoyed great influence at Constantinople.

A.D. 431. When Aspar and Bonifacius had united their forces, they gave battle to Genseric; but neither the skill of these generals nor the valour of their legions were of any avail; and after a very severe conflict they were compelled to embark. The Roman cause then became desperate; and Hippo, abandoned by the inhabitants, fell into the hands of the victors.

A.D. 432. Bonifacius, nevertheless, on his return to Italy, was cordially received by Placidia, and entrusted with the command of the army.

Aetius, meanwhile, had been alike successful in war and in diplomacy. He had defeated the Franks, and gained over their youthful king, Merovius, to the Roman alliance. When he received the decree that deprived him of his command, he stood on the defensive; Bonifacius marched against him, and in a battle, the locality of which is unknown, obtained the victory, but received from the hands of his rival a wound of which he died.

Aetius then betook himself to his old allies the Huns, and was able to assemble such an army as, under his direction, was deemed irresistible. With that army he threatened to invade Italy, but only with a view to enforce his own re-establishment. The court of Ravenna, in its dread of the Huns, submitted to all his demands, conferred upon him the rank of Patrician, and named him, for the second time, Consul.

Having the absolute control of the army, like Stilicho, he monopolized power, leaving to Placidia the enactment of salutary laws, the administration of ecclesiastical affairs, and the construction of beautiful churches. Though, in persecuting the relations and adherents of his fallen adversary he betrayed a deplorable want of generosity, his services, especially in Gaul, were highly appreciated. He compelled the Burgundians to acknowledge the Roman supremacy: his successes, the terror of his name, and the prowess of his Huns, caused the ambitious but astute Vandal to lower his pretensions. For the settlements already acquired by his people in Africa, A.D. 435. Genseric submitted to pay tribute; and, for a security against any attempt to possess himself of Carthage, he sent his son Hunneric to reside at Ravenna as a hostage. Yet these advantages were dearly purchased: for the maintenance of the confederated Huns entailed heavy burthens on Gaul, and the Khans who commanded them acquired a dangerous acquaintance with the localities and condition of that tempting region.

A.D. 437. Meanwhile, between Ravenna and Constantinople the most cordial relations were kept up. Valentinian III, when he had attained his eighteenth year, went to Constantinople[1] for the celebration of his marriage with his affianced cousin Eudocia, whose father, Theodosius II, on occasions of state ceremony was able to act his part with dignity, but who left all weightier affairs to be administered by Pulcheria.

A.D. 438. In A.D. 438 Pulcheria caused to be promulgated, in her brother's name, the celebrated digest of Roman Law known as the Theodosian Code, a work of great and permanent utility; for this code, being adopted in the West, conferred a signal benefit on both empires, and also on the semi-barbarous races settled within their pale. But while under the auspices of the benevolent Augustas, Pulcheria and Placidia, just laws were enacted and public interests advanced, there was no security for the maintenance of peaceful blessings.

The fear of a Vandalic conquest of Carthage was not the only one: the Huns, under the brothers Attila and Bleda, had become a terror. They had

[1] Chronicon Paschale, in Niebuhr's collection.

occupied Thrace, and had approached, with impunity, the walls of Constantinople. Meanwhile, in the West, Aetius, profiting by his intimacy with some of their chieftains, availed himself of their aid against the Burgundians and Visigoths; though the resort to such an alliance was humiliating, its permanency doubtful.

The military genius of Aetius was undisputed: in the liberation of the Gallic provinces he had done good service; but his relations with the Huns were such that he could rely upon their aid against, as well as in favour of, Roman interests: the loss of Africa was justly ascribed to his selfish machinations; but proconsular Carthage, with its adjacent territory, was still Roman, and might, on some favourable opportunity, have served to facilitate a re-conquest; an advantage which, ere long, was needlessly thrown away.

Genseric, by artful protestations, aided perhaps by his gold, obtained the liberation of his son: he then, by an unexpected attack, gained possession of the port and city. A.D. 439.

Carthage, since the sentence 'Delenda est' was executed by Scipio Aemilianus, had risen from her ashes, and, as the capital of Roman Africa, had attained a second greatness. She was now doomed to a second destruction. The horrors of the sack are related by a contemporary, Salvianus of Marseilles. Salvianus dilates on the splendour of the public establishments and especially of the institutions for the promotion of learning and science; but describes the inhabitants as equal to those of Rome in luxury, and their superiors in vice[1]. Thus the great proconsulate, whence Rome derived her sustenance, and her nobles their wealth, was allowed to fall into the hands of the Vandals, in whose possession it remained until they were driven out by Belisarius.

A.D. 441. The following year, Genseric, having undisputed command of the Mediterranean, established his power in many of the Sicilian cities, and the progress of Vandalic conquest roused the pacific government of the East to action. Pulcheria, acting on behalf of her brother, despatched a considerable army to Sicily; but dangers nearer home demanded its recall. The Huns, whose power and whose insolence were ever on the increase, had commenced hostilities.

Since the fabric of the Roman world began to crumble, there seems to have existed amongst the barbarian aggressors a feeling that it was their interest to encourage and facilitate each other's aggressions. It was on the instigation of Genseric that the Huns, though in Gaul they had assisted Aetius against the Visigoths, renewed their attacks on the Eastern Empire, and effected such a diversion as enabled the Vandals to retain their conquest.

A.D. 442.

A.D. 444. Attila, when he had slain his brother Bleda, became sole autocrat of the Huns, and the fame of his victories attracted to his standard hordes of migratory

---

[1] See the collection of Baluze.

Attila insults both Empires. 51

warriors. Boasting himself to be the possessor of the sword of Mars, he assumed the title of King of kings, and claimed to be the descendant and legitimate successor of Nimrod. The East Roman generals made a brave but unsuccessful attempt to cope with his overwhelming numbers: but Sirmium, now Belgrade, and other flourishing Roman cities of Pannonia fell into his grasp; and the court of Constantinople, as the price of peace, consented to pay a subsidy, and to surrender all deserters or fugitives who might seek its protection. **A.D. 446**

By Cedrenus, a Greek monk of the eleventh century, a legend is preserved that Pulcheria, desiring to check her brother's habit of affixing his name to unread documents, let him sign one which ordained that his Empress should be sold for a slave; and that Eudocia, as a retort, obtained his signature to another unread decree, whereby Pulcheria, to prevent her meddling in public affairs, was commanded to take orders as a deaconess. Whatever may be the credit attached to this story, it appears certain that Pulcheria, about this time, ceased to possess her previous influence, and also that the remaining three years of her brother's reign were years of deep humiliation.

During that interval Attila did not cease to harass the pleasure-loving court of Theodosius with inconvenient demands, accompanied by threats, for the surrender of fugitives. In 448 or the following year Edecon and Orestes, barbarian chieftains who had been employed as his envoys, were about to return. **A.D. 449.**

It was then that Theodosius, already sufficiently abased, sank to a still lower level, and yielding to the persuasions of a vile favourite, sanctioned a plot for the assassination of his too powerful opponent. Edecon, to whom the prospect of enormous wealth was exhibited, joined or pretended to join in the conspiracy. As if for the purpose of satisfying all the demands of Attila a specious embassy was named, with Maximin, an officer of rank, for its chief. Maximin took with him the historian Priscus, and, accompanied by Edecon and Orestes, proceeded on the arduous journey, without the least suspicion that he had disguised assassins in his train. When they reached their destination Edecon, the sole depository of the guilty secret, instead of acting as he had promised, revealed the plot to its intended victim. Bitter and contemptuous were the taunts launched by the royal Hun against the imperial delinquent; yet we do not read that Theodosius II died of shame, but of an injury received while hunting.

A.D. 450.

In the West, the death of Placidia, which took place the same year, left Valentinian free to indulge, without restraint, his follies and his vices, while in the East, on the decease of her brother, Pulcheria, by an unprecedented mark of attachment and confidence, was invited to resume the direction of affairs. Yet the management of the army was more than she could undertake. Aspar had the command of the forces; and Aspar, like most of the northern converts, was an Arian,—a circumstance which gave additional strength to the bond between him and his confederated legions. It was felt that, to prevent military dictation, the authority of an Emperor was requisite; and Pulcheria therefore consented to a Platonic marriage with the veteran general, Count Marcian, who, with the approbation of the Western government, was proclaimed. Marcian had long enjoyed the respect of his fellow-citizens, and he was able, when invested with the purple, to exercise, without offence, a needful control over the army, and to restore its efficiency. When called upon by Attila for the payment of a subsidy, he refused to be bound by the weak concessions of his predecessor, and, in courteous language, told the envoys that if their master desired war, he would not find the Romans asleep. Before Attila came to a decision as to which of the two capitals should be the first object of his attack, he transmitted to each of them, as an ultimatum, a summary of his demands. Of these the foremost and the most strongly urged was that which he put forward for the hand of the Emperor Valentinian's sister, Honoria. The levities of Honoria had made it necessary that she should be kept in seclusion, but the guardians to whom she was entrusted failed to intercept entirely her communication with the outer world. In the hope of regaining, on any terms, freedom and greatness, she sent her ring to Attila, together with an intimation that, in obtaining her for his wife, he might one day establish a claim to the Western sovereignty.

The politic Hun, willing to profit by such an overture, assumed the character of an affianced suitor, and champion. It was in vain that the ministers of Valentinian assured his envoy that marriage with a Roman princess would not confer a claim to the imperial succession, and that, in point of fact, Honoria had already become the wife of an obscure husband. The autocrat of the Huns, who was also the leader of a great confederacy, no longer hesitated; he resolved, in the first instance, to overwhelm his old opponents the Visigoths, and then to assail the Romans of Italy, of whose unprepared condition he could not fail to be cognizant.

Amongst the races that had acquired a permanent footing within the pale of the empire, the Visigoths now held the first place. During the long and successful reign of Theodoric, their fourth king, they had greatly risen in national importance; but prosperity had not effaced the memory of wrongs inflicted on their fathers by the Huns. The danger to which they were exposed was identical with that which threatened the Romans; and the only way of safety for either lay in an alliance for mutual defence. But the Visigoths could not readily bring themselves to trust Aetius, who had only lately been their enemy, and who had throughout the whole of his career been on friendly terms with the Huns. They therefore preferred to stand or fall alone, rather than incur the perils of an alliance that might prove to be insidious.

By the timely intervention of Avitus, a wealthy

Roman colonist, this difficulty was overcome. The conduct of Avitus, when he held the office of pretorian prefect for Gaul, had entitled him to general respect. At the court of Theodoric he was no stranger; and on the present occasion the counsels of which he was the bearer were trusted. He warned the king of the overwhelming numbers of the enemy, and finally prevailed with him and with the chieftains to make common cause with the Romans; a decision which induced the minor independent tribes to accept the imperial gold and to thicken the ranks of Aetius with a needful supply of combatants.

The great Germanic race of the Franks was A.D. 451 divided; a part being devoted to Aetius, while another section, that held extensive settlements on the lower Rhine, afforded to Attila facilities for crossing the river. The march of the invaders, when they reached the left bank, was one of destruction. Metz was amongst the 'civitates effractae,' and Treves, so long the capital of Roman Gaul, underwent a ruin which, to this day, is visible. Attila, when he had trodden down the opposition of the Burgundians, crossed the Loire, intending to attack the Visigoths; but Orleans (Aurelia), where the inhabitants had erected fortifications, stayed his progress. Attila, informed of the junction of Aetius with the Visigoths, abandoned the siege; and, when his forces were sufficiently concentrated, chose for his battlefield the wide open country of Champagne. His entire army, composed of heterogeneous races, is said to have numbered seven hundred thousand combatants[1]; an estimate which may appear fabulous; yet it ought to be borne in mind that, with the northern nations, armed emigration had become a habit of life, and Attila himself declared that by no other means could they obtain subsistence.

As to the details of the great conflict, called in history the battle of Chalons, little could, even at the time, have been known. The extent of the ground occupied was far too vast to be scanned by any eye. 'Bellum atrox, multiplex, immane, pertinax'—such are the words, few but pregnant, employed by Cassiodorus to describe the ferocity of the contest, the multiplicity of the distinct yet simultaneous conflicts, and the obstinacy wherewith they were maintained.

The forces of Aetius, weakly supported by his doubtful allies, the Alani, were overmatched, and King Theodoric had fallen; when Theodoric's son, Thorismond, with his unbroken phalanxes, renewed and maintained the conflict, until Attila found himself compelled to seek the protection of his fortified camp. Conscious of his danger, he caused a funeral pile to be raised, on which he declared his resolution to die rather than survive a defeat. Thorismond had already commenced an attack on his defences when called back by the authoritative voice of

---

[1] 'Dicebat enim suae gentis multitudinem veram necessariorum inopia ad bellum se convertisse.' Priscus. Byzant. Script. 1, p. 208.

Defeat, and unmolested retreat of Attila.

Aetius, who allowed **the invaders an unmolested** retreat.

The Visigoths, as the successful defenders **of** civilisation, had now attained their highest renown: but Aetius regarded their power with apprehension, and that of the Huns as a necessary counterpoise; a policy of which the bitter fruits were, before the year had elapsed, experienced in Italy; for Attila, having ascertained the comparative weakness of the Roman forces, persisted in his design. During the A.D. 452. winter he repaired his losses, and, when its rigour abated, he began to move in the direction **of the** Alps. We read of no attempt on the part of Aetius to guard the passes; and the first opposition encountered by the invaders was from the fortified and populous city of Aquileja, 'Aquileja praedives,' the emporium of commerce between upper Italy and the East. After a prolonged and brave defence Aquileja was taken by assault, and underwent a destruction from which it never accomplished more than a partial recovery. Altino, Concordia, and Padua were rased to their foundations; the citizens of these and the neighbouring **towns, who, by a timely** flight, escaped death or slavery, found a refuge amid the sand-banks **of** the Rio **Alto or** in the neighbouring islands. There, after a long struggle with privations, they succeeded in obtaining sustenance for their families; and these were the men whose children's children became the founders of Venice.

The ruin extended to **the** whole of the Aemilia: **the citizens** of Milan, **Bergamo**, Pavia, **and Vicenza,** if allowed to purchase the lives of their children, did so at the sacrifice of all that they possessed. Valentinian fled from Ravenna to Rome and there awaited the end, prepared in case of need to abandon Italy.

Attila would seem to have paused before he decided on a course which, however flattering in its commencement, had in the end proved fatal to Alaric; and when it was desired to try the effect of negotiation, or, rather, of a deprecatory appeal, Leo the Great[1] consented to head a deputation, consisting of himself, the pretorian prefect, and Avienus, a senator of consular rank. During these years of humiliation and weakness, the papacy exhibited such signs of vital energy as formed a singular contrast to the weakness of the civil government. When the first Leo commenced his Pontificate (A.D. 440), a variety of circumstances contributed to the exaltation of his See. That of Milan had, since the death of St. Ambrose, ceased to compete with Rome; and the patriarchs of Alexandria and Constantinople, when, by unseemly contentions, they had impaired their dignity, were fain to submit to Leo as an arbiter. While, in ecclesiastical rank, the primacy of the Roman patriarchate was undisputed, its superior wealth, derived from vast possessions in Italy and Sicily, could not fail to invest the possessor with influence, social and political.

If Roman captives were to be redeemed from slavery, if hospitals were to be endowed, or works of

[1] Leo I, 440-461 A.D.

public utility executed, the Pontiff, with more than princely liberality, provided the funds: **as the chosen** of the Senate and people no less than of the clergy, he came, during the habitual residence **of the Emperor at Ravenna**, to be regarded as head of the state; and though not yet invested with temporal dominions, he possessed, in the bishops and abbots of Western Christendom, ecclesiastical proconsuls and pretors, on whose intelligence and willingness to promote his wishes he could rely. To the moral influence of their Pontiff as head of Western Christianity, the Senate and people of the old capital were mainly indebted for the preservation of that 'nominis umbra,' which was still theirs.

When the embassy reached the **Hunnish encampment** on the shores of lake Benacus (Garda) its arrival would not seem to have been otherwise **than** acceptable to Attila, inasmuch as it afforded him an excuse for the relinquishment of an enterprise which his Huns were longing to undertake. In reply to Leo's appeal, he consented to spare Rome; **but as some** explanation of this change of purpose was required, he declared that he had seen a vision of a **man with** a drawn sword, who stood beside the Pontiff, ready to support his demands [1]; **a** myth which may admit of a non-miraculous explanation; for Aetius having by this time received from the Emperor Marcian a timely reinforcement [2], was prepared to take advantage of such opportunities as the destitution or sickness of the invading host might offer.

[1] Historia Miscella.   [2] Idacius, Chron.

Before Attila commenced his retreat, he reiterated his claim for the princess Honoria and her dowry, and declared that, unless his demand was complied with, he should return the following year; a threat made nugatory by his own death and by the consequent collapse of the great Hunnish confederacy.

The terror of the Huns being at an end, the predominance of Aetius was no longer acquiesced in as a necessary evil. His failure to save the richest provinces of Italy and many of her noblest cities from devastation and ruin, destroyed his prestige. While his influence and power were at their height, he had aspired to secure for his descendants the imperial succession, and had been promised for his son, Carpilio, the hand of Valentinian's daughter.

A.D. 455. When, under altered circumstances, he claimed the fulfilment of that engagement, an altercation ensued; Valentinian struck him with his sword; and, in a moment, the most gifted leader of his day fell under the cowardly blows of the courtiers.

Ere this eventful year ended, Valentinian himself was assassinated by the adherents of the fallen dictator; and the unlamented fate of the last Theodosian emperor left the throne of the West without an hereditary claimant.

The accounts, handed down by Latin authorities, of the circumstances and motives connected with the death of Aetius and that of Valentinian seem natural and consistent, but the Greek writers give a totally different version. If Procopius is to be credited, the wife of Maximus had been violated by

Valentinian; and her outraged husband, by his machinations, brought about the death of Aetius, but only with a view to remove an obstacle to the gratification of his revenge on the Emperor. This story, whatever may be its probability or improbability, is accepted by Gibbon, who has made it the subject of an elaborate paraphrase; yet it rests on the sole and somewhat doubtful authority of Procopius, who was not born until after the commencement of the sixth century, and, though repeated by subsequent Greek writers, it is altogether ignored by contemporary historians. Yet, to the latter, it must, if true, have been well known; and the matter was of too great interest to be disregarded or passed over in silence.

CHAPTER IV.

From the Death of the last Theodosian Emperor to the Extinction of the Western Empire.

A.D. 455–476.

Proclamation and fall of Maximus. Sack of Rome by Genseric. Inability of the Romans to control Ricimer, the Suevic commander of the forces. Defeat of their efforts to restore and uphold the imperial government. Death of Ricimer. On the nomination of the Eastern emperor Leo, Nepos, Governor of Dalmatia, obtains the Western empire. His employment of Orestes, by whom he is betrayed and driven from Italy. Orestes usurps power, and proclaims his son. Overthrow of Orestes by Odoacer. Odoacer, with the title of Patrician and the acquiescence of the Romans, bears rule at Ravenna as protector.

A.D. 455. AFTER the long succession of ills caused or aggravated by the imbecility of Honorius and Valentinian, it cannot excite surprise that the Romans of the West should have desired an Emperor of their own choice. In Petronius Maximus they had a fellow-citizen in whom illustrious birth was combined with hereditary wealth, and one who had discharged with credit the highest offices. Maximus had twice been pretorian prefect, had twice served as consul for the West, and to him, 'adhuc viventi,' a statue had been erected, of which the base is still to be seen, in the Forum.

The hopes that led to the election of Maximus soon came to an end. An enemy whose approach was easier, and consequently more to be dreaded, than that of Attila, was on the watch. The possession of Africa, and of settlements on the coasts of Spain and of Sicily, gave Genseric such a supply of seamen, and such ample materials for shipbuilding, as enabled him to make his naval superiority absolute. The violent death of his ally Valentinian relieved him from his engagements, and furnished him with a pretext. The sharers in the spoils of Carthage were athirst for those of a still nobler city.

Maximus had neither galleys to defend the Tiber, nor soldiers to man the walls. No longer the idol of the multitude, he became the object of unmerited scorn and aversion. After a reign of a few weeks, while attempting to escape from the city, he perished in a tumult, and his body was thrown into the river.

When Genseric approached the unguarded gates, Leo, then in the sixteenth year of his great Pontificate, went out to meet him.

The present circumstances differed widely from those which, three years before, had conduced to the success of his mission to Attila; yet he obtained a promise that no massacre should be permitted, that the churches and public buildings should be respected, and that no citizen should be subjected to torture.

During fourteen days and nights, galleys laden with all manner of spoil descended the Tiber.

Statues of heathen deities which, until then, had been permitted to adorn the deserted temple of the Capitol were carried off; and with them went emblems of a purer worship—the Golden table and the Candlestick [1], brought by Titus from Jerusalem.

On leaving Rome the Vandals and Moors spread themselves over the South; but, after they had destroyed Nola and Capua, they re-embarked for Africa, without venturing to approach self-reliant Naples.

Of the customs which in these days aggravated the horrors of war, that of selling captives for slaves was the most deplorable. From Rome and from the Southern cities, men, women, and children were carried off, and doomed, when separated from their kindred, to become the property of barbarian masters. In all cases when liberty could be purchased, or intermediate sufferings alleviated, the bishops were on the alert. Most conspicuous for their Christian charity were Deogratias of Carthage and Paolinus of Nola, who grudged neither personal risks nor the wealth of their churches. The circumstances related in connection with this subject show that, even amongst the Vandals, feelings of humanity were not altogether extinct. The fact that a Catholic bishop obtained permission to reside and exercise his functions without molestation at Carthage, is a remarkable one: ruthless as was Genseric, there must needs have been amongst those who bore rule,

[1] Idacius, Chron.

or had influence, some men or women of a **superior** stamp.

The self-sacrifice of Bishop Paolinus, and the return which it elicited, lead **to a similar conclusion.** Of Paolinus we learn that, when he had spent all he possessed in the redemption of prisoners, and was unable by any other means to obtain the liberation of a widow's son, he surrendered himself; **but when,** after his arrival at Carthage, the case became known, **his bonds were removed and** he was permitted to carry back with him to **Nola all prisoners belonging to that** city.

The widowed Empress Eudoxia, if really **guilty** of having sent an invitation to Genseric, received **an** ungrateful return. Stript of her jewels, she **was** carried off to Carthage, where, with her daughters Eudocia and Placidia, she remained a prisoner, until Genseric, who, like other barbarian kings, coveted alliances with the imperial family, bestowed the hand of Eudocia on his son, Hunneric, to whom she bore a son, Ilderic, who after the death of an elder brother became king of the Vandals. **Eudoxia** effected her escape **to** Jerusalem, where **she ended** her days[1], and her younger **daughter Placidia,** through the intervention of the **Emperor Leo,** became the wife of the patrician Olybrius, who in A.D. 472 reigned for a few months as Emperor of the West.

The spoliation of Rome by Genseric was only a beginning of sorrows; for, during the sixteen years

---

[1] Theophanes, Chron. rep.

that ensued, Italy remained at the mercy of her own paid leader, **Count Ricimer,** by birth and family alliances a barbarian, who defeated every attempt to re-establish legal government.

After the fall of Aetius, Ricimer obtained the command of the Western forces and the patrician dignity. The father of Ricimer belonged to the Teutonic race of the Suevi; and his mother was a daughter of the Visigothic king, Wallia. The career of Ricimer resembled in some degree those of Stilicho and of Aetius; for though his delinquencies were more numerous and of a far deeper dye than theirs, like them he possessed great military abilities, and like them he had personal interests that could not be reconciled with those of the 'Respublica Romana.'

After the fall of Maximus, **Avitus** the ex-prefect of Gaul, who had nobly sustained the Roman cause in that country, and who secured to that cause the support of the Visigothic king, Theodoric, was proclaimed at Arles. His acceptance of empire was hailed by the Senate as a happy termination of anarchy. The prostration of Rome, after the Vandalic sack, may more easily be imagined than described. Though Genseric had been warned by the Emperor Marcian to desist from further hostilities, the piratical descents of the Vandals on the defenceless coasts of Italy continued, until Ricimer, by his skilful use of such galleys as he was able to collect, gave the corsairs a lesson, by the utter destruction of one of their fleets. This gleam of

A.D. 456.

success sufficed to inspire new hope and exalted the prestige of Ricimer, while the past services of Avitus were either ignored or forgotten.

Meanwhile the Teutonic race of the Suevi, having during the decline of Roman power in Spain possessed themselves of Gallicia, were preparing to add Portugal to their dominion, when Avitus induced the Visigothic king, Theodoric, to commence hostilities against them, which effectually checked their advances,—a policy which, however strictly in accordance with his duty as emperor, gave deep offence to Ricimer, the Suevic commander of the imperial forces. The following year Avitus, finding his position at Rome untenable, fled to Placentia, resigned the greatness that he had never coveted, and, as a security against any change of purpose, consented to be made bishop of that city[1]. The Roman colonists in Gaul were at this time under the direction of their governor Egidius, whom they honoured as their king and who resided at Soissons, unaffected by the prepotency usurped by Ricimer in Italy.

For about ten months after the dethronement of Avitus, Ricimer, with the title of patrician, governed; but, in April 457, this interregnum was terminated by an unanimous election of Majorian, a Roman officer whose services had scarcely been inferior to those of Ricimer himself, and who, like him, had been thought worthy of the patrician dignity. Nor

A.D. 457.

[1] The only child of Avitus was the wife of Sidonius Apollinaris, the poet and orator.

could a better choice have been made; for in Majorian were combined with the aspirations of a Roman patriot, enlightened views and indefatigable energy.

A few months prior to his elevation, the throne of the East became vacant by the death of Marcian, who outlived by four years the sainted Pulcheria. Marcian's firm yet pacific policy had conferred on the Eastern empire unwonted prosperity. In A.D. 452, during Attila's invasion of Italy, he afforded essential aid; and the arrival of Roman succours from the East was one of the circumstances that weighed with Attila, when, after the destruction of Aquileja, he gave up his design against Rome. It is therefore difficult to discover the grounds on which Gibbon hazards the assertion, 'Marcian seemed to behold with indifference the misfortunes of Rome.' The blow inflicted by Genseric was much too sudden and unexpected to have admitted of any intervention.

7 Feb., A.D. 457. As there now existed for the Eastern throne no hereditary claimant, the long services of the patrician Aspar, and his position 'Magister utriusque militiae,' might in those perilous times have justified his elevation; but Aspar, like Ricimer, was an Arian, a circumstance which he felt would have rendered his elevation inexpedient and perhaps hazardous. He therefore prevailed with the Eastern Senate to elect Leo, an officer of good repute, who had been indebted to his merit for advancement, and on whose subserviency Aspar thought he might rely.

Aspar had mistaken his man; and yet Leo, in the first instance, was unable to resist the dictation of his too powerful patron; so that, at Constantinople, as at Ravenna, the reigning Emperor was liable to be overawed and kept in check. It yet remained to be seen whether the virtue and the fortune of Majorian would so far prevail as to relieve both himself and his imperial colleague from this thraldom, and enable them to employ, for the defence and redintegration of the dual empire, its great remaining resources.

Of Majorian's efforts to reform and purify the administration there is ample evidence: his enactments testify a sincere desire to elevate the moral and physical condition of the people; he relieved the oppressed provincials from a grinding system of taxation; to the municipalities he restored their ancient right of self-government; and when, after the sack of Rome, a diminished and degraded population had ceased to take interest in the public buildings, and leave was readily obtained for their demolition, Majorian, by a timely decree, put an end to the worse than Vandalic sacrilege.

The success of his first military operations raised to an unwonted pitch the hopes and aspirations of the Italians. He inflicted on the Vandal and Moorish plunderers a signal defeat, re-captured their spoil, and chased the survivors to their ships. So long as Genseric held possession of Africa, it was impossible to prevent a repetition of descents; but to the Romans, the re-conquest of Carthage, and the re-establishment of a naval superiority, did not seem more than was within their reach.

The time was gone by when, in Classe, the harbour of Ravenna, there rode a fleet of galleys ready for any emergency; and, on application being made to Constantinople to supply the deficiency, Leo, still in subjection to Aspar, pleaded engagements to Genseric. Every nerve was then strained to construct war-galleys; but then, as now, an efficient fleet could not be extemporized.

A.D. 461. In placing on foot land forces superior to those of the Moors and Vandals, there was no difficulty: Franks, Goths, and Burgundians filled up the roll.

Carthagena, the queen of Mediterranean ports, was the general rendezvous. There, under the protection of a chain of forts, the remains of which still exist, the entire armament assembled; but, when all was prepared for an embarkation, Genseric, by an unexpected attack, threw the unwieldy armada into confusion, sank or captured the vessels of transport, and rendered any immediate prosecution of the enterprise impossible. Genseric, nevertheless, convinced of his inability to withstand the forces of the empire, when vigorously employed against him, sued for peace. Thus time was gained for the prosecution of needful reforms, and Italy had a respite from Vandalic depredations: but only a brief one, for the days of Majorian were numbered:

During the spring of 461, as he was returning from a celebration of the Circensian Games, at Arles, Ricimer, to whom any superiority was unbearable, under pretence of doing him honour, went to meet him with a body of troops, and, in conjunction with a servile coadjutor, Libius Severus, circumvented him and put him to death.

Scanty as are the records of Majorian's energetic career, they sufficiently show that the resources of the Western empire were still such as might have sufficed for its defence, if the personal objects and barbarian sympathies of Ricimer had not stood in the way. Severus, as the nominee of Ricimer, next wore the purple, and decrees were registered in his name; but his appointment obtained no confirmation at Constantinople, and the usurped power of Ricimer himself never extended beyond the limits of Italy. In Gaul and in Dalmatia, the Roman governors, Egidius and Marcellinus, continued to hold their respective provinces in trust for the 'Sancta Respublica,' acknowledging no emperor but Leo; and Leo nominated both consuls.

After four years of confusion and misery, Severus A.D. 465. died; and when Ricimer, as patrician, had exercised for above a year the powers of the executive, he appears to have become satisfied that, without a combined effort, in which the naval resources of the East should be brought to bear, the plague of Vandal descents could not be stayed. Yielding, it would seem, to necessity, he concurred with the Senate in a request to the Emperor Leo, that he would name an emperor of the West.

In this attempt to establish closer relations with A.D. 467. the East, the Senate appears to have acted in conformity with the original constitution of the two empires; and at the same time to have adopted a policy that might, under favouring circumstances, have relieved the Roman world from its besetting danger, namely, that of a military despotism exercised by men who derived their wealth and importance from Roman sources, and yet failed to entertain any exclusive attachment to Roman interests.

The choice of Leo fell on Anthemius, who, some years previously, had served as consul, and whose hereditary influence placed him at the head of the Eastern magnates. It was agreed, as part of the treaty, that Ricimer should marry the daughter of Anthemius,—an arrangement by which it was hoped to secure his permanent support; and when, accompanied by his daughter, the new Emperor approached the gates, Ricimer, attired as a senator, went out to meet them, great was the exultation of the Quirites.

The unprecedented task entrusted to the Emperor Leo, of selecting the man with whom he was to share the administration and defence of the whole Roman world, makes it requisite to consider his actual position. Leo had now attained the eleventh year of a reign which, from the first, had been beset with difficulties. Aspar, with his barbarian satellites, overawed the Eastern Senate; and it was only by compliances savouring of duplicity that the government could be carried on. Leo could do no more than turn to advantage any opportunity that might arise for the extension of his influence. When the Huns invaded Thrace, he gained a battle in which one of Attila's sons was slain; a success which increased his influence. By enlisting the services of an Isaurian prince, whose barbaric name he changed to that of the Stoic, Zeno, he at length obtained a counterpoise to Aspar. The Isaurian, though no philosopher, and though in his manners a barbarian, had at his disposal a considerable array of hardy combatants, whose services Leo secured by accepting their leader for his son-in-law. The resources of the Eastern empire were then freely devoted to an enterprise, on the success or failure of which the weal or woe of Italy depended. Coins were struck representing the two Emperors with joined hands, and sanguine hopes were once more entertained that, by their combined efforts, Africa, with the command of the Mediterranean, would be regained.

In fitting out an armada of fabulous magnitude, A.D. 468. the sum expended by Leo exceeded five millions sterling. Marcellinus, under whose government Dalmatia had prospered, and who had refused to obey Ricimer, declared his allegiance to Anthemius; and the successes which his galleys obtained over those of the Vandals enabled him to liberate the island of Sardinia from their oppression. About the same time, the prefect Heraclius landed at Tripoli, re-conquered the adjacent settlements, and commenced his march to co-operate with the main expedition in an attack on Carthage. Such were the signs of an irresistible superiority with which the war commenced[1], and which so far shook the confidence of

[1] Procopius de bello Vandalico, 1-6.

Genseric that he protested his willingness to submit to whatever terms the two Emperors might dictate; and there appears to be no doubt that his apprehensions were shared by his co-religionists, Ricimer and Aspar, to whom a subversion of the Arian ascendancy in Africa would have been fatal.

Fortunately for them, the chief command was given to Basiliscus, a brother of the empress-consort, Verina. As Leo had no son, Basiliscus, if Procopius is to be relied upon, already aspired to the imperial succession, and was anxious to stand well with Aspar.

The landing took place at a small seaport about forty miles from Carthage; and while the disembarkation of stores and other impedimenta was in progress, envoys from Genseric arrived. Basiliscus, whether yielding to a desire to gratify Aspar, to the allurements of Vandal gold, or to the suggestions of his own weak judgment, lent a willing ear to their assurances. They asked and obtained a truce of five days, during which the terms of submission might be arranged.

The panic, which would have made the re-conquest of Carthage an easy achievement, subsided; and Genseric, having time for a careful examination, took note of the crowded order in which the Roman armada lay at anchor. His fire-ships, the torpedoes of ancient warfare, were in readiness, supported by galleys, which, however inferior to those of the Romans in number, were the best manned and the most efficient in existence.

Destruction of the Roman fleet by Genseric. 75

At nightfall the fire-ships were so placed that they drifted on the very centre of the unsuspecting enemy: the flames spread, and when the confusion was at its height, a bold and well-timed attack did the rest. The store-ships, on which the army depended for subsistence, were captured or sunk; and acts of individual heroism on the part of the Roman commanders, of which there were many, were of no avail. A hopeless resistance was for a while maintained, but the losses were irreparable. Basiliscus saved himself by an early flight. On arriving at Constantinople, he took refuge in the church of St. Sophia, until he obtained a reprieve from capital punishment through the intercession of his sister.

Such was the disastrous ending of the combined effort made for the recovery of Africa. Its success would have consolidated the power of the two Emperors: by its failure, Ricimer and Aspar were relieved from their fears, and their arrogance became greater than ever.

Leo found it necessary to pacify Aspar by A.D. 471 investing his son Patricius with the dignity of Caesar, a title which conferred on its bearer a prospective claim to the throne. To Aspar and his family, whose unpopularity was already great, the acquisition of this dangerous honour brought no advantage, but only an increase of hostility; for, to the orthodox East Romans, the idea of an Arian Emperor was insufferable. Owing to the losses incurred during the late disastrous expedition, the forces on which Aspar formerly relied were no longer at his beck; and, rightly or wrongly, he and his son were charged with treasonable designs against the government, over which they had long domineered, and against the life of the Emperor.

The circumstances preceding and attending their assassination are variously and obscurely related; but no plea of state necessity can relieve the memory of Leo from the stain of participation in the death of his benefactor.

In Italy, the reckless energy of Ricimer led to a very different result. Having resolved to break up the alliance of the Emperors, he fixed his head-quarters at Milan, enlisted forces, while Anthemius, relying on the cordial support of the Senate and the bulk of the people, remained inactive at Rome.

The Milanese, wishing to prevent a civil war, employed Epiphanius, bishop of Pavia, as negotiator; and from the account given by Ennodius of the bishop's embassy, some estimate may be formed of the difficulties that stood in the way of any attempt on the part of the West Romans to re-construct their dilapidated empire.

The pacific exhortations of the bishop resulted in a truce, which gave time for Ricimer to engage the requisite number of Sueves and Burgundians. Having done this he threw off the mask, and making the death of Aspar his plea, refused to acknowledge either Leo or Anthemius, proclaimed Olybrius, an

Death of Ricimer and elevation of Nepos.

enemy of his father-in-law, emperor, and commenced his march to Rome.

When the Roman governor of Gaul brought an army to support Anthemius, he was defeated and slain. Rome nevertheless held out bravely until reduced by famine, when with the exception of a few streets, occupied by his own adherents, Ricimer condemned it to be sacked. He then added to the list of emperors whom he had put to death the name of his own father-in-law, and died the same year. {A.D. 472}

The reign of Olybrius was as uneventful as it was brief. Having survived his patron for about two months, he died a natural death, and the nephew of Ricimer, having obtained the command of the forces, set up Glycerius, one of his own officers, as emperor. The hopes so long cherished by the Romans of Italy, and by the Gallic, Spanish, and Dalmatian provincials, that the disjointed limbs of the empire might be re-united, and that, after a re-conquest of Africa its power might be restored, were now on the verge of their final extinction. But they still looked to the East for a plank in the shipwreck, and obtained from the Emperor Leo the nomination of Julius Nepos, governor of Dalmatia. Nepos had succeeded in that office his patriotic uncle, Marcellinus, who had never submitted to Ricimer; and Nepos, like his uncle, possessed in the military and naval resources of his government sufficient means for its defence. {A.D. 473} {June 24. A.D. 474.}

Nepos was proclaimed, Glycerius who fled took orders as bishop of Salona; but at this time, Euric, king of the Visigoths, the seventh and most powerful of Alaric's successors, was reigning at Toulouse, and having conquered Roman Spain, became intent on adding the Auvergne to his possessions in Gaul. He therefore laid siege to Clermont, the capital, the episcopal seat of the poet-orator, Sidonius Apollinaris. Ecdicius, the Roman governor, made a gallant defence, and compelled the Visigothic forces to withdraw, but their king persevered, and Nepos, when appealed to for aid, having no disposable troops, engaged the services of Orestes, a chieftain residing in Pannonia, who had at his command an army of mercenaries. Whether this was the Orestes who in the year 448 was serving as secretary of state and ambassador to Attila seems very doubtful. If the same he re-appeared, after a lapse of twenty-seven years, in unabated health and vigour, but acting a very different part in the great drama of life, that of a daring but faithless *condottiere*. Be this as it may,

A.D. 475. the Orestes of whom we are now treating, instead of marching to the defence of Clermont, turned against his employer. It was vain for Nepos, since the decease of his friend and patron, Leo, to look for aid to Constantinople, where disputes as to the succession were still unsettled. He therefore

Aug. 28, A.D. 475. took ship and resumed his residence at Salona, where, for the ensuing five years, he maintained himself as Emperor of the West, *de jure*, his actual sovereignty being limited to the Dalmatian provinces.

Orestes, when in possession of Ravenna, caused

his son, a youth of goodly exterior, whose name was Romulus Augustus, to be named Emperor, intending to retain for himself the reality of power; and, on the 31st day of October, Romulus Augustus, or Augustulus, the last Emperor of the West, was proclaimed. His father, meanwhile, contented himself with the title of patrician, and essayed to strengthen himself by an alliance with Genseric. But in less than a year his triumph came to an end. When his mercenaries called upon him to reward their services with a third of the land, they found him unwilling, or, more probably, unable to satisfy their expectations, they abandoned his standard for that of another soldier of fortune, Odoacer.

As to the parentage and early life of Odoacer great ambiguity prevails. But we have the authority of Theophanes that he was brought up in Italy, and that of Procopius, for his having served in the imperial body-guard,—statements which appear to be confirmed by the tact which he subsequently displayed in his dealings with Pope Simplicius and the Senate, and which argued considerable acquaintance with Roman institutions.

By Jornandes he is said to have been the leader of Teutonic combatants of various races from Pannonia, but the object of his march and the cause of his hostility to Orestes are unexplained. Muratori is of opinion that he was invited and retained by the friends and supporters of Nepos. To Nepos, after his early success and victory over the nominee of Ricimer's party, the Romans of Italy might naturally look with hope for the commencement of a more peaceful and happier future. By the treason of Orestes that hope was extinguished; and the prospect of having Augustulus for their emperor and the traitor Orestes for their actual ruler, must needs have been odious. Odoacer came too late to benefit the fallen and fugitive Emperor, but in time to relieve the Romans of Italy from their greater anxiety, by the defeat and punishment of Orestes.

Before the Romans are accused of tame submission to Odoacer, the actual condition of affairs should be considered. Barbarian leaders, with interests of their own to consider, had long possessed the supreme direction of the imperial forces[1]. Ricimer had crushed every attempt to reform and re-invigorate the government. The ports and estuaries, once the receptacles of a world-wide commerce, had become inlets for the Vandal pirates who, under the protection of Genseric, had reduced the inhabitants to beggary, and sold their children for slaves. The population of the country had so dwindled that many even of the most fertile districts were destitute of cultivators. The last chance that remained to the Roman authorities of averting the continuance of these, or the approach of still greater calamities, depended on the possibility of engaging some protector, of sufficient power, whose interests were not at variance with their

[1] Magistri utriusque militiae.

own, and on whose fidelity to his engagements they could rely.

Of what passed before the peaceful admission of Odoacer into Rome there is no record. The supposition that the gates were thrown open to him without previous compact would seem alike inconsistent with the character of Pope Simplicius, a pontiff of Roman birth and of resolute disposition, or with the abstention, constantly observed by Odoacer, from all interference with the civil government.

The Emperor Zeno, after his deposition and banishment, had recently regained the Eastern throne; but neither the stability of his power nor the tenour of his policy were such as to inspire confidence. His career from first to last had been marked by cowardly compliance and cruelty; and from him it was in vain to look for advice or succour. A.D. 477.

The surrender of a third of the depopulated land to be held by foreigners on the tenure of military service, indicates a very low stage of national degradation; but Odoacer might have insisted on still harder conditions, and his followers would not have been satisfied with less. The crisis, moreover, was one that admitted of no delay. Troops of barbarian invaders, encouraged by the success of Odoacer, were spreading themselves over the country, and it was only by consenting to his demands and by investing him with some title that implied legitimate authority, that the work of devastation could be arrested. An embassy was sent to Constantinople, ostensibly for the purpose of congratulating Zeno on his restoration. But the envoys were charged with the more important commission of announcing to him that the West Romans no longer desired an emperor of their own, that they deemed the majesty of one Augustus a sufficient safeguard, that in Odoacer they had acquired a protector distinguished alike for valour in arms and by political discretion, to whom they prayed the Emperor to confide the defence of Italy, with the title of patrician.

Such was the diplomatic form of words under which the Roman authorities concealed their contempt for Zeno.

The reply of Zeno was guarded and seemed to betray a consciousness of weakness. He admitted the meritorious conduct of 'the barbarian' in his dealings with the Romans, and recommended that he should receive from Nepos the desired dignity. Yet he himself soon afterward indited a letter, inscribed 'To the Patrician Odoacer.'

The course adopted by the Romans, with a view to obtain a breathing time for their ruined country, appears to have been politic. Zeno was soothed and flattered with the title of sole emperor, and the position of Odoacer being that of a subject, the prescriptive right of the 'Sancta Respublica' to supreme dominion was preserved. The regalia of the West were then sent to Constantinople : after an inglorious existence of eighty years, the dual empire,

established by Theodosius the Great, came to an A.D. 477.
end; and the decade of centuries, denominated the
Middle Ages, began[1].

[1] From the establishment of Odoacer to the taking of Constantinople by Mahomet II. Sismondi, Introduction to his History of the Italian Republics.

CHAPTER V.

A.D. 476–534.

Odoacer patrician and protector, but never king of Italy. His Italian minister, Cassiodorus, obtains from Genseric a cessation of piratical descents. The Ostrogoths under their king, Theodoric, with their families and moveables, make good their exodus in winter. After a war of four years they take Ravenna, and accomplish the destruction of Odoacer. The great Romanized Ostrogoth becomes king of Italy. His family alliances. Requires for himself and the Arian Ostrogoths nothing more than toleration. His visit to Rome and zeal for the preservation of the historical monuments. Cassiodorus, his secretary and friend, is *Princeps Senatus.* Revival of Italian prosperity. Fame of Theodoric as an impartial arbiter, a lover of peace and protector of the weak against the tyranny of the strong. The circumstances which, after he had attained his seventieth year, led to a complete change in his conduct. His illness, last injunctions to his daughter Amalasunta, whom he appoints regent, and death. Affairs of the East. Belisarius subdues the Nika insurrection and reconquers Africa. Murder of Amalasunta.

A.D. 476. ODOACER, having been elected by his own countrymen and by their companions in arms for their king, has not unfrequently, but incorrectly been called the first barbarian king of Italy, a title to which he never laid claim. With the rank of patrician and the powers of a military protector entrusted with the conclusion of treaties, he established himself at Ravenna; but never presumed to enact laws, to coin money, or to interfere with the civil administration. The collection and expenditure of the public revenue remained, as of old, under the direction of the pretorian prefect. The civil constitution underwent no change; Odoacer, though an Arian, appears to have regarded the see of Rome with veneration, and no record exists of any act or claim of his that caused disquietude to the able and vigilant Pontiff, Simplicius[1].

During the term of Odoacer's power, the country enjoyed a grateful interval of peace, and other advantages, which could not have been secured had he not placed his confidence in advisers who knew the wants of their country and were devoted to its service. Of these the most able and best known was Cassiodorus, who belonged to a family that had held important offices, and possessed considerable influence in Calabria. Relief from the long-standing misery of piratical descents was a first necessity, and Cassiodorus became the negotiator of a treaty which secured that boon. Genseric bound himself to desist from hostilities, and showed his respect for Odoacer's power by giving up to him, in consideration of an annual subsidy, the whole or nearly the whole of the Vandal possessions in Sicily. The advantage thus gained was permanent, for with the death of A.D. 477.

---

[1] Ennodius.

Genseric, which took place the following year, the decadency of the Vandalic nation commenced. By Hunneric, his son and successor, it was accelerated. Hunneric was no sea-king, and in his preference for a life of luxury and self-indulgence, the nobles followed his example.

Nepos, when driven from Italy, applied in vain to Zeno for aid, and continued for upwards of four years to reside in a palace near Salona, retaining Dalmatia, until slain by two of his own
A.D. 480. nobles; when Odoacer, who had always treated the ex-emperor with respect, punished his as-
A.D. 481. sassins and annexed the Dalmatian provinces to his government.

During the reign of **Leo I**, Theodoric, a scion of the great Gothic family of Amali, was gaining knowledge of the world, and of medieval politics, while detained at his court as a hostage. When elected to succeed his father as king of the Ostrogoths he became engaged for a while in hostilities against the empire, until the honours and advantages proffered to him and to his people by the Emperor Zeno, who found him too strong to be coerced, induced him to desist. After this he continued to rise in favour until Zeno conferred upon him an honorary sonship, placed his equestrian statue in front of his own palace, and conferred upon him the consular dignity. For an interval Theodoric served as a prop to Zeno's tottering throne, but his people became weary of inaction and desired a less dependent position, while at Constantinople their numbers, and the nearness of their location, was a cause of alarm.

When the Rugi, from Upper Danube, made a predatory irruption into Italy, Odoacer drove them back, and took their king, a relation of Theodoric, prisoner, and put him to death. It was under these circumstances that Theodoric asked and obtained the consent of Zeno to an enterprise, which had for its objects the destruction of a family foe, the expulsion of his people from their Italian settlements, and the substitution of the Ostrogoths.

It was late in the autumn when the Ostrogoths, A.D. 488. with their wives, their children, and their parents, with supplies of corn, with hand-mills and such moveables as they possessed, began their exodus from their Eastern settlements. The approach of winter did not deter them, and its rigours facilitated the passage of their waggons over the frozen plains.

In February 489, when they had accomplished a march of nearly 700 miles, and when provisions were beginning to fail, they reached the river Ulca[1], of which the Gepidae disputed their passage, but only to encounter a defeat. Odoacer, meanwhile, concentrated his forces in a fortified position on the Sontius (Isonzo), and, when driven from his entrenchments, fell back on the Adige ; but a second overthrow compelled him to relinquish the defence of Verona. While on his retreat to Rome, he

[1] Historia Miscella.

ascertained that the gates would be closed against him; the northern cities having already espoused

A.D. 489. the cause which had the imperial sanction, the Pontiff Felix III, and the Senate came to a like decision.

At this critical time, a considerable number of the Ostrogothic warriors perished in an ambuscade, and the prospects of Odoacer seemed to brighten. Theodoric, with his diminished strength, found it necessary to remain for some months on the defensive at Pavia, until the arrival of reinforcements sent from Toulouse by Alaric II, king of the Visigoths, restored his superiority and enabled him to gain a decisive victory. Odoacer, with the remainder of his army, took refuge in marsh-girt Ravenna, where by vigorous sallies he kept the enemy at bay until, after a siege of more than two years, famine compelled him to surrender.

A.D. 493. The anonymous chronicler of de Valois states that his life was guaranteed; a promise, it would seem, only made to be broken; for at a banquet to which he and his nobles were invited they were all perfidiously slain. The anonymous writer referred to agrees with Cassiodorus and Procopius in attributing this massacre to the discovery of a traitorous plot; but Muratori rejects such a plea as improbable and only put forward with a view to palliate the crime of Theodoric. It seems probable that the vengeful spirit displayed in these atrocities may have been inspired or exasperated by the reigning king of the Rugi, who had joined the Ostrogoths for the express purpose of assisting in the destruction of his hereditary enemy.

During the sixteen years of Odoacer's patriciate, the only war from which Italy suffered was that into which he was driven by the instinct of self-preservation. Even by the admission of his enemies, his leading characteristic was benevolence, 'Homo bonae voluntatis [1],' and he has left a name unstained, with the exception of his treatment of the Rugian king, by any recorded act of cruelty.

Theodoric, when established at Ravenna, did not omit to strengthen his position by family alliances with other barbarian rulers. On Hunneric, king of the Vandals, he bestowed his sister. On Alaric II, king of the Visigoths, one of his daughters, and on the king of Burgundy's son, another, while for his own consort he had a sister of Clovis. While the conflict with Odoacer was still undecided Zeno died, and during the long reign of his weak and unwarlike successor, Anastasius, Theodoric was left free to accomplish, without any serious interference, the objects of his ambition.

Reign of Theodoric the Great. A.D. 493-525.

Of the new kingdoms formed out of provinces once Roman, that of the Visigoths, was the earliest and the most extensive, including as it did, since the conquests of Euric, their seventh king, southern and central Gaul, from the Loire to the Pyrenees, and the whole of Spain, with the exception of Gallicia. But Alaric II, the son and successor of Euric, did

---

[1] Anon., Valesianus.

not inherit the abilities, still less the courage of his father.

Of the Teutonic races the Franks had long been the most numerous. But until united under Clovis, the founder of their monarchy (A.D. 481), their tribes had not been amalgamated; and though frequently engaged as auxiliaries on the side of the Romans, in the great conflict at Chalons they were divided, and a part fought under Attila. In 486, Clovis, encouraged by the distracted state of the empire, invaded northern Gaul and defeated Siagrius, the last Roman governor. Siagrius, like his father Egidius, had maintained an independent position at Soissons, and having refused to recognise Odoacer was looked up to by the colonists as their king. When unable to make head any longer against the forces brought against him by Clovis, he threw himself on the protection of Alaric II; and Alaric, yielding to the threats of Clovis, gave him up to be slain. Such was the miserable termination of the Roman dominion in Gaul.

The heathen Clovis, having married a Catholic princess, Clotilda of Burgundy, declared himself a convert to his wife's religion, and the majority of his countrymen followed their king's example. Thus the Franks, in the commencement of their career as a united nation, obtained the sympathy and support of the Pope and of the Catholic clergy, an advantage which, as years went on, was found to be of great and constantly increasing importance.

The Emperor Anastasius, regarding with mingled

feelings of discontent and fear the independent powers acquired by the great Ostrogoth, did not refuse to recognise him as king of Italy,—a recognition which by no means implied any surrender or abatement of the imperial supremacy, which in fact was undisputed; for the barbarian rulers, however great their power, aspired to no higher honour than that of being acknowledged members of the 'Sancta Respublica Romana'; and as such they were pleased to have conferred upon them the honorary dignities of patrician and consul, which were valued as a confirmation of their right, no less than as a personal distinction [1]. That they acknowledged the seignory-in-chief of the Emperor is evident from the fact that their coins bore the imperial effigy in conjunction with their own; and the rooted impression, which had existed since the time of Constantine, that the authority of all Christian rulers was derived from the head of the Roman empire, still prevailed [2].

When the Alemans sought in Italy an asylum from the persecutions of Clovis, Theodoric encouraged an immigration which in some degree supplied the scarcity of cultivators; and is said to have sent to the court of his brother-in-law an accomplished minstrel, in the hope of mitigating his ferocity, and that of his nobles, by the humanizing influence of poetry and music.

In his relations with the see of Rome, Theodoric,

[1] Gregory of Tours, Historia Francorum, L. ii. c. 38.
[2] Procopius, de bello Gothico, iii. c. 33. Muratori, Au. 508.

for himself and for his Arian people, asked for nothing more than toleration. From whatever might give offence to the Catholic clergy he carefully abstained; and, such was the confidence reposed in him that, on the occasion of a disputed papal election, he was asked to be arbitrator, and his decision in favour of Pope Symmachus was accepted as final.

A.D. 499.

A.D. 500. When for the first time he visited Rome, the Pope, the Senate, and the people went out in procession to meet him; and after he had shown his respect for the established faith by kneeling at the shrine of St. Peter, he pledged himself by a public declaration to respect the laws and institutions of the Roman Republic, as a citizen of which he possessed in fact a distinction of the first order, since fourteen years previously he had worn the palm-embroidered toga, as consul for the East.

During a stay of six weeks in Rome, he showed his appreciation of her historical monuments, by procuring the appointment of a professed architect as their curator, and by the assignment of funds for their maintenance[1]. For much of the tact and intelligence shown in his transactions with the Romans, Theodoric would seem to have been indebted to Aurelius Cassiodorus, a member of the same family that had already done much to promote the prosperity of his countrymen. The established reputation of Cassiodorus led to his

[1] Cassiodorus, Var. i. 21-25.

appointment as the secretary to the great Romanized Ostrogoth, of whom he became the trusted friend and confidential adviser. To Cassiodorus was accorded by universal consent the title of 'princeps Senatûs,' and in A.D. 514 he served as sole consul.

So secure was the basis of Theodoric's government, and so constant the progressive increase of his power, that he might, had his ambition been less under the control of his judgment, have been tempted to assume complete independence; but that was a course which would only have impaired his power, inasmuch as the Romans of Italy had become accustomed to regard the Emperor enthroned at Constantinople as their only legitimate suzerain.

Yet the pains that he took to allay the jealousy A.D. 505 of the imperial court were not always successful; and (A.D. 505) a collision, which he could neither have intended nor foreseen, took place in Illyria between a Gothic force and a body of imperial troops, in which the latter were routed. In order to revenge himself, Anastasius sent an armament to ravage the southern coast of Italy, and his ships returned to Constantinople, laden with spoils extorted, not from the Goths, but from unoffending Roman citizens. Yet Theodoric would not allow himself to be provoked, and on this, as on other occasions, his moderation presented a remarkable contrast to the restless ambition of his brother-in-law, Clovis.

Clovis, encouraged by the orthodox zeal of Queen Clotilda, and by the weakness of Alaric II, declared in an assembly of his nobles that it grieved him to see a nation of Arians in possession of the fairest provinces of Gaul[1]. Theodoric employed every art that friendship might suggest to prevent a conflict; but in vain. When hostilities became imminent, he warned both parties that the first aggressor would have him for an enemy, an announcement which only induced Clovis to commence operations before his brother-in-law had time to intervene.

A.D. 507. Alaric II, in accordance with his uncle's wish, remained on the defensive, until he beheld his territories reduced to a state of ruin, and until the Franks declared that they would undertake to lay aside their arms and drive the Visigoths before them with roasted apples. A conflict then took place on the plain of Vouillé, ten miles south of Poitiers, which resulted in the breaking up of the Visigothic power in France, and in the death of Alaric himself, whom A.D. 508. Clovis slew with his own hand. Toulouse, with nearly the whole of the Visigothic territory in Gaul, became subject to the Franks; but the Visigothic governor of Arles defended the bridge over the Rhone, and stayed their further progress until Theodoric sent an army to the rescue, and the Franks, in their turn, sustained an overthrow.

Alaric II left, by the daughter of Theodoric, an infant son, Amalaric; and he also left a natural

---

[1] Gregory of Tours.

son. The latter, having attained manhood, was preferred by the Visigoths to the infant heir. But Theodoric vindicated the right of his grandson to the whole of Provence, with Arles, the 'little Rome' of Ausonius, and the beautiful Roman city of Nismes. The Visigoths, who contrived to hold nearly the whole of Spain, then acknowledged Theodoric, not merely as regent during the infancy of his grandson, but as their elected sovereign; and, for the remainder of his life, the two great sections of the Gothic race were combined. The death of Clovis (A.D. 511) put an end to the anxieties caused by his restless greed for territorial acquisitions; and though he left a memory stained by acts of heinous cruelty, he has been honoured with the appellation of 'Eldest Son of the Church.' A.D. 511.

Under Theodoric, whose justice was acknowledged, and whose power was feared, nationalities that had suffered from continual warfare, discord and misrule, willingly placed themselves under a protector who thus summed up his own desires and the scope of his ambition : 'Leaving others to pride themselves in deeds of violence and spoliation, I desire that my government shall be conducted in such a manner that the people who submit to my rule may regret that they have not done so sooner[1].' When relieved by the death of his brother-in-law from a turbulent and unscrupulous neighbour, he employed a long and grateful interval of peace in removing the impedi-

---

[1] Cassiodorus, vol. iv.

ments to public prosperity. Having created a navy sufficient for the purposes of defence, he made Ravenna an emporium of commerce, renowned for the grandeur of its public buildings and sumptuous works of utility. At Verona and Pavia he built palaces, porticoes, and amphitheatres, of which the remains are extant. Under him the diminished and impoverished population enjoyed, during the third of a century, immunity from invasion. With true liberality of mind, he placed his confidence in the men who, in the time of Odoacer, had laboured successfully to mitigate calamities; and left the civil administration to be conducted by Romans. The cities retained their ancient municipal freedom, and their prosperity revived; the cultivators of the soil, no longer liable to spoliation, resumed their industry; and a cheapness of provisions, long unknown, diffused contentment.

A.D. 515. Theodoric, having no son, bestowed his only child, Amalasunta, on Eutaric, a kinsman of his own, and a scion of the royal house of Amali, whose death
A.D. 523. preceded his own. When, in conjunction with his nephews, the sons of Clovis, Theodoric succeeded in breaking up the Burgundian kingdom, he received for his share Avignon, Carpentras, and Geneva, his last territorial acquisitions. Yet Theodoric lived to justify the saying that no man can be pronounced happy on this side the grave. During the last two years of his life and the thirtieth of a singularly prosperous reign, his mind and whole disposition underwent a change; and, when subjected

to the test of a crucial provocation, the most considerate and tolerant of rulers became a **tyrant** and a persecutor.

The ignorant and decrepit Emperor, Justin, published a decree which debarred Arians from holding any office, and deprived them of their churches. A reservation was made in favour of Goths in the imperial service; but the saving clause did not extend to those who were settled in Italy. In the hope of preventing an outbreak of animosities, Theodoric despatched an embassy, of which he compelled Pope John I. to be the head, to demand from Justin a reversal, or at least a mitigation, of his decree. Nothing could be more flattering than the reception accorded to the first Roman Pontiff who had visited Constantinople; and he returned laden with gifts for the Catholic churches; but having failed to bring any concession to the Arians, he was thrown into prison, where after a short confinement he died. The people cried, Sacrilege! and Theodoric, urged by the fears of his Arian courtiers, deprived them of their arms. **It must** not, however, be supposed that apprehensions of a revolt were altogether groundless; **for the Goths had never ceased to be regarded as** barbarians, aliens **in blood, and** heretics in religion, **of whom** it would be well to be relieved. A.D. 524. A.D. 525.

While under the beneficent sway of Theodoric, and the wise administration of Cassiodorus, prosperity had increased, along with that prosperity longings for independence had also increased. The permanent establishment of a Gothic dynasty at Ravenna, and of Goths as lords of the Italian soil, had never ceased to be contemplated with horror, and hopes of an approaching deliverance were entertained. But though Theodoric had attained his seventieth year, and had no son, he regarded Italy, and the whole of his dominions, as the rightful inheritance of his daughter's descendants, and of their children's children; by him the existing discontents were accounted treasonable, and, on the charge of being engaged in secret plottings, a sentence of death and confiscation was pronounced against the ex-consul, Boethius. Combined with the advantage of ancestral wealth and honours, Boethius was possessed of great abilities and considerable literary attainments; and, while confined in the tower of Pavia, he beguiled an interval of suspense which preceded his cruel execution, by the composition of his celebrated treatise, 'De consolatione Philosophiae,' which King Alfred translated into Anglo-Saxon. Symmachus, the friend and father-in-law of Boethius, and, like him, universally esteemed, gave vent to his grief and indignation in words that were judged treasonable; he was dragged in chains to Ravenna and put to death in prison.

A.D. 526. During the autumn of 526, Theodoric, while engaged in drawing up an edict for the prosecution of the Catholics, was attacked by the first symptom of a fatal illness. When at table with some of his friends, he was observed to shudder at a fancied resemblance between the head and eyes of an enormous fish and those of his strangled victim, Symmachus. Before his death, he exhibited deep contrition for the crimes into which his passions, worked up by selfish counsellors, had betrayed him; and, having commended his daughter, Amalasunta, and his grandson, Atalaric, then in his tenth year, to the protection of the Gothic magnates, he conjured them, with his latest breath, to love the Roman Senate and people, to give no provocation to the Emperor, and to cultivate his goodwill[1].

The kingdom of Theodoric embraced the whole of Italy, Dalmatia, Sicily, Sardinia, Corsica, the Mediterranean provinces of France, the Visigothic kingdom of Spain (which he held during the last fifteen years of his life), the greater part, if not the whole, of modern Hungary, the cities of Augsburg, Ulm, Constance and the Tyrol, with the district of Trent. Under him Italy had become once more the centre of a vast empire. Procopius, though hostile to the Goths, concludes his eulogy on their king in these terms: 'In name Theodoric was a king, in reality a true emperor, and not inferior to any who, in that high station, from the commencement of the Roman empire itself, attained distinction[2].'

On the death of Theodoric, the union of the two

---

[1] Jornandes, de rebus Geticis, Rerum Ital. Scriptores, i. p. 221

[2] 'Verbo tyrannus fuit Theodoricus, re-ipsa verus Imperator, coram nemini postponendus, qui ab ortu Imperii in illo honoris gradu excelluerunt.' Procopius, de bello Gothico, L. i. c. 1. Latin translation.

main sections of the Gothic race, which rendered it so formidable, came to an end, and the Visigothic kingdom, embracing nearly the whole of Spain, reverted to the heir for whom it had been held in trust. But this was not the only cause of weakness; for when Amalasunta, the widowed daughter of Theodoric and regent of the kingdom, desired to educate her son Atalaric and to bring him up in the habits of Roman civilisation, she encountered a formidable opposition; and the Gothic magnates, by whom those habits were despised, faltered in their allegiance to a female regent. Their Arianism combined with anti-Roman tastes to forbid the hope of any permanent amalgamation between Goths and Italians.

Cassiodorus, when the great intellect of Theodoric became obscured by resentment and enfeebled by age, withdrew from a court where his counsels had lost their efficacy; and the lamentable events that ensued justified the prudence of his retreat. For a while he occupied himself with experimental philosophy, with the collection of manuscripts, and with historical studies; but when Amalasunta, as regent, required his assistance it was not withheld. Under his direction the last injunctions of Theodoric were carried out; the supremacy of the Emperor was recognised; and to the sons of Symmachus and Boethius their confiscated estates were restored.

A.D. 527.   The ignorant and intolerant Justin only survived Theodoric for a year and was succeeded by his nephew Justinian, who as his coadjutor had become conversant with public affairs, and who is described by his contemporaries as a man of abstemious habits and a diligent administrator. As such he could not fail to be aware of the confusion which still prevailed in the laws of the Empire; and when, in the second year of his reign, he undertook the responsibility of a reform, the same intuition that in after years led him to choose Belisarius and Narses for his generals, enabled him to select the learned jurisconsult, Tribonian, to be head of the commission entrusted to draw up his Pandects. A.D. 528.

Justinian at the time of his accession had attained his forty-third year, yet his recent choice of a consort betokened an excess of youthful folly. He nevertheless succeeded in obtaining his uncle's consent to his marriage with the celebrated Theodora—a woman of low extraction and depraved habits— though endowed by nature with intelligence, beauty and courage.

Between Justinian and the Ostrogothic government amicable communications were kept up, and Amalasunta in all her difficulties looked to Constantinople for support. Her Romanizing tendencies may be accounted for by the circumstance that from her youth she had been liable to the influence of her father's Roman friend and trusted counsellor, Cassiodorus. But her position was one of constantly increasing difficulty. In the eyes of the Gothic nobles her desire that her son should be an educated man was a crime, and the mere fact that she was a woman unfitted her for rule. Amalasunta herself could converse with equal facility in Greek and Latin; but the defenders of her son's throne preferred that their sovereign when he received ambassadors should require an interpreter.

A.D. 531.

A.D. 527.

We are told that Atalaric when ten years of age committed some fault, for which his mother boxed his ears, and that he ran off crying; that the Gothic nobles became indignant that their king should be so treated, and that they sought an interview with Amalasunta, in which they complained of the way in which Atalaric was brought up, and of the attempts that were being made to give him literary instruction. In support of their argument that for a prince learning was not required, they instanced his grandfather Theodoric, who though unlettered had been the successful ruler of an extensive empire, and ended by declaring their conviction that a boy who had been taught to fear the schoolmaster's rod, would fail to be an intrepid leader of men. Amalasunta, being unable to withstand the determination of her feudatories, surrendered into their hands the management of her son, and then, writes Muratori, began the ruin of Atalaric[1].

For a short interval peace was maintained, but in A.D. 531 the Gothic magnates conspired to depose the regent and take the government into their own hands. Amalasunta, hoping to break up the combination, relegated the three leading conspirators to remote stations, on the pretence that their services

[1] Di qui venne la rovina di Atalarico.

were required for the protection of the frontier. But when they **continued**, by their **letters**, to foment disaffection, she resolved to try the effect of a *coup d'état*, and gave orders that their lives should be A.D. 531. taken, having first ascertained that in **case** of necessity she would find an asylum at Constantinople. For a while intimidation prevailed, and Amalasunta was **able to retain the** regency, but the outraged malcontents only awaited their opportunity.

Meanwhile the Emperor Justinian, having made peace with Persia, commenced his efforts for the redintegration of the empire, by the re-conquest of Africa from the Vandals.

In 530 Ilderic, **king of Vandal Africa, whose** relations with the empire had been amicable, **was** dethroned and imprisoned by his relation and next heir, Gelimer. When Justinian asked for explanations, the usurper only replied to his remonstrances **by** increasing the rigour of Ilderic's confinement, and by putting out the eyes of his nephew. Justinian then demanded that the imprisoned king and his blinded relation should be suffered **to** live out the rest of their days at Constantinople, and when he threatened war as **the** alternative received an insulting defiance. Justinian, though impatient to execute his threat, found his most trusted advisers averse to an undertaking that involved the risks and A.D. 532. sacrifices of a **distant war.** Nevertheless being encouraged by the bishops with assurances of divine favour, he had already commenced preparations when his throne and **even his life were** imperilled by one of those outbreaks of popular violence—which at Constantinople constituted the only check to absolute government.

By a custom of old standing, the races of the hippodrome afforded to the malcontents an opportunity of meeting, and of backing their arguments by physical force. The blues and the greens alike were sure to be reinforced by crowds of sympathizers or idlers from the neighbouring district, who, like themselves, were prepared with concealed daggers to shed the blood of their opponents, or, if the opportunity offered, to declare the deposition of the reigning Emperor and to proclaim a successor.

Justinian, though he had formerly belonged to the blues, had of late become anxious to support the judges in an impartial administration of the law, and had thus incurred the dislike of both parties. The greens renounced their allegiance and compelled the patrician Hypatius, a nephew of the Emperor Anastasius, to accept against his will their offer of sovereignty. The insurrection soon became irresistible, and it was in vain that Justinian offered to dismiss his unpopular ministers and to admit his own fallibility. The attempts of his guards to limit the fury of the insurgents only increased their madness. With Nika for their watchword, there was no excess of destruction in rapine from which they refrained. Convicted prisoners were set at liberty, private houses pillaged, public buildings and even hospitals were set on fire. The noble cathedral built by Constantine was reduced to ashes, and for five days the condition of Constantinople was that of a city taken by storm.

Justinian, regarding the recovery of his power as hopeless, was preparing to embark when the firmness of Theodora saved him from the ruin of an ignominious flight. Belisarius, a Thracian by birth, who in the recent war with Persia had won distinction as an able though not always a successful leader, and who had under his command three thousand disciplined troops which the hesitation of Hypatius had given him time to assemble. He received orders to act, and having chosen his opportunity when the arena was densely crowded sent his lieutenant, Mundus, to secure one of the two gates while he forced his own way in by the other. There was no escape, and thirty-five thousand persons are said to have fallen, of whom the greater part were crushed or trampled to death in the panic.

Notwithstanding the desolation and misery caused by the Nika insurrection, Justinian persevered in his resolution to attempt the re-conquest of Africa; for which before the autumn of the following year he was A.D. 533. able to place ten thousand infantry and five thousand cavalry under the command of Belisarius. On this, as on most of his subsequent expeditions, Belisarius was accompanied by his wife, Antonina, a widow with two grown up children, to whom he had been recently married. Antonina, like her friend and patroness, the empress, had been nurtured in an atmosphere of vice. Yet the abilities of these congenial spirits enabled them to make their influence felt in matters of public concern.

The fleet being assembled in the Bosphorus, Belisarius, with the historian Procopius for his secretary, and Archelaus who had served as pretorian prefect for paymaster, embarked in the presence of the Emperor, and of the Patriarch who invoked a blessing on the enterprise. The forces, being detained by calms and contrary winds, endured great privations, until they reached Sicily, where the representative of Amalasunta gave every facility for re-victualling of the galleys and for the purchase of horses. By this time the soldiers were longing to quit the ships on which they had embarked with reluctance, and where they felt that in case of an attack no valour on their part could be of much avail. Belisarius, when they approached the African coast, rejected the timid counsels of the patrician, Archelaus, and having assembled a council of his officers, listened with patience to their opinions, but over-ruled objections, and ordered an immediate landing. Without more delay than was necessary, he then commenced his march in the direction of Carthage. Forbidding and punishing all approach to pillage, he omitted no precaution that might tend to conciliate the inhabitants and to gain their confidence; while amongst the men of a higher grade he circulated a proclamation wherein Justinian disavowed all hostility to the Vandals, pointing to the usurper of Genseric's throne and the remorseless persecutor of Genseric's descendants as the sole object of his enmity.

The Vandals after their conquest of Africa, with a view to secure the permanent submission of the colonists, dismantled their towns,—a circumstance that greatly favoured the rapid advance of Belisarius, to whom delay might have been fatal. His entry into the city of Sullecte, one day's march from his landing-place, being unopposed, he obtained there refreshment for his troops, and an additional supply of horses; and from thence he pursued his way along the coast, his right being protected by the sea, and the fleet having orders to keep pace with the army. Gelimer, when informed of his approach, ordered the imprisoned king and all who shared his captivity to be executed. Though the prompt decision of Belisarius had taken him by surprise, he assembled forces sufficient in point of numbers to have surrounded and crushed the invaders. A recital of the complicated arrangements whereby he vainly hoped to accomplish such a result would be tedious to the reader. Suffice it then to say that the battle which took place at Decimus, ten miles from the capital[1], was preceded by various skirmishes, in one of which Ammatus, the brother of Gelimer, was slain. The principal conflict ended in an entire rout of the Vandals, who, together with their king, fled in the direction of Numidia. The victors slept on the battle-field, and on the morrow Belisarius, when he reached the capital, found that the in-

[1] Procopius, de bello Vandalico.

habitants, relieved from all further anxiety, had opened their gates, that they had removed the chain from the mouth of the harbour, and that a propitious east wind had enabled the Roman fleet to enter. Yet he deemed it better to encamp outside the walls until the following morning, when at day-break he marshalled the whole of his surviving and unscathed combatants, and summoned those who had been left on board ship to rejoin their comrades, when horse and foot, in gallant array and adorned with emblems of victory, defiled through the streets of liberated Carthage. The descendants of the men who first colonized the great pro-consulate, though for nearly a century compelled to bear the yoke of Vandal and Arian masters, were still in heart and mind Romans and Catholics; perfect order was maintained: there was much rejoicing, but no tumult; the citizens were able to follow without interruption their accustomed occupations; the panic-stricken Vandals, who had taken refuge in the churches, were re-assured; and Belisarius gave a banquet to his officers in Gelimer's palace.

Although the Vandals, when they destroyed the fortifications of the African towns, excepted those of Carthage, they had allowed them to fall into a state of ruin; and Belisarius was no sooner in possession than he engaged a number of well-paid workmen to repair the mouldering walls and to deepen the ditches; being determined not to quit the city until its defences were restored.

Gelimer meanwhile was preparing to renew the

conflict; and collected an army composed partly of Moors and partly of raw levies from the rural population. Belisarius, after a sojourn of three months at Carthage, having provided for its security against secret conspiracy no less than against open attack, went forth to meet the enemy, and, when about twenty miles from the city, ascertained that the Vandals were encamped in his front at Tricameron. During the night no movement took place, but the following day, while the Romans were cooking their dinner, Gelimer's whole army was seen to approach. Belisarius at once directed an attack on its centre, and when he had overcome a brief and ill-sustained resistance, entered the Vandal encampment. In the centre of that vast area, Gelimer, with a view to secure the fidelity of his nobles, and to give them a motive for courageous efforts, had commanded their wives, their families and their moveable wealth, to be placed. Yet Gelimer himself, without uttering a word, fled; and when his departure became known, any further hope of a prolonged conflict, or even of an orderly retreat, came to an end. When the victors entered the camp, all that they saw or heard was the hasty and confused flight of those who ought to have been its defenders, the shriek of mothers, and the wailing of children. The stores of money and valuables exposed to the grasp of the victors were such, says Procopius, as had never before been collected in one locality; and before a temptation like this all efforts to maintain discipline or enforce forbearance failed; so that, as night advanced, darkness concealed, but did not terminate, unbridled license and rapine.

To Belisarius that night was one of ceaseless anxiety; if only a tenth part of the Vandal army had been rallied, and led by some competent officer against the pillagers, who, intent only on spoil, were widely disseminated, a serious reverse must have been the result. In the early dawn he betook himself to the needful task of restoring order, and to the painful one of reproving, with impartial severity, the misconduct of the officers and men. Though the return of Belisarius to Carthage was eagerly looked for, the accidental death of his gallant leader of cavalry required him to follow up his victory in person. On arriving at Hippo Regius, he found that the fugitive king had betaken himself to the mountain fortress of Pappua, where, with the Moors at his devotion, he might hold out for an indefinite time. He therefore left the task of reducing the Mauritanian strong-hold to an officer in whose ability he could confide; and who ultimately succeeded in making the fugitive king his prisoner.

Belisarius after his return to Carthage obtained the surrender by the Vandal governors, of Sardinia, Corsica, the Balearic Islands and Mauritanian Cesarea, at that time a flourishing centre of commerce. The dreaded power of the Vandals was permanently abated. Dominions most essential to its safety and prosperity were restored to the Roman empire, and prophecies that the African expedition would be a failure were belied.

Only eight months had elapsed since **Belisarius** A.D. 531. was called upon to stay the progress of destruction and to quell the ruinous excesses of party madness at Constantinople, and resentments were still fresh. A conspiracy, got up at Algiers for the accomplishment of his ruin, found numerous partisans even amongst his own officers. Of Roman governors who had sought, and for a time maintained an independent position in Africa, instances were by no means rare. The imputation of such a design to Belisarius was easily made and the charge was one which, however ungrounded, it was difficult for him to disprove. When the accusation was reduced to writing and submitted to Justinian, he kept it to himself, either 'because he regarded it with contempt, or because he deemed it politic[1].' But he sent Saloman, a general in whom he had confidence, to inform Belisarius that he might either return with Gelimer and his suite as his prisoners, or remain at his post and send them to Constantinople.

Belisarius, when this option was offered, had been for some time aware of the plot. The conspirators, to guard against the risks of a sea-voyage, had allotted to distinct messengers and ships full particulars of the charges to be laid before the Emperor. Of the messengers, one accomplished his mission; the other, having fallen under suspicion, was stopped at the outport and gave up the document. Belisarius, after he had read it, at once commenced preparations for his voyage; and, on the arrival of

[1] Procopius, de bello Vandalico.

Saloman, handed over to him the government of Africa, together with the task of bringing the Moors into subjection.

When, with king Gelimer and the rest of the Vandal captives, and with the spoils of the Vandal kingdom, he landed at Constantinople, envious tongues were silenced, false accusations abandoned; and, the obsolete custom of rewarding brilliant services with a triumph, was revived, though in a form somewhat different. Instead of being borne on a car, he walked from his own residence to the Circus, where the imperial throne was erected; on his way he was surrounded by recovered trophies carried off from Rome by Genseric; and amongst them were the golden candlestick and table from Jerusalem that had graced the triumph of Titus. Gelimer in his kingly robe, and accompanied by Vandal nobles, followed. Gelimer as he went, repeated once and again the words of King Solomon, 'Vanity of vanities, all is vanity.' On approaching the throne, he was stripped of his royal trappings and compelled to prostrate himself before the Emperor, a ceremonial in which Belisarius himself acted a similar part. Justinian and Theodora then made provision for the progeny and kinsfolk of Ilderic, while to Gelimer and his dependents they allotted estates in Galatia. To complete the honours accorded to Belisarius, he was named sole consul for the ensuing year (A.D. 535). Though not absolutely the last, he was one of the last subjects on whom this honour was conferred.

While Belisarius was engaged in completing the

conquest of the Vandal dependencies, the aspect of affairs in Italy underwent a change. Atalaric still a minor, having set his mother and his mother's ministers at defiance, became the victim of dissolute habits, and by his death in the eighteenth year of his age the regency of Amalasunta came to an end. Theodatus, the son of one of Theodoric's sisters, being the nearest remaining representative of the Amali, might have looked for the preference of his countrymen. But though the possessor of great estates in Tuscany he had been convicted of wrongful violence, in attempts to appropriate the lands of others, and though described by Procopius as versed in Platonic philosophy, had made the acquisition of lucre the main object of his life.

Amalasunta's first idea when no longer regent was to leave Ravenna and obtain leave to reside at Constantinople, while the aim of Theodatus was to purchase at any cost the Emperor's support. But while negotiations for these objects were pending, the ministers and adherents of Amalasunta hit on an expedient whereby they vainly hoped to retain the power, which during the last eight years they had exercised with credit to themselves and advantage to the country. Theodatus was sent for to Ravenna, and encouraged to assume the title of king, but with a proviso that Amalasunta should continue to direct the administration of affairs. Having sworn to abide by this condition, Theodatus had no sooner obtained his proclamation, than he joined his cousin's enemies, and by his order, or with his consent, she was carried off to an islet of lake Bolsena, and strangled.

Theodatus retained the title of king for a year. But though a scion of the house of Amali, he possessed none of the qualities required in the head of a brave and high-minded people, and it was in vain that he sought to retain his position by offering Justinian to retain it as his vassal.

Justinian, when he undertook the re-conquest of Africa, acted in accordance with the advice and with encouragement from the clergy. The success that had attended their counsels strengthened their influence; it was again brought to bear, and the liberator of Africa from the Arian Vandals was commissioned to liberate Italy from the Arian Ostrogoths.

CHAPTER VI.

The first six years of the Gothic war: From the landing of Belisarius in Italy to his return to Constantinople bringing with him King Vitiges.

A.D. 535-541.

Motives and encouragements of Justinian. Belisarius, received as a liberator by the Sicilians, celebrates the termination of his consular year at Syracuse. The Ostrogoths choose Vitiges for their king. Belisarius crosses the Straits, overcomes the Gothic garrison at Naples. His joyful reception at Rome. Reparation of the defences and storing of provisions. Vitiges with his enormous army arrives. The various actions wherewith Belisarius while awaiting reinforcements keeps him at bay. Failure of provisions and despair of the famishing citizens. Conspiracy for a surrender. Deposition and cruel treatment of the Pope. The difficulty of obtaining reinforcements and of securing their introduction, together with supplies of food, are at length overcome. Belisarius sends forward Johannes with one thousand horse into the Picenum, and Johannes contrary to his orders takes possession of Rimini, a loss which decides Vitiges to raise the siege. Johannes when hard pressed at Rimini owes his relief to the remonstrances of Narses. Revolt of Milan from the Goths, and sanguinary recapture. Recall of Narses. Belisarius having cut off the supplies of the Ostrogoths has them in his power, when Justinian offers them acceptable terms of peace. Belisarius refuses to sign the treaty. His feigned acceptance of the Ostrogothic sovereignty. The arts by which he is enabled to carry off Vitiges as his prisoner and his reception at Constantinople.

THE re-conquest of Carthage and the plenary success of the Vandal war, revived the hopes of the Roman world. The Pope and the Catholic clergy of Italy began to entertain expectations of a

A.D. 535

deliverance from the Arian Ostrogoths, not less complete than that which had been obtained for their African brethren from the Arian Vandals. That their exhortations had weight cannot be doubted. Yet the wide scope of Justinian's ambition, as a law-giver, may seem to strengthen the supposition that his views for the redintegration of the Roman empire, were, from the first, no less comprehensive; and if so, his abstention from any attempt in Italy until he had first crushed the Vandals, would seem to have been in accordance with a judicious and far-sighted policy.

When the long and destructive conflict, called the Gothic war, commenced the Ostrogothic lords of the Italian soil were possessed of land forces numerically superior to any that could be brought against them, and capable of being recruited to an almost unlimited extent. Yet a variety of circumstances contributed to diminish the risks of the undertaking. Justinian, having transferred to the empire the naval resources which had been employed by Genseric with such terrible effect against it, had a fleet that enabled him to select and to vary his points of attack, as circumstances might require. The murder of Amalasunta furnished him with a plea for hostilities, the dastardly weakness of Theodatus an opportunity.

Soon after the declaration of war, the imperial forces expelled the Ostrogoths from Dalmatia, and obtained possession of Salona, its maritime capital. During the autumn Belisarius, accompanied as before by Antonina, left Constantinople with instructions to land in Sicily, alleging some temporary necessity, and holding out Carthage as his destination, but to feel his way and, if it could be done without serious risk or delay, to secure the submission of the whole island. The sanguine expectations with which these instructions would seem to have been dictated were not disappointed; for, although Sicily had for nearly a century been separated from the empire, the re-union presented no difficulties. The government of Theodoric had been one of invariable gentleness, and he had been at pains to conciliate a population on whose industry he was dependent for supplies of corn: yet the Sicilians, and especially those of the towns, had never ceased to regard their barbarian masters with aversion; and it was only at Palermo that the Gothic garrison offered a brief and ineffectual resistance.

When the year of his consulate expired, Belisarius, finding himself at Syracuse, went through the accustomed ceremonies of its resignation, and scattered his gold amongst the populace in the streets of that ancient city. Having possessed himself of the re- A.D. 536. sources of Sicily, he effected without hindrance his landing at Rhegium (Reggio), and the Calabrians, Apulians, and Beneventans, having no Goths to restrain them, joyfully proclaimed the Emperor; but the Gothic garrison of Naples held out with great determination, and, when the besiegers at length obtained an entrance, the unoffending citizens were subjected to all the horrors of a sack, a cruelty from the blame of which Procopius would fain exculpate Belisarius; yet Belisarius did not escape the reproachful censures of the newly-elected Pope, Silverius.

Theodatus, meanwhile, dismayed by the loss of Dalmatia and Sicily, delegated to Vitiges, a Gothic chieftain of high rank and good reputation, the defence of his kingdom, but at the same time sued for peace on the most humiliating conditions. The Goths, despising a ruler who shunned danger, elected Vitiges in his place.

Vitiges proceeded at once to Rome, and exhorted Pope Silverius and the Senate to trust the Goths, reminding them of the great advantages that Italy had enjoyed under Theodoric. He then compelled them to swear allegiance, and, having provided the city with a garrison, returned to Ravenna, taking with him several of the senators as hostages[1]. At Ravenna, he forced Matasunta, the young and beautiful daughter of Theodoric, to accept him for her husband, a marriage whereby he vainly hoped to strengthen his position.

The provinces acquired by Theodoric in Gaul being threatened by the Franks, a considerable part of the Gothic forces was engaged in their protection; and Vitiges, with a view to conciliate a dangerous enemy, gave them up,—a surrender for which he obtained no compensation, and one which, as the event proved, did not add to his security.

Belisarius, meanwhile, accomplished without fur-

[1] Procopius, L. ii.

ther hindrance his march to Rome, and entered the city by one gate, while the Gothic garrison, too weak to hold its ground against the popular feeling, withdrew through another. Justinian, when informed that Rome was already his, and that Vitiges **had** retreated to Ravenna, appears to have flattered himself that the reign of the Goths in Italy, like that of the Vandals in Africa, was doomed to a speedy **extinction.**

Belisarius omitted no precaution whereby time might be gained for the arrival of reinforcements which he knew to be essential; and in order to retard the advance of Vitiges, sent Bessas and Constantian, two of his ablest officers, to garrison and secure the fortified cities of Tuscany that lay in the line of the enemy's march.

Christmas was kept with more than the accustomed festivity; but ere long, the storage of corn from Sicily in the public granaries, and repairs of the defences, showed too clearly that a siege was expected. During the remainder of the three months that elapsed between his entry and the arrival of Vitiges, Belisarius, by strengthening the dilapidated walls, by deepening the ditches, and rebuilding the **turrets,** made the city tenable against an assault. The Romans, says Procopius, while they commended his energy, did not refrain from murmurs, being of opinion that the difficulty of obtaining food for the vast population of their city rendered it unfit for the prolonged endurance of a siege.

The Goths, in the meantime, responded to the call

of their king for a strenuous effort in defence of all that was most dear to them. Italy for more than a generation had been their adopted country, and the hearths around which all but the aged of them had been nurtured were at stake. So numerous were their combatants that Vitiges was able to detach forces for the re-conquest of Dalmatia, while with an enormous army he hastened to Rome, thinking to surround and exterminate the scanty forces of the invaders. The position of Belisarius, though apparently one of imminent danger, had not been taken up without consideration. He was no doubt correctly informed as to the ignorance and incapacity of the Gothic warriors in all matters connected with siege operations, and in the hastily repaired walls he possessed the advantages of a fortified camp where he might keep the enemy at bay and await reinforcements. When the approach of Vitiges was no longer doubtful, he recalled Bessas and Constantian, directing them to leave garrisons in the Tuscan places of strength. Bessas, having lingered in Narnia, became engaged with the enemy's van-guard; but, after a successful skirmish, he made good his way to Rome, bringing sure tidings that the Goths would shortly be there.

Feb., A.D. 537.

Vitiges, who according to Procopius only prayed that he might reach Rome before Belisarius had run away, left the Tuscan fortresses behind him, and on the 11th of March reached the Milvian bridge, which Belisarius had fortified with a tower and gates. The garrison of the tower, on beholding the

Gothic numbers, fled by night to Campania, and the following day the Goths crossed the river.

Belisarius, being taken unawares, was making a reconnaissance at the head of one thousand horse, when he found himself engaged in a hand-to-hand fight. He routed the Gothic cavalry; but when their infantry came up he was driven back with heavy loss —a result which confirmed the apprehensions of the citizens.

Vitiges, in order to increase their despondency, sent an embassy with the offer of an unmolested retreat. The chief envoy, having obtained permission to speak in the presence of the Senate, extolled the justice and generosity of the Gothic government, and claimed for his master as the successor of Theodoric a just title to the crown. Belisarius in a haughty reply denounced the Goths as usurpers, and declared that the day was not distant when Italy, having been restored to her ancient owners, the intruders would seek to hide their heads in bushes.

Of the memorable siege which then commenced it would be beyond the scope of this work to describe the vicissitudes and to give an account of the numerous actions[1]. By his personal heroism, by the almost uniform success of his skirmishes, and still more by the display of an intelligence immeasurably superior to that of his opponent, Belisarius kept up the drooping spirits of the citizens and raised the confidence of his soldiers to an unwonted pitch. Procopius, a

March, A.D. 537.

---

[1] According to Procopius there were no less than sixty-seven distinct engagements.

deeply-interested eye-witness, has handed down the details. For these, the glowing paraphrase of Gibbon, or the less ambitious rendering of Lord Mahon, may be referred to; but of the siege and of the ultimate failure of Vitiges the clearest understanding may perhaps be gained from the narrative of Procopius himself, either in the original Greek, the Latin version of Niebuhr's edition, or even in the quaint English translation made by Sir Henry Holcroft in the reign of Charles II.

The end of March arrived and reinforcements were still looked for in vain. On the 30th of that month, after an arduous and prolonged conflict, a general assault was repulsed, and imminent danger for the time averted. After this, Belisarius, in a manly appeal to the Emperor, recapitulated the various successes which his skill or fortune had enabled him to achieve. 'We must not,' he said, 'in the absence of reinforcements and supplies, trust any longer to fortune. If the Goths beat us, we shall lose Italy and our army also. The Romans are as yet well affected; but provisions are failing, and famine may force them to do what they would not. Nothing, be assured, will draw me out of this place alive. My life, which I owe to you, is in your hands; but think, sir, what sort of glory the death of Belisarius, under circumstances like these, would bring you!'

On the receipt of this letter, Justinian assembled troops and ordered their prompt embarkation. He was able, moreover, to inform his general that a body of Hunnish and Slavonian cavalry had been embarked for Italy during the winter solstice, but had been delayed by stress of weather.

Though the battle of the 30th March saved Rome from capture, increasing scarcity made it necessary that non-combatants should be constrained to leave the city. Vitiges could not fail to be aware of the straits to which it was reduced. With a view to push this advantage, he sent troops to take possession of the port, (Portus Romanus,) which at the distance of about twelve miles commanded the northern entrance to the Tiber, and guarded the only convenient access to the city by land, the opposite harbour of Ostia being in a state of ruin, and the road along the southern bank impracticable. The port of Rome, being well fortified, might have been held by a garrison of three hundred; but Belisarius had not a man to spare, and its loss made it necessary for any store ships that might be sent from Naples to deliver their cargoes at Antium, fifty miles from the city.   2 April, A.D. 537.   22 April.

When the summer solstice drew near, Euthalius, an officer who had been sent from Constantinople with an all-important supply of money, landed at Terracina. Belisarius, when informed of his approach, drew out the whole of his forces as if for battle, and effectually diverted the attention of the enemy while Euthalius with his escort entered the city.

For a time Belisarius, having received a small addition to his cavalry, was able to send out foraging

A.D. 537. parties, and to cut off those of the enemy; but these precarious supplies did little to meet the daily increasing want, or to avert its concomitant evils. The solstice had only commenced when sickness and misery generated despair, and a conspiracy was formed which had for its object the termination of a resistance which to the majority seemed hopeless. Of complicity in this treasonable design several men of senatorial rank, and Pope Silverius himself, were declared to be guilty. The senators, though condemned to banishment, were, after the abandonment of the siege, allowed to return[1]; but for the Pope, who in the discharge of his duty had incurred the ill-will of the Empress Theodora, a more cruel fate was in store[2]. Belisarius and Antonina were only too ready to execute Theodora's commands. Having deprived Silverius of his pontifical vestments and compelled him to wear the habit of a monk, they banished him to Greece, and procured by corrupt means the elevation of Vigilius, Theodora's nominee. The following year the unfortunate ex-Pontiff was sent back to Italy, but only to be transferred to an uninhabited island in the Tuscan sea, where he died of want.

Belisarius had still in his magazines such provisions as enabled him to supply his soldiers with half-rations, the deficiency being made up for in money; but it was evident that without some unlooked for change this miserable state of affairs must soon

---

[1] Procopius, de bello Gothico, 1–25.
[2] Baronius, Annal. Eccl. quoted by Muratori.

give place to a worse ; and a tumultuous assemblage of the starving inhabitants demanded immediate action, in which they declared the readiness of every Roman to take part. Belisarius, while he praised their resolution, deprecated untimely zeal, and was able to comfort them by assurances that the Emperor's fleets, with ample means, not for relief only, but for a complete victory over the barbarians, were already coasting the Campanian shore. He then despatched Procopius to Naples to collect and provision galleys, to withdraw all available combatants from the southern garrisons, and to expedite the embarkation of the reinforcements that were under orders to assemble there. Meanwhile he sent such cavalry as he possessed to cut off the enemies' supplies, and so effectually was this done that the Goths soon began to suffer even greater privations than the Romans. Antonina then went with an escort to join Procopius at Naples, and being provided with a supply of money did good service in collecting provisions.

Five hundred combatants were promptly gathered from the garrisons of Southern Italy; and a fleet having on board three thousand Isaurians anchored in the bay, whilst a body of eighteen hundred horse led by experienced officers of whom the most distinguished was Johannes the nephew of Vitalian[1],

[1] Johannes, erroneously surnamed 'The Sanguinary,' like his uncle Vitalian was of Gothic extraction, both being descendants of Aspar, who in the time of Leo I ruled, though he did not reign, at Constantinople. The ability, and on some occasions the disobedience of Johannes, when acting as the lieutenant of Belisarius, had no inconsiderable influence on the subsequent progress of the war.

having landed at Otranto, joined the troops collected by Procopius. In addition to these, three hundred cavalry had already reached Rome by the *Via Latina*.

The contest had now reached a stage when the arrival of five thousand disciplined troops was sufficient to turn the scale; but the numerical superiority of the Goths still made them formidable. It was arranged that the Isaurians should proceed in their ships to the mouth of the Tiber, whilst the other forces, under the direction of Johannes, were to march along the shore to Ostia. In doing so, they were liable to be attacked and delayed. Belisarius, desiring as far as possible to prevent any such interference, organised a diversion; and by a surprise, planned and executed with consummate skill, he gave full occupation to his besiegers.

Nov.   Vitiges, discouraged by a fresh defeat, by exaggerated accounts of the imperial reinforcements, and by the increasing difficulty of obtaining food, offered to give up Sicily and Campania with Naples, and to pay an annual tribute for the rest of his dominions.

Belisarius replied that he was not commissioned to surrender the imperial rights, but only to vindicate and defend them; but he did not refuse to allow time and facilities for access to the Emperor.

Dec.   Negotiations for a truce were then commenced, and soon afterwards Johannes with his forces arrived at Ostia, while the Isaurians, having disembarked from their galleys, took up and fortified a position near the port of Rome. Belisarius, when aware of this, set out during the darkness of a December evening with an escort of an hundred horsemen, and rode to Ostia for the purpose of imparting to the commanders needful information as to the actual state of affairs. Having informed them of his recent victory and of the fact that negotiations for a truce were in progress, he enjoined them to push forward, and to convoy the supplies with the least possible delay to Rome, assuring them that should any difficulty arise they might count on his protection. This done he took his departure, and before the break of day accomplished his safe return.

His directions were well carried out, and the Goths who held the port, from unwillingness to disturb the negotiations, refrained from opposition; but as the truce was not yet signed, the utmost caution was required, and the difficulties of the transit seemed at first insuperable. The overworked oxen that had drawn the waggons from Campania lay prostrate, and were unable to tow the provision-boats up the river, in the windings of which sails were but of little avail. It was only by intense labour that the rowers could stem the currents and maintain a slow advance, escorted on the right bank by a portion of the army.

At the time when the introduction of troops and provisions into Rome was accomplished her besiegers were dying of hunger. The treaty for a truce, 21 Dec.

while it was in progress, had secured to Belisarius all the advantages he required, and, when ratified, failed to withhold him from acts of hostility.

A.D. 538. Vitiges, relying on the agreement for a cessation of hostilities, permitted the half-starved Gothic garrison of Portus Romanus to withdraw in quest of subsistence; but no sooner was this done than the town and fortress were occupied by Belisarius. Alba and Centum-cellae (Civita Vecchia) were in like manner evacuated and captured.

Belisarius was not the man to let slip an opportunity, however unfairly gained, or to heed the remonstrances of an outwitted opponent. To him it signified little that the truce from which he had already obtained all that he desired should be set aside. Foreseeing and perhaps desiring a rupture, he sent Johannes with one thousand horse to his newly-acquired fortress of Alba, with orders that, in case hostilities were resumed, he was to persecute and rob the Gothic families resident in the Picenum.

Vitiges gave vent to his resentment by repeated attempts to gain an entrance into the city; but the failure of his desperate efforts only confirmed his people in their despair of the war.

Meanwhile Johannes, moved by the prayers and promises of the inhabitants, pushed forward to Rimini, and succeeded in gaining possession. This was done in direct contravention of his orders, but it was followed by important consequences, since the loss of Rimini with its sea-port within a day's march of Ravenna, decided Vitiges to raise the siege of Rome.

When, at dawn of day, Belisarius saw the columns of his late besiegers defiling over the Milvian bridge, he doubted as to the course that it might be safe to pursue, the greater part of his cavalry being with Johannes; but he warned the whole of his remaining troops to be in readiness, and having waited until more than half the Goths had crossed, he attacked their rear-guard. After an obstinate conflict, Roman discipline prevailed: the bridge became choked with fugitives; many were crushed to death, whilst others were forced into the river, and being encumbered with their armour sank.

Such was the termination of the siege which, including the armistice, had occupied more than a year and had proved fatal to a third of the Gothic army,—a result which fully justified the bold resolution of Belisarius, and irretrievably ruined the prestige of his opponent.

As Vitiges with his still numerous, though demoralised, army fell back in the direction of Ravenna, he entrusted the defence of Auximum to one of his ablest generals with four thousand of his best troops, and was able to leave garrisons in other defensible places, while with the rest he undertook in person the recapture of Rimini. Procopius records the skill and unflinching resolution whereby his attempts to take the place by escalade were defeated by Johannes, and also the bitter complaints of that leader, for Johannes conceived that the importance of his acquisition would not only secure for him a full condonation, but prompt and adequate support.

June.   Leaving only a small garrison in Rome, Belisarius followed Vitiges in the direction of Ravenna. On arriving at Firmo, about a day's march from Auximum, he fell in with reinforcements, amounting to seven thousand men, that had landed on the coast under the command of Narses. Narses, from humble beginnings, had risen to be the Emperor's chamberlain and treasurer, and, though a eunuch, he lived to prove his fitness for command. At Firmo a general council of war was assembled, in which the state and prospects of the contest were discussed. The gallant but hazardous action of Johannes was blamed, as inconsistent with his instructions and disturbing to the plans of Belisarius; since, by hastening to the relief of Rimini, the Romans it was said would leave the Gothic forces stationed at Auximum in their rear, and the Roman families in that neighbourhood without protection.

Narses, who entertained a great affection for Johannes, then spoke. He cautioned the commanders to beware lest they punished the Emperor for the involuntary offence of an officer. If Rimini were allowed to fall, her brave defenders would be at the mercy of the barbarians, and a city devoted to the Roman cause would be sacrificed. The mischief, moreover, would not end there; for such a catastrophe would not fail to revive the broken spirits of the enemy; and the Goths, availing themselves of their numbers, would renew the conflict with dangerous energy[1].

At this stage of the debate, a soldier who had escaped brought a letter from Johannes, declaring that he could not possibly hold out for more than seven days. On the receipt of this intelligence Belisarius is said by Procopius to have been troubled, and for the moment undecided; but his fertile genius soon devised a plan of operations by which he kept the garrison of Auximum in check, while, by a night attack at Rimini, he caused a fatal panic in the camp of the besiegers. The demoralised army of Vitiges, believing itself to be surrounded, fled in confusion to Ravenna. Ildiger, a son-in-law of Antonina, was the first to enter the trenches; and Belisarius, accompanied by Narses, came up later. Belisarius, when he beheld the emaciated countenance and wasted form of Johannes, remarked, 'You have something to thank Ildiger for'; but Johannes would acknowledge no deliverer save Narses, implying that Belisarius had not willingly relieved him.

After this there was an end of harmonious action, for Johannes, with his followers and the forces that had lately arrived from Constantinople, would obey no orders that had not the fiat of Narses; and yet while acting independently of each other, Belisarius was able to win Urbino, and Narses Imola.

Before Belisarius left Rome, the Bishop of Milan and a deputation came with assurances that the

[1] Procopius.

Milanese, if aided by a small body of troops, would undertake to expel the Goths, and to gain over the whole of Liguria for the Emperor. Relying on their assurances, Belisarius sent a small force under Mundilas, a distinguished officer of his guard, by sea to Genoa ; and Mundilas having made his way across the Po without opposition, took formal possession of the city. Vitiges, when aware of what had happened, sent his nephew Uraias with a large part of his army to punish the rebels, and with the connivance of king Theodebert, obtained ten thousand Burgundians as auxiliaries. It was in vain that the Milanese manned their walls, for the waste of war and the neglect of agriculture had caused a general scarcity, and the populous city was unprovided with food ; and it was in vain also that Belisarius despatched for its relief a considerable body of troops, for his commanders, when they reached the Po, could not venture to cross in the face of overwhelming numbers, unless they were supported by Johannes, whose force was within reach. But Johannes awaited instructions from Narses, and in the meantime Milan surrendered and was sacked. When informed of the catastrophe, Belisarius wrote to the Emperor a full account of the dissensions by which it had been preceded ; Justinian, in reply, confirmed his appointment as head of the whole of his forces, and recalled Narses.

A.D. 539. The recapture and sack of Milan by the Goths, though a grievous discredit to the imperial cause, brought no advantage to Vitiges. His Burgundian mercenaries, sated with spoil, recrossed the mountains, and he looked in vain for others. The warlike Lombards, being indebted to Justinian for their settlements in Pannonia and Noricum, though tempted with high pay, refused to bear arms against him; while on the Franks neither party could rely. Their faithless king, Theodebert [1], had recently made an incursion into the northern provinces, and had allowed his followers to attack and pillage assailable stations, whether Roman or Gothic, until subsistence could no longer be obtained, and sickness had more than decimated his forces.

Vitiges, though without an ally in Europe, obtained one in Asia. By means of a secret embassy he induced Chosroes, king of Persia, to renounce his recent agreement for a perpetual peace with the Romans, and to resume hostilities [2] on the most vulnerable side of the empire.

Belisarius, after having supplied the towns with garrisons, had now an effective body of eleven thousand combatants; but Auximum, by the strength of its position and of its garrison, presented an obstacle to his onward progress. It was on Auximum that Vitiges relied for the preservation of his kingdom, until the progress of the Persian invasion should compel Justinian to negotiate; and he had promised the defenders that, in case of difficulty, he would march with his whole army to their aid.

---

[1] A grandson of Clovis, and an inheritor of his restless energy, reigned in Austrasia from 535 to 548 A. D.

[2] Procopius, de bello Persico, ii. 2.

After an interval of successful defence, the provision of food came to an end, whereupon the governor reminded Vitiges of his promise, and informed him that they were contending, not with Belisarius only, but with famine. But the dearth of food had by this time become universal. Vitiges, having no commissariat, was unable to move. Belisarius, by contaminating their only water-supply, at last compelled the defenders of Auximum to capitulate; and so disgusted were they with their king that they transferred their allegiance to the Emperor, and mingled in the ranks of his army.

The result of the conflict was no longer doubtful. To the Goths, neither their superior numbers, nor the inaccessible ramparts of their marsh-girt capital, were of any further avail: the imperial fleet prevented the arrival of supplies by sea, and such as had hitherto been obtained from Liguria were stopped ere they reached their destination.

Having received additional reinforcements from Dalmatia, Belisarius was enabled to occupy both sides of the Po; and, by an unusual subsidence of the river, several barges laden with supplies for Ravenna were stranded. These were immediately captured, while the approach of others was prevented.

Vitiges, after he had rejected a proposal from Theodebert to join him in driving the Roman forces from Italy, and to divide the country between them, opened negotiations for a partition with the Emperor. This was in fact to sue for peace, and Belisarius affected to treat, but only to gain time, in order that the stringency of his blockade might have its effect. At this crisis, two senators arrived from Constantinople with instructions to conclude peace. This change in the imperial counsels had been caused by grave events in Syria. King Chosroes, at the instigation of Vitiges, had thrown his engagements to the winds, and, with an innumerable army, had crossed the Euphrates, laid waste the country, and taken Antioch by storm. Antioch, some fourteen years before, had suffered greatly from earthquakes; but having been rebuilt at the cost of Justinian, it had regained its position as the most beautiful and most prosperous of Eastern cities, when it was condemned by Chosroes to be burned.

The envoys, having first made known their instructions to Belisarius, were conducted into Ravenna. Vitiges, already reduced to despair, joyfully accepted the proffered conditions which left him the title of king with the provinces beyond the Po and a moiety of the contents of the palace and treasury; the rest of Italy being restored to the empire.

Belisarius, meanwhile, had time to meditate with bitter disappointment on the proposed termination of the war. To him the terms conceded to the Goths seemed alike inconsistent with imperial interests, and injurious to himself as robbing him of the honours and rewards to which he felt himself entitled; and, when the treaty was brought back to him, he refused to sign it.

This refusal was regarded by his officers with

suspicion, and thought to indicate disloyal intentions. Being aware of these feelings, he invited the commanders to a conference, where, in the presence of Justinian's envoys, he announced to them the Emperor's resolution to terminate the war, and the willingness of Vitiges to accept the proffered terms. He then required each one of them to declare and put in writing his views as to the probable result of continued hostilities. Their decision was unanimous. They all recorded their opinion 'that the Emperor's instructions were the best that could have been given,' and that further efforts to subdue entirely the resistance of the Goths would be fruitless. Belisarius expressed himself satisfied; but the course which he would have followed, had not an important change of circumstances occurred, can only be conjectured.

In the meantime at Ravenna a treaty for which Belisarius refused to be guarantee was regarded as worthless; and the Gothic magnates, pressed on the one hand by an inevitable famine, and on the other by the fear that submission to the Emperor would lead to their removal from Italy, had come to an unforeseen and extraordinary resolution. With them the valour, the genius, and above all the fortune of Belisarius had won unbounded admiration; and, by conferring on him their sovereignty, with the promise of unanimous aid in winning for himself the imperial crown of the West, they thought to obtain relief from present miseries, combined with the prospect of a not inglorious future. Vitiges himself joined in the offer, exhorting him in private to grasp a prize which no one, he said, would venture to dispute; and Belisarius feigned acceptance. His fertile genius suggested to him a scheme for turning this overture to account, and for the attainment of such great and unlooked for advantages as might excuse, and even render commendable, an act of disobedience. Having again assembled his commanders, together with the Emperor's legates, he asked them whether the capture of Vitiges with his nobles, the appropriation of their national treasure, and the recovery of all Italy for the Romans, would not justly be considered a great and memorable achievement. To this they assented, and urged him, if he saw his way to such a result, to proceed without delay in the execution of his plans [1].

He then informed Vitiges and the Gothic leaders that it would be well for them to do at once what they had offered to do; and to this invitation they replied by an immediate acknowledgment of him as their king; but they required that he should enter in secret into an engagement, confirmed by an oath, for their indemnity, and also for his acceptance, of their offer of their crown. As to the rest he readily complied, and with regard to the kingdom, he promised to take the requisite oath when he could do so in the presence of Vitiges and the magnates.

His deceitful assurances were accepted, and the A.D. 540. gates were opened to him, but to several of his own officers his conduct in refusing to sign the Emperor's treaty seemed indefensible. Being aware of their

[1] See Procopius, L. ii. c. 25.

suspicions, before he entered the city he dismissed Johannes and the other commanders of whose goodwill or of whose acquiescence in the extraordinary course that he was following he doubted, with orders to conduct their troops to distant and distinct stations, assigning as a reason the difficulty of providing food[1].

Having thus secured himself against any hostile combination or interference on the part of his commanders, and having gratified the famishing Raven-

[1] This dismissal of Johannes, resting as it does on the authority and clear statement of Procopius, is important, inasmuch as it proves, if proof were wanting, the grossly erroneous character of a paragraph respecting Johannes in the Historia Miscella, which appears to have been relied upon by Gibbon, in order to fix on Johannes the disgraceful nickname of 'The Sanguinary.' The passage referred to is as follows :—

'Vitiges vero, coacto rursus in uno magno Gothorum exercitu, cum Belisario conflixit, factaque magna suorum strage, in fugam conversus est. Quem Johannes, magister militum, cognomento Sanguinarius, noctu fugientem persequens vivum comprendit, Romamque ad Belisarium adduxit.' L. xvi.

Now there is not a statement in this paragraph—the production of some unknown compiler of a subsequent age—that is not at variance with the testimony of contemporary and reliable authorities, from whom it appears that Johannes is incorrectly styled Magister Militum; that he never took King Vitiges prisoner, or carried him to Rome, and presented him to Belisarius. Throughout the Gothic war Johannes bore a conspicuous part, and Procopius relates in detail, with apparent impartiality, his achievements, his sufferings, and his differences with Belisarius. But while praising his energy, and the fortitude with which he bore the severest privations, he makes no allusion to his having acquired the nickname of Sanguinarius, or to any act whereby he might have deserved it. Yet Gibbon adheres to the appellation, and, while he describes it as one that might do honour to a tiger, seems grateful to Anastasius, the translator of the Historia Miscella, for having preserved it!

nati by causing his provision **galleys to enter** the haven with supplies of corn, he made his entry into the city, took possession of the palace, with its accumulated store of treasure, and treated Vitiges with respect, but took care that he should be placed in honourable confinement. The troops that he had with him were comparatively few, and Procopius, an interested eye-witness of all that was done, relates that the Gothic women, having gazed with astonishment on the inferior stature and number of his troops, spat **in the** faces of their own **soldiers, who** had allowed such unequal opponents to prevail.

Justinian, **being** aware that Vitiges **had** already sued for peace, had no reason to doubt that the favourable conditions he had offered would **be accepted** and that the war in Italy was terminated. It was therefore only natural that he should desire to have the advice and services of his ablest general **for** the war which was raging in the East. Certain generals of the imperial forces had accused Belisarius of being engaged in a conspiracy to usurp for himself the Italian crown: yet it was not, says Procopius, by these calumnies, but by the pressure of the Persian war that Justinian was induced to sign his recall[1].

The commanders of cities and fortresses still held by the Goths, when they saw **the** capital of their kingdom in the possession of Belisarius, and Vitiges his prisoner, accepted his assurances of immunity and sent in their submission. The Goths, whose location was beyond the Po, and who still possessed

[1] De bello Persico, ii. 30.

some means of resistance, though informed of his recall by the Emperor, could not be persuaded that he would obey a mandate which would have deprived him of Theodoric's crown. But when his preparations for departure became manifest, they at once resolved to elect another king, under whose auspices the conflict might be renewed.

They first applied to Uraias, by whom the recapture of Milan had been accomplished, assuring him that had they not confided in his valour and energy as a counterpoise to the weakness of Vitiges, they should have applied to him before. Uraias, being sister's son to Vitiges, declined, and on his recommendation they elected Ildebadus, governor of Verona, a magnate of great influence. Ildebadus, before he was proclaimed, joined his electors in a last attempt to overcome the scruples of Belisarius: exhorting him to keep faith with the Goths, they assured him of their persistent desire to lay at his feet the insignia of royalty, and to salute him as king of the Goths and of Italy; but the time for further deception was passed, and Belisarius replied by a declaration that never, during the lifetime of Justinian, would he accept that title.

A.D. 541. When Belisarius with Vitiges and the nobles of his court as his prisoners embarked for Constantinople, the Gothic cause was at its lowest ebb, and Pavia was the only city of note which had not sent in its submission. Ildebadus, when he took the field, had at first no more than one thousand followers, but his Ligurian countrymen flocked to his standard; and when Vitalius, the Roman commander in the Venetia, ventured to attack him, he encountered defeat. This victory had acquired for Ildebadus at Constantinople and elsewhere no small consideration, when his career was cut short; for, having in a private quarrel slain his benefactor Uraias, he fell by the hand of an avenger.

Belisarius, in the meantime having with him Vitiges, the children of Ildebadus, and a numerous accompaniment of Gothic nobles, accomplished his voyage to Constantinople. Justinian beheld with wonder and pleasure the groups of captives, admiring their lofty stature and beauty of form. He received the rich collection of treasures taken from the palace of Theodoric, and allowed the senators a private view of them; but he neither permitted these trophies to be seen by the public, nor did he accord to Belisarius, by whose double dealing and contravention of his own orders and policy they had been acquired, the honour of a triumph, as he had done when king Gelimer and the spoils of the Vandals were brought from Africa. The cases had, in truth, no similarity. In Vitiges the Emperor beheld a prince with whom he had recently been engaged in negotiations for peace, who had accepted his conditions, and who, but for the condoned disobedience of his captor, would then have been reigning in Transpadane Italy. The conduct of Justinian on this occasion was such as might be expected from a superior who felt ashamed of advantages, gained as these had been gained by his subordinate, but which were, nevertheless, too great and too specious to be safely disapproved.

Meanwhile from the citizens, Belisarius, whose martial aspect and invariable courtesy made him the admired of all beholders, received a prolonged ovation ; and the liberator of Africa from the Vandals was greeted without doubt or reservation as the deliverer of Italy from the Goths, while the presence of Vitiges as his captive was accepted as an all-sufficient proof of the fulness and finality of his victory.

In Italy itself no such delusion prevailed, for there hostilities were already resumed, and there the baneful conflict called the Gothic war continued during the twelve ensuing years to devastate the country.

Vitiges, having received from Justinian the rank of patrician and senator, together with a grant of estates, continued to reside at Constantinople until his death. Belisarius, when on the return of spring entrusted with chief command against Chosroes, proceeded in all haste to the Persian confines, and the Goths whom he had brought from Ravenna took service under him.

The Ostrogothic nobles when called upon to elect a successor to Ildebadus, chose for their leader and their King, the young duke of Friuli, best known by his acquired cognomen of Totila—'the Victorious.'

CHAPTER VII.

RECOMMENCEMENT, CONTINUANCE, AND FINAL RESULT
OF THE GOTHIC WAR.

A.D. 541–567.

The Imperial forces, having **no** Commander-in-chief, retreat from Verona, and **are defeated by Totila at Faenza**. Failure of their attempt to relieve **Florence**. Reduction of Naples by Totila. Belisarius sent back to Italy. **His letter to the Emperor.** Failure of his endeavours to relieve Rome. **Totila, having** obtained an **entry**, dismantles and **abandons the city**. Reoccupation of Rome **by** Belisarius, who **holds it** against **Totila**. His subsequent misfortunes and recall. Totila, for the second time, **becomes master of Rome. Johannes and Narses commissioned to act against him.** Totila, **after** the destruction **of his fleet, is defeated, and, after a successful** reign of twelve years, **dies of his wounds. Narses** enforces the departure of the Ostrogoths **from Italy. Death of Justinian, and succession of Justin II, who** rewards Narses with insults. Longinus, the **first Exarch** of Italy.

IN Totila the confidence of his countrymen was A.D. 541. not misplaced, and concurrent circumstances favoured his efforts. Of these, the most important was the total inadequacy of the imperial revenue to meet the cost of two contemporary wars. Yet Justinian delighted in the construction of magnificent buildings, and appears to have cared little as to the means by which supplies were obtained. With him the most ingenious inventors, and the most reckless exactors of taxes, were the surest of favour; and, when pressed by the necessity of defending the Eastern provinces from the Persians, he would fain have extracted from Italy herself sufficient funds for terminating the conflict with the Goths, the difficulties and duration of which he did not foresee. With this object he sent to Ravenna one Alexander, who was generally believed to have enriched himself by coin-clipping; and Forficula, as he was called, being invested with full powers, fabricated debts to the treasury, and enforced their payment; even the soldiers, by whom some better reward for wounds and long service might have been expected, being subjected to Forficula's extortions.

After the departure of Belisarius no one was appointed to command; but the officers left in charge of the towns, eleven in number, were equals. When reproached for allowing Totila to make head and to renew the war, they assembled a heterogeneous army of twelve thousand men and invested Verona. Through an act of treason they obtained possession of one of the gates; but, while engaged in a dispute as to the expected spoil, they lost their opportunity, the garrison recovered from its panic, and Verona proved too strong for the investors. During their retreat, Totila, with five thousand Goths, fell in with them at Faenza and succeeded, by the employment of a well-executed stratagem, in throwing their dense ranks into confusion. His victory was complete: since the commencement of the Gothic war, no such reverse as that of Faenza had befallen the imperial arms.

It was not long before the result of another action proved the demoralised condition of the troops. In answer to the urgent appeal of Justinus, the governor of beleaguered Florence, the commanders undertook the relief of that city. On their approach the Goths abandoned the siege and took up a strong position near the Tuscan city of Macella. Johannes, on account of some jealousy as to the leadership, attacked them at first with his own troops only. The Goths made a gallant resistance, but must soon have yielded, when, a body-guardsman of Johannes being killed at his side, a cry pervaded the ranks of the other leaders that Johannes himself had fallen, upon which the whole army fled in confusion, and a belief spread far and wide that the most gifted and the most successful of the Roman leaders had been defeated and slain.

After this, the Roman commanders, whose ill-paid mercenaries were given to desertion, confined themselves to their respective head-quarters ; and Totila, with whom no further interference was attempted, pursued his way to Southern Italy. Leaving Rome on his right, he gathered as he went from amongst his countrymen additional combatants ; and, encountering no opposition, occupied Beneventum, where, as in the other walled cities of which he gained possession, he broke down the fortifications, lest the Romans, with whom he preferred to contend in the open country, should avail themselves of their protection.

While thus engaged he visited the newly-established monastery of Monte Cassino, and had an interview with its founder, St. Benedict, from whom he received exhortations to Christian kindness and forbearance.

A.D. 543. Meanwhile the Neapolitans, who held out against him until the attempts made by the imperial government to introduce supplies from Sicily had failed, surrendered; and the conduct of Totila, when he entered the city, seemed to show that he had not forgotten the humane counsels of Benedict; for he not only supplied the famishing multitudes with food, but insisted with parental solicitude on the observance of needful caution against the danger of too sudden repletion.

A.D. 544. After the submission of Naples, Totila sent troops to invest Otranto, while with the rest of his forces he marched in the direction of Rome. Being informed of the disgust caused by the want of discipline and the exactions of the imperial troops, who, according to Procopius, 'left no insolence unpractised,' he sent an address to the Senate, wherein he contrasted the present condition of their country with that which existed during the reign of Theodoric. When Johannes, who commanded the garrison, would not permit the senators to reply, Totila caused placards to be posted by night in the principal thoroughfares, in which, after a repetition of the same suggestions, he alluded to the malversations of Alexander the coin-clipper, and pledged himself that, when he became established as king, no act of oppression nor any deviation from impartial justice would be tolerated.

Urged by a sense of responsibility Constantian, the governor of Ravenna, resolved to furnish his sovereign with a correct account of the deplorable condition of Italy, and the other commanders joined him in a confession of their total inability to stay the progress of Totila. On the receipt of this appalling statement, Justinian decided to send back Belisarius to the scene of his former triumphs ; but the dangers which threatened the Eastern frontiers were undiminished, and from thence not a cohort could be withdrawn. All that Belisarius could obtain was money for the enlistment in Thrace of untried combatants ; and with these he proceeded to Salona, intending to embark for Ravenna and to ascertain there in what way his slender means might best be employed. Before his departure he was able by timely succour to save Otranto from the Gothic besiegers, but when he reached his destination, neither the influence of his name nor his offers of free pardon were of any avail either to bring back deserters or to confirm the waverers. Totila, having ascertained his weakness, continued to advance, obtained possession of Tivoli, crossed the Apennines, and laid siege to Auximum.

Belisarius, though unable to relieve Auximum, the object nearest his heart, obtained possession of Pesaro, where the port and adjacent pastures presented facilities for the importation and sustenance of cavalry horses ; the walls having been broken down by the Goths, he obtained from Ravenna iron palisades, with which he so far strengthened the defences that Totila failed in an attempt to regain possession.

When the loss of Ascoli Firmo and other places

had convinced Belisarius of his inability to check the advance of the enemy, he wrote to Justinian a letter of which the following is the substance :—

A.D. 545. 'I find myself in Italy without either troops or money, having only a handful of untrained recruits. To levy taxes is impracticable, the country being held by the enemy; and amongst the soldiers, want of pay has produced insubordination, for a debtor cannot expect obedience from his creditors. The better part of your army, Sire, has taken service with the Goths. If the appearance of Belisarius in Italy could secure success, I am here in obedience to your command; but if you wish to conquer, the means of conquest must be provided, and a body of veteran soldiers, with my own guards, should be sent me; and money also provided for the regular payment of the Huns and other mercenaries, without which their services cannot be relied on.'

This letter was confided to Johannes, who engaged to impress upon the Emperor the urgency of the crisis, and to return. But Johannes lingered at Constantinople to celebrate his marriage with a daughter of Germanus, the Emperor's nephew, and Totila meanwhile took Placentia, the chief city of the Emilia, whilst his forces surrounded Rome, where Bessas, having succeeded Johannes in the command, made no effort to diminish the stringency of the blockade.

The relief of Rome being now the primary object, Belisarius left a garrison in Ravenna, re-crossed the Adriatic with the remainder of his troops, and awaited at Epidamnus the arrival of adequate forces. Soon after his landing there he despatched reinforcements to the Portus Romanus, with the twofold object of giving additional security to that all-important station, and of encouraging Bessas to disturb by desultory attacks the operations of the besiegers. But Bessas refused to stir, and his inaction is attributed by Procopius to the most sordid motives; for to him the prolongation of the blockade brought ill-gotten gain, and, having the public granaries at his command, he was able to sell their contents to the senators and wealthy citizens at fabulous prices, while the people were famishing. Pope Vigilius had already effected a timely escape; for, as the nominee of the Empress Theodora and the intruded successor of Simplicius, he would have been obnoxious to the Goths. Vigilius, though his elevation was uncanonical, proved himself a good citizen, by sending from Sicily a supply of corn in the hope that it might reach Rome before the completion of the blockade. But no sooner had his well-stored galleys reached the mouth of the Tiber, than they fell into the hands of the enemy, and after this misfortune the famine assumed a frightful aspect. Bessas, meanwhile, though he permitted those who offered him money to leave the city, refused to capitulate.

Before the end of the year, Johannes arrived at Epidamnus with an army composed in part of Roman troops and partly of barbarian mercenaries. Belisarius overruled the proposal of Johannes that they should land on the opposite coast, and expose themselves after a long march to the risks of a pitched battle against superior numbers. He therefore set sail at once with the bulk of his forces to the mouth of the Tiber, having directed Johannes, with a body of cavalry and a small force of mercenaries, to land in Calabria, to re-establish the imperial authority in the southern provinces, and, having accomplished this important diversion, to join him as soon as possible in the neighbourhood of Rome.

In emancipating the Italians of the south from the Goths, Johannes performed his task with ability and success; but Totila, desiring to prevent or delay his junction with Belisarius, sent a force to Capua, with orders to its commander that when Johannes commenced his march to Rome, he was to hang upon his rear; and Johannes, disliking to be placed between two enemies, made no attempt to execute his orders. In this way, Belisarius, when he reached Portus Romanus, found himself deprived of the co-operation of Johannes, and of an efficient body of cavalry.

A.D. 546.
Failure of Belisarius' attempt to relieve Rome. He returns to Portus Romanus.

At Rome famine was doing its work, and Totila omitted nothing that might keep up and increase its severity. To guard against attempts to throw in supplies, he cast an iron chain across the Tiber, and, nearer the city, he spanned the stream with a wooden bridge, flanked at either end with a capacious tower. It was only by the prompt removal of these obstacles that the city could be saved, and on no occasion was the energy of Belisarius or the fertility of his genius more strikingly displayed than in organising suitable means.

Having caused two barges of the largest dimensions to be linked together, on the basis thus obtained he caused a tower to be constructed exceeding in height those by which Totila's bridge was defended, and on its summit was placed a cock-boat filled with combustibles. When the day of action arrived, the attack was commenced by a flotilla of two hundred loop-holed pinnaces laden with provisions and manned with archers. To guard the approaches to Portus Romanus, which constituted the only refuge in case of a reverse, and where Antonina was staying, bodies of horse and foot were placed in advantageous positions; and the command of the harbour and fortress itself was intrusted to Isaaces the Armenian, an officer of tried valour, with injunctions that he should on no account stir from his post, even though informed that Belisarius himself had fallen.

These arrangements being completed, Belisarius took his place in front of the flotilla. With infinite toil the rowers stemmed the current, broke the iron chain, and with a well-directed shower of missiles drove the Goths from the right shore. The floating castle was then towed to the front and placed in contact with the tower which on that side projected into the river, and upon whose summit the cock-boat, with its cargo of combustibles, was overturned. In a few moments the whole of that wooden structure was enveloped in flames, and for two hundred Goths closely pent up within it there was no escape. The horrors of this catastrophe, combined with an incessant discharge of arrows from the pinnaces, caused a panic, during which the entrance of the Roman forces and of the supplies would easily have been accomplished, when a well-meant disobedience to orders turned the scale.

Tidings having reached the Portus Romanus that Belisarius, having overcome every obstacle, was on the point of entering Rome, Isaaces, in his eagerness to secure for himself a share in the triumph, crossed the river and surprised a Gothic force stationed at Ostia. His success was, in the first instance, complete; but when the Goths discovered the smallness of his force they returned to the charge, put his troopers to flight, and made him their prisoner. Belisarius, when informed that Isaaces was in the hands of the enemy, at once concluded that they had taken the Port, his only base of operations, and that Antonina was their prisoner; whereupon, thinking to take the captors unprepared, he ordered an immediate return; and, when he found that he had been misled, the mortification was more than he could bear; he was attacked by a fever, and for many days lay prostrate.

Illness of Belisarius.

By deaths that had taken place during the siege and, still more, by the escape of fugitives, the population of Rome was by this time greatly reduced; for Totila, though successful in preventing the entrance of provisions, had not been able to prevent the nightly egress of the poorer citizens, while the senators and those who had much to lose, being unwilling to abandon their possessions, continued to purchase subsistence from Bessas, whose avarice and neglect of his duty, if not credibly attested, would exceed belief. At length, the treason of four Isaurian sentinels provided Totila with an unopposed entrance. Bessas, though warned of his danger, was taken by surprise and fled, leaving behind him his accumulated wealth. In his hasty retreat he was accompanied by such of the senators as had retained their horses, while those who remained in their houses or took refuge in the churches were sent, with their wives and children, as prisoners and hostages to Campania. Totila then renewed his proposals for peace and alliance, and, when they were again rejected, declared his resolution to make Rome a sheep-pasture; a project which the grave and persuasive remonstrances of Belisarius eventually led him to renounce, but not until he had broken down about a third of the walls and removed the gates.

Having encamped a considerable part of his army at Algidus, fifteen miles west of the city, with orders to watch the movements of Belisarius and to prevent his advance from the Portus Romanus, Totila, with the rest of his forces, took his departure, being bent on the recovery of Southern Italy. Johannes, who was in Apulia, found it necessary to betake himself in all haste to Otranto, and was joined on his way by three hundred Roman soldiers who were on their retreat from Antium. While the Goths reoccupied the adjacent districts of Calabria, Johannes, from his secure position at Otranto, continued to harass them by desultory attacks, until, urged by the Tarentines, he consented to aid them in their defence. On reaching Tarentum he found that the city, though unprovided with defences, could only be approached on the land side by a narrow strip, across which he built and fortified a wall, and thus secured for the expected Roman forces a safe and convenient place of assembly.

In the meantime Totila surprised and garrisoned Acherontis (Acerenza), a fortress of Lucania, and leaving a small force in Campania to guard the senators who, together with their families, had been brought from Rome, returned to Upper Italy, intending to make himself master of Ravenna.

A.D. 547. Belisarius, when restored to health, became intent on a re-occupation of Rome; and, with an escort of one thousand men, was on his way to inspect the actual state of the walls, when he found himself opposed by the Goths stationed at Algidus, and inflicted on them a severe defeat. Soon afterwards, leaving a garrison in the Portus Romanus, he occupied the dismantled city with the rest of his army; and for five and twenty days the soldiers laboured to fill up the breaches of the walls, the stones of which had not been carried off, and lay at hand.

Successful defence of dismantled Rome by Belisarius.
When informed of what had happened, Totila brought back the whole of his forces from Ravenna, and having encamped them on the Tiber, commenced the following morning a furious attack, in full assurance of success. The gates had been carried off, but the open spaces were held by men who could be trusted, and showers of missiles from the adjoining walls were well kept up, until darkness and weariness compelled the assailants to fall back

on their camp. During several weeks similar attacks were repeated, but without any different result; the Roman forces, having ample store of provisions brought from the Portus Romanus, could afford to wait, while those of their opponents being exhausted, Totila was obliged to withdraw and fell back on Tibur. This abandonment of an enterprise confidently undertaken lowered his prestige, and exalted that of Belisarius, who, making the city his winter quarters, had leisure to provide new gates, the keys of which he sent to the Emperor, together with an urgent demand for reinforcements.

When the thirteenth year of the Gothic war began Perugia was still strictly blockaded by the Goths, and Totila was about to undertake the siege in person, hoping that by the capture of the chief city of Etruria he might mitigate the discontent of his people; when he allowed a daring and successful exploit of Johannes to turn him from his purpose.

Johannes, with his small force, had done much to regain Southern Italy for the Romans, but had failed in an attempt to recapture Acherontis, and he now conceived the project of rescuing the senators and their families whom Totila had carried off from Rome and confined in Campania. With a chosen troop of horse, and by dint of forced marches, he accomplished his object, and convoyed the liberated captives, together with seventy Goths by whom they had been guarded, to Sicily. With Totila, impatience to punish this affront got the better of his judgment; and, relinquishing the prospect of a triumph at Perugia, he pursued Johannes, who nevertheless made good his retreat to Otranto.

At this stage of the war, Belisarius, in obedience to orders from Constantinople, left Rome; and, having entrusted the command of the garrison to Conon, the defender of Naples, he embarked, accompanied by Antonina, with a selected body-guard of seven hundred horse and two hundred foot, for Tarentum, where it was intended that an army should be assembled under his orders. Before he reached his destination, a succession of hurricanes compelled him to disembark at Cotrone and to send his cavalry inland for the pasturage and refreshment of their horses. Being surprised by the vigilant Totila the men were slain, and the horses carried off. The loss of his body-guard compelled Belisarius to hasten, like a fugitive, to his galleys, and to await in the less exposed position of Messina the course of events. At this time the Slavonians crossed the Danube in force and their predatory invasion extended itself to Epidamnus, the accustomed place of embarkation for forces intended to serve in Italy; an occurrence that may account for the Emperor's delay in fulfilling his engagements with Belisarius.

A.D. 548. It appears, however, from the impartial narrative of Procopius, that before the Slavonian invasion, Justinian sent two thousand infantry to Sicily and had ordered Valerianus with his cavalry to cross the Adriatic and proceed without delay to the headquarters of Belisarius. It also appears that Valerianus, when in the beginning of 548 he landed at

Otranto, found Belisarius there, engaged in the despatch of his wife to Constantinople, where he hoped to obtain, through her influence with the Empress, such an army as might enable him to cope with Totila. The fortress of Rossano, where many Romans of distinction had found an asylum for their families and their wealth, was at this time surrounded by the Goths, and the garrison had already treated for a surrender. Belisarius, supported by Johannes and Valerianus, resolved to embark with such forces as could be mustered and to strike a blow for its relief; but, after they had come within sight of the castle, they were driven back by a tempest and were obliged to make for Crotone, the only harbour on the coast. From thence they renewed their attempt, but Totila, being informed of their intention, had caused the shore to be occupied by bodies of horse and foot in such a manner as to render a landing impracticable, and he subsequently obtained possession of Rossano on terms dictated by himself.

Before Antonina reached Constantinople, Theodora had ceased to live; but Justinian, though unable to comply with Antonina's request for the prompt despatch of an army to Belisarius, consented, as an alternative, to his recall, on the specious pretence that his services were required in the East. The truth appears to be that Justinian had little or no choice in the matter, and that the dangers which beset the Empire during this and the two following years, rendered the despatch of an army adequate to the re-conquest of Italy impracticable; for obedience

Belisarius recalled from Italy.

to the imperator was at that time by no means implicit, as may be inferred from the fact that, when the garrison of Rome put their commander Conon to death and declared that they intended to join Totila unless they received their arrears of pay together with a free pardon, their mutiny was overlooked and their demand complied with.

When, after the humiliating affair of Rossano, Belisarius took his final leave of Italy and reached Constantinople, his reception amounted to a public acknowledgment that his ill-success was attributable to no other cause than a total want of means. By Justinian he was honoured with the rank of 'Magister Militum,' together with the appointment of a bodyguard, whilst his seniors in consular dignity relinquished in his favour their right of precedence, and he was recognised by universal consent [1] as 'First of the Romans.'

A.D. 549. At this time the barbarian powers had obtained an undisputed predominance in the West [2]. Italy was re-conquered by the Ostrogoths; Gaul, with Marseilles and its other principal seaports, belonged to the powerful Germanic nation of the Franks; who celebrated at Arles, once the Roman capital, their Circensian games, and whose money no longer bore the impress of Caesar, but only that of their truculent king Theodebert. Theodebert had established his power in the Venetia, and neither Goths nor

---

[1] 'Id quod valde Imperatori placebat.' Procopius, de bello Gothico, iv. 21.

[2] Procopius, de bello Gothico, iii. 33.

Romans, while engaged in an internecine war, **could** venture to incur his hostility. Justinian had allowed the Lombards to settle in Noricum and Pannonia, while he acquiesced in the occupation of Sirmium by the Gepidae; but these surrenders had failed to purchase immunity from incursions, and, while the Persian war continued, there existed at home no force that could afford protection.

Totila, when he had re-established his power in Calabria and overcome the resistance of Perugia, secured the port of Rome, and commenced the blockade of the city, where Diogenes, an officer of ability who had been appointed by Belisarius as second in command under Conon, maintained with great perseverance and ability a long but **hopeless** defence until, as on a former occasion, the Isaurian sentinels at one of the gates betrayed their trust.

Totila, when elated by his successes, demanded of Theodebert the hand of one of his daughters, and received a disdainful reply, being told that the man **who,** having Rome **in** his possession had failed to keep it, could have no right to call himself king of Italy. Theodebert was in truth disinclined to recognise either **a** Gothic king or a Byzantine emperor as sovereign of a country which he hoped to call his own. He had already usurped the title of Augustus; and such was the increase of his power that his threatened march to Constantinople could not be regarded as improbable, when his accidental death, while hunting, relieved Justinian from his A.D. 550. greatest anxiety.

On Totila, it would seem, the reproaches of the Frank had a salutary influence; for, no sooner had he supplied the wants of the starving population than he ordered the damage inflicted during his former possession to be repaired; invited absentees to return; released the senators whom he detained as prisoners; and gratified all classes by the celebration of the equestrian games. With a just estimate of his own position, he had two objects in view; to conciliate the Italian people and to obtain from the Emperor peace on any terms consistent with a continuance of the Gothic occupation.

A.D. 549. His re-conquest of Rome had filled Constantinople with refugees and suppliants, whose entreaties for aid, and perseverance in the war had no small influence; and, when the envoy of Totila would have expressed his master's desire to act under the imperial sovereignty as the guardian of the peace, he did not obtain a hearing. The refugees, headed by Pope Vigilius and the Patrician Cethegus, received a promise from Justinian that Italy should be cared for, and, in their patron Germanus, Justinian's nephew, they had a guarantee that the promise would be kept.

Germanus, when the vices of the colonial government had driven Africa into rebellion, had given proof of ability as a general and an administrator, and his considerate treatment had won back the native population. For his second wife he had married Malasunta, the widow of King Vitiges, the grand-daughter of Theodoric the Great; and a belief

Death of Germanus, succeeded by Johannes.

was entertained, that if Germanus went to take the command in Italy, accompanied by Malasunta, her presence would have its influence, and that the Goths would hesitate to take arms against the only lineal descendant of Theodoric.

When the hope of peace was at an end, Totila crossed the Straits and punished the Sicilians for their hostilities and then abandoned the island, taking with him an enormous store of corn.

Germanus, when appointed to take the command in Italy, was furnished with a good supply of money, which, with his reputation as a leader who paid his soldiers punctually, enabled him to assemble and bring into a state of efficiency a large army. Before his departure, his presence in Illyricum had saved the country from an invasion of the Slavonians; while in Italy the mere expectation of his coming changed for a while the current of feeling. A.D. 550.

His decease after an illness of a few days overclouded the prospect; but the confidence in an ultimate deliverance, which his example and preparations had restored, continued.

By a former marriage Germanus had two sons, Justinian and Justin, who inherited their father's abilities, and had already done good service in defeating a barbarian incursion which had reached the long wall; and when, on the death of Germanus, Johannes succeeded to the command of the army, Justinian was named to accompany him to Italy.

In the meanwhile Totila had spared neither pains nor money in the formation of a navy, being convinced that while the enemy commanded the seaboard, any permanent defence of the Gothic kingdom was impossible. He had now at his disposal a fleet of three hundred war-galleys which, being sent to the coast of Greece, intercepted vessels laden with provisions for the imperial army; and the Gothic crews having landed at Corcyra, despoiled the inhabitants.

A.D. 551. When the winter was past and Johannes was preparing to embark, an order reached him at Salona which charged him to await there the arrival of Narses, who was to take the chief command; but, while Narses was still expected, Johannes received intelligence from Valerian the governor of Ravenna that Ancona was besieged by land and sea, together with urgent exhortations for help.

To Totila the fortified port of Ancona would have afforded an invaluable station for his fleet, with facilities for its more complete organisation, while to the new-born hopes of the Italians its loss would have been a heavy discouragement. Johannes did not hesitate to incur the responsibility. It was not the first time that, with a palpable advantage in view, he had ventured to act in contravention to orders; and, in the affair of Rimini, Narses had been his supporter, and had approved of such contravention. There was no time to hesitate. With a chosen body of combatants and forty war-galleys he hastened to the rescue, and being joined on the way by Valerianus with twelve more, drove off the hostile fleet from before Ancona.

The Goths showed no want of courage; but, after the first brunt of the battle, their inexperienced seamen fell into such disorder as rendered personal valour useless. Their fleet, with the exception of eleven vessels, was either captured or sunk; and the troops that had invested Ancona by land abandoned their camp and fled. Johannes, when he had supplied the garrison of the castle with provisions, sailed back to Salona, and Valerianus returned to Ravenna. 'This overthrow,' writes Procopius, 'greatly abated the power of Totila.' His hope of getting up a serviceable navy was at an end. The blow inflicted by his old enemy Johannes was decisive.

Narses, being well supported by Justinian, and provided with the sinews of war, brought with him large additional forces consisting chiefly of cavalry, and conspicuous amongst these were two thousand five hundred Lombard warriors, accompanied, like the men-at-arms of a subsequent age, by their attendants. Yet serious difficulties arose in the deficiency of means for transport of so large an army. With Narses the primary object was to reach Ravenna, his proposed base of operations, without delay; and for this the local experience of Johannes enabled him to suggest the means. By his advice the whole army marched along the coast of the Adriatic, accompanied in its progress by such a fleet of ships and galleys as served to ferry horse and foot across the creeks and estuaries, until, without loss or hindrance, the whole army reached its destination.

A D. 552. When Totila, advancing from Rome, had effected at Verona his junction with his able lieutenant Teja, he took up a position at Tagina on the western slope of the Apennines, and there the conflict which decided the fate of Italy took place. The Goths, though outnumbered, fought with their accustomed valour, but were eventually routed. When all was lost Totila escaped from the battle-field, but only to die of his wounds. During a reign of twelve years he had exhibited a character and endowments scarcely inferior to those of Theodoric himself, and had well sustained the right of his countrymen to a primacy amongst the barbarian races. The remnant of his forces were rallied at Pavia by Teja, whom they proclaimed their king.

Narses, when he had compelled the Gothic garrison of the mole of Adrian to surrender, fixed his head-quarters at Rome, and sent the keys of the city to Justinian. His success being assured, he desired to conciliate the people; and with this view he dismissed to their settlements, with good words and liberal rewards, his Lombard auxiliaries, whose cruelty and license he had witnessed with pain. But the Lombards while serving under him had not failed to appreciate the superiority of the Italian sky over that of Pannonia, and had acquired a dangerous knowledge of the nakedness of the land no less than of its advantages.

A.D. 553. From Rome Narses sent forces to invest the fortress of Cumae, where a large amount of Gothic treasure was deposited. Teja, with his remaining forces, hastened to the south, being resolved, if possible, to relieve the garrison. When unable to cope with Narses he entrenched himself and retained an unassailable position on the banks of the Sarno, until the desertion of the fleet, on which he depended for supplies, destroyed his last hope of successful resistance; and, after an heroic display of courage, the sixth and last of Theodoric's successors died with arms in his hands.

The following day, after a second obstinate conflict, the Gothic leaders offered to lay down their arms, on condition that they should be allowed an unmolested departure, taking with them their moveable property; and when Narses hesitated, Johannes, on whose judgment and knowledge he could rely, advised him to consent. Cumae and the other places of strength were then surrendered, and on these conditions the eighteen years' war, of which the history has been written by Procopius, was brought to a close[1].

On Narses now devolved the task of pacifying the cries of a ruined population, of repairing the broken walls of the cities, and of defending the country from barbarous inroads. The following year, when his available forces were reduced by furnishing garrisons, he was unable to stem a predatory invasion of Franks and Alemans, who, when they had exhausted Liguria, swept over the south. When famine and disease had facilitated the destruction of these marauders, evils of a more permanent nature beset the imperial

[1] Procopius, de bello Gothico, L. iv. c. 35.

representative, whose efforts to restore prosperity obtained neither aid nor encouragement from Constantinople, where he was expected to make of devastated Italy a self-supporting dominion.

Justinian, during his ten remaining years, reigned without credit over an empire whose redintegration brought weakness rather than strength. From the ocean to the Tigris the boundaries of the Roman world had been regained; but no attempt was made to revive Roman patriotism. While the sanguinary faction-fights of the circus, in which the Emperor allowed himself to be made a partisan, assumed the proportions of a civil war, the Huns and Avars approached with impunity the gates of Constantinople, and a cessation of hostilities with Persia was purchased by the payment of an annual tribute to Chosroes. Justinian died in the eighty-third year of his age, and the thirty-eighth of his eventful reign.

Nov. 14,
A.D. 565.

By Justin II his nephew and successor endeavours to benefit Italy were unappreciated; and the difficulty of collecting an adequate revenue exposed the administration of Narses to the charge of being more oppressive than that of the Goths. Before two years had passed he became the victim of a palace intrigue, and received a letter of recall couched in terms of insult. Whilst hesitating whether he should obey the mandate, he died.

A D 567.

The supposition that, stung by a sense of injustice, he invited the Lombard king, Alboin, to cross the Alps, appears to rest on no sufficient evidence. On every side of the unwieldy empire the barbarian powers were making advances in union and strength : the Franks under Clothair possessed the whole of Gaul: a decisive victory over the Gepidae had given to Alboin such military renown as attracted to his standard a host of combatants, whilst the death of Narses relieved him from the discredit and danger that he would have incurred, had he taken arms against his benefactor.

The civil and military administration of Italy was entrusted by Justin to the patrician Longinus, the first of a succession of exarchs, who for more than two centuries were located at Ravenna as representatives of the imperial government. The authority of the exarchs extended in theory to the whole peninsula, but how unequal the powers possessed by these functionaries were to the realisation of such a theory will appear in the sequel.

CHAPTER VIII.

ITALY UNDER THE LOMBARD KINGS.

A.D. 568-605.

The Lombard Conquest. Weakness of the Emperor Maurice and his exarch. Rome indebted for preservation to Pope Gregory I. Enlargement of the Lombard boundary by King Agilulph. Destruction of Maurice and elevation of Phocas. Death of Gregory the Great. Monza and the iron crown.

A.D. 568. WHEN Alboin, elated by his recent victories over the Gepidae, undertook to win for his people settlements on the south of the Alps, neither he nor his chieftains required the treasonable invitation falsely ascribed to Narses. While engaged in the imperial service they had realised the superiority of Italy over Pannonia, and had bidden adieu to her vine-clad hills with longings for a return: to a race whose habits of life were migratory no additional incentive was requisite.

The fame of Alboin's successes had attracted to his standard a host of auxiliaries; but the flower of his army consisted of his own nobles who, in their equipments and in the number of their personal attendants, resembled the men-at-arms of a subsequent age. The opportunity too was well chosen; for though Justinian in his declining years had been willing to purchase peace at any cost, his successor Justin II, with a courage akin to rashness, had by a withdrawal of the stipulated subsidies provoked hostilities with Persia, and also with the Avars, so that Italy was left defenceless.

Alboin, when he had surmounted the Carnic Alps, is said to have halted on a promontory, afterwards known as 'Mons Regis,' and gazed in ecstasy over the fair region which he had already accounted his own[1]. When, without opposition, he had established himself in Friuli he conferred the government on a nephew, and among the settlers in that fertile province were the ancestors of the Lombard historian Paul Warnefrid, better known as the Deacon, from whose work the following brief sketch of the Lombard occupation is mainly derived. A.D. 569.

The Lombards, to use the words of Mr. Finlay, 'occupy an important place in the history of civilisation.' Their settlement in Italy, like that of the Romans in England, was permanent. During a self-sustained occupation of two hundred and five years, their manners, habits of life and religion underwent a marvellous alteration. To them the overthrow of their last king by Charlemagne brought little more than a change of dynasty, desired by many and acquiesced in by all. Throughout the wide limits of their dominions they remained lords of the soil. Under the Carlovingians, Lombards and Italians were alike eligible to offices of trust and distinction; long cherished animosities

[1] Paulus Diaconus, L. ii. c. 7.

were forgotten and intermarriages took place. The blood of the once abhorred nation, the 'gens nec dicenda,' now flows in the veins of princes, and even the illustrious house of Este is shown by Muratori to have originated in a Lombard ancestor[1].

Although, compared with the Ostrogoths, the Lombards were uncivilised, their twilight Christianity in some degree mitigated the horrors of their invasion; for when Alboin had crossed the Piave, the bishop of Treviso repaired to his head-quarters, and the Arian king did not refuse to the Catholic prelate immunity for his churches, with an exemption of church property from the general confiscation.

However formidable in the field, the invaders possessed neither the knowledge nor the appliances required for the reduction of walled towns. Verona and Vicenza succumbed during the first panic; but Mantua, Cremona, Padua, Montselice and other fortified places maintained an isolated independence.

From the surrender of imperial Milan, Paul Deacon dates the commencement of the Lombard kingdom; yet Pavia, having been fortified by the Goths, still presented an obstacle, and while Alboin undertook the siege, his dukes carved out for themselves and their followers settlements in Liguria, which in those days comprehended Novara, Montferrat and Piedmont. Pavia, after a siege or blockade of three years, surrendered, and the palace built by Theodoric became the residence of the Lombard kings.

A.D. 572.

[1] Muratori, Annali, An. 651.

Death of Alboin.

The provinces first occupied fared the best; for, as the wave of conquest rolled southward, resistance increased and the victors became more relentless. While many Roman garrisons were compelled by famine to surrender, Rome with her duchy continued to form an independent oasis; and though of the means by which this result was accomplished nothing is known, it is certain that the invaders, who repeatedly surrounded the city, failed to obtain an entrance. That all communications between Old and New Rome was at this time cut off is proved by the fact that on the death of John III the succeeding Pope, Benedict I, could not receive the imperial fiat for his consecration until the following year. Meanwhile, the old republican institutions and the authority of the Senate acquired, from the very necessity of the case, a partial revival; and the Pontiff whose wealth, derived from estates in Sicily and elsewhere, supplied the cost of the defence, came to be regarded more and more as immediate head of the state. The determined attitude of Rome, the prolonged resistance of Pavia, and the wide dissemination of the Lombard forces might have enabled a leader like Belisarius, with a small disciplined force, to turn the scale; but Justin, hard pressed on the Euphrates by the Persians, and on the Danube by the Avars, made no attempt to uphold the Roman cause in the West. [A.D 573.]

Alboin did not long survive his capture of Pavia; and the circumstances which formed the prelude to his violent death sufficiently show that, though endowed with abilities which enabled him to found a monarchy, he was still in mind and habits a barbarian. After the death of his first wife he had married Rosamunda, a daughter of Cunimund, king of the Gepidae, whom he had himself slain in battle. As a trophy, he caused the skull of his vanquished adversary to be set in gold for a drinking cup, and, while feasting with his nobles at Verona, he sent for the unfortunate Rosamunda and compelled her to drink wine from this hideous goblet. The outraged queen devised a prompt revenge; and having, without scruple as to the means, suborned an assassin, she took part as an accomplice in her husband's murder by tying his sword into the scabbard [1].

The opinion formed by Narses of the Lombards when, on account of their ferocity, he dismissed them from his service, was now justified. Happy were the proprietors who, abandoning their possessions, made a timely escape to Rome, Ravenna, Genoa or Corsica. For the protection of the vanquished, Alboin had neither the inclination nor the time to legislate; and the rule of Clepho, his elected successor, was one of barbarous violence; the owners of the soil were put to death or driven into exile, churches were pillaged, priests slain, and flourishing towns reduced to ashes [2].

The dominion exercised by Odoacer was, at least

[1] For the last act of the tragedy see Paulus Diaconus, de Gestis Lungobardorum, L. ii. c. 28.

[2] 'Multos Romanorum viros potentes alios gladio interfecit, alios ab Italia exturbavit. Multi nobilium interfecti sunt.' Such is the admission of a writer in descent and predilections a Lombard. Paulus Diaconus, L. ii. c. 31.

in its commencement, consented to and approved by the Roman Senate as a protection against greater evils: that of Theodoric was legalised by an imperial commission; he had served as consul, had resided as an honoured guest at Constantinople, and many of his people were to a certain degree Romanized. On both these occasions the established laws were maintained, the old republican forms respected, and the flattery of self-love might succeed in persuading the Romans of Italy that though fallen they were not enslaved. But the Lombard domination was palliated by no modifying circumstances; it involved, wherever it prevailed, a total abolition of the existing laws and the enforcement of a social system, new to the Latin race, the essence of which was feudality.

While in Italy oppression was at its height, terror reigned at Constantinople. The Persians had overrun Syria and consigned to slavery a large portion of the inhabitants; the Avars were assembled in menace on the Danube; and the Emperor Justin, driven to despair if not to madness, transferred to his son-in-law Tiberius the responsibilities of power, A.D. 574. —and in this he did well, for the virtues of the second Tiberius belied a hateful name.

Clepho, when he had reigned eighteen months, fell by the hand of an assassin, leaving a son Autharis. A.D. 575. An interregnum followed, (A.D. 575-585), during which the Lombard dukes, six and thirty in number, exercised each within his own district uncontrolled authority: and yet, in one respect, the working of this many-headed tyranny appears to have been uniform, for the 'civis Romanus,' if allowed to exist, was divested of every right. It is impossible to read the proofs adduced by Carlo Troja[1] without arriving at the conclusion that, throughout the conquered districts, the inhabitants who failed to make good their escape were reduced to the condition of 'tributarii,' a phrase which implied personal subjection to some Lombard chief by whom they were held responsible for a third of the produce obtained from the land.

The dukes, when in their preference for personal rule they dispensed with the advantages of a central executive, incurred the risk of some fatal reverse. Many places and districts, together with the whole of the sea-ports, were still in the possession of the empire, and opportunities for a re-conquest were not wanting; but the struggle in the East continued to engross the attention and absorb the resources of the government at Constantinople, for, although during the latter years of Justin his adopted colleague Tiberius succeeded in repulsing the Persians, Hormisdas, the son and successor of Chosroes I, persevered, and the war continued. When, on the death of Justin II, Tiberius became sole Emperor, the Pope and Senate in reply to their entreaties received a supply of money together with reinforcements, which, however inadequate, served to keep alive the spirit of resistance.

A.D. 578. About this time the Lombard Duke of Spoleto

[1] Storia d' Italia del medio evo.

succeeded in obtaining possession of Classe, the port of Ravenna; and although the invaders, having neither ships nor commerce, derived but small advantage from this acquisition, the fact that they were allowed to retain for three years a station so important, affords proof of the straits to which the empire was reduced. Though foiled in their attack on Rome, the Lombards, having extended their occupation to nearly the whole inland of Magna Grecia, destroyed the great Benedictine establishment at Monte Cassino[1]; but the monks escaped, and were enabled by Pelagius II to live at Rome according to the rule of their order. *A.D. 581-582.*

Naples, with her surrounding duchy and the maritime cities of Calabria, enjoyed under the sovereignty of the Emperor virtual freedom, but Tiberius II during his reign of four years was unable to afford relief to the defenders of the inland cities; and his successor, Maurice, though a man of cultivated mind and generous disposition, possessed neither the determination nor the tact requisite for the accomplishment of those civil and military reforms of which the empire stood in need. His reign of twenty years, ushered in by an earthquake which laid Constantinople **in ruins**, ended in the murder of himself and his descendants by the tyrant Phocas. *A.D. 583.*

Maurice, having no disposable forces, enlisted the Franks against the Lombards,—a weak and hazardous expedient, for the barbarian powers that had

---

[1] **Restored by** Gregory II after it had lain for 135 years in ruins.

become established around or within the confines of the empire, though willing to receive subsidies, were fickle allies, swayed by a feeling of common interest, which disinclined them to persist in any undertaking that might lead to a re-establishment of Roman power. The dukes nevertheless, urged by the dread of a combination between the Emperor and the Franks, consented to a partial surrender of independence by the election of Autharis, the son of Clepho, for their king, and placed at his disposal a portion of their revenues. The danger which this arrangement was intended to meet was at the door; for King Childebert, having accepted from Maurice an enormous subsidy, pledged himself to expel the Lombards, and had already crossed the mountains when Autharis, through the liberality of his dukes, was able to out-bribe Maurice; and the Franks, without striking a blow, retraced their steps[1].

A.D. 584.

To the crushing yoke of the illiterate Lombards may be ascribed the dearth of contemporary annals; and hence arises the necessity of relying mainly on Paul the Deacon, whose history was compiled about two centuries after the first settlement of his countrymen in Italy, and who admits that he depended for his dates and the earlier portion of his narrative on the history of the Franks by Gregory of Tours. When the exarch Smaragdus was replaced by Romanus, the change boded no good to Roman interests. According to Gregory of Tours[2], it was

A.D. 588.

---

[1] Paulus Diaconus, L. iii. c. 17.
[2] Ibid., L. ix. c. 25.

during this year that **Autharis, in the hope of securing** himself from the **hostility of Childebert,** sent an embassy with costly presents **to demand the hand of** his sister. Childebert, **in the first** instance, encouraged the overture; but ecclesiastical, **no less than political, influences were brought to bear against it, and the** Arian suitor was rejected though **his presents were retained.**

Until the twentieth year of the Lombard occupation the island of Comacina, on the **Lake of Como,** which in the twelfth century **became the scene of** obstinate contests between **the Comaschi and the** Milanese, had been held by a **Roman garrison, and** had served as a place of security where **valuables might be deposited.** After **a siege of six months,** however, by the forces of Autharis, the **governor** was forced by famine to capitulate, and **a rich booty** fell into the hands of the captors.

The following year Autharis found a suitable **consort in** Theodelinda, daughter of Garibaldo, duke of **Bavaria, and the incidents connected** with this marriage **show** that there existed amongst the Lombards **a taste for knight-errantry** altogether unknown **to the Romans. Under the** assumed character **of an ambassador,** Autharis **presented** himself at the Bavarian **court. After an audience** with the Duke, he **obtained an interview** with Theodelinda, and declared in the presence of the courtiers that in her he beheld a princess such as King Autharis desired for his wife, and the Lombards for their queen. At the command of her father and in

A.D. 589

token of his consent, Theodelinda then offered a cup of wine to her unknown suitor, who, as he gave back the goblet, contrived, without being observed, to kiss her hand,—a circumstance which Theodelinda thought it well to confide to her nurse, who advised her to keep the secret, inasmuch as the man who had so presumed could be no other than the king himself.

Childebert, in his animosity against Autharis, whom he had already injured, invaded Bavaria, in the hope of being able to carry off the affianced bride; but Theodelinda, whose destiny it was to reign in the hearts of the Lombards, evaded the toils, and escorted by her brother, arrived in safety at Verona, where the marriage was solemnized with great rejoicings.

May 15.

The dukes, during the nine years of their independence, had consulted mainly their separate interests; but Autharis, when invested with supreme power, began to contemplate a more complete conquest, and soon after his marriage he visited, as liege lord, the great Lombard fief of Beneventum, from whence he proceeded to the Straits of Messina, where he pointed to a column which stood by the shore as the future boundary stone of his kingdom. Yet before a year had elapsed, not the limits only, but the very existence of that kingdom became doubtful.

A.D. 590.

A revolution in Persia had relieved the Emperor Maurice from the greatest of his difficulties: King Hormisdas having been put to death by his subjects, it was through the aid of the Roman forces that his son, Chosroes II, ascended the throne, and the rival empire was converted for a time into a friendly power. This turn of events enabled Maurice to equip an armament for the expulsion of the Lombards, an enterprise for which he once more engaged the support of the Franks and Alemans.

Autharis, unable to contend simultaneously with these enemies, shut himself up in Pavia. His dukes, leaving the cultivators of the soil to the mercy of the enemy, betook themselves to places of strength, while Franks and Alemans continued to consume and lay waste until, urged by famine and sickness, they secured their retreat by separate conventions. At the time of their departure the prospects of Autharis were gloomy, the imperial generals had already possessed themselves of Modena, Altino, and Mantua, and the Lombard Dukes of Parma, Reggio, and Placentia, regarding the struggle as hopeless, had proffered their adherence to the 'Sancta Respublica.' Meanwhile the Romans of Italy were beginning to hug themselves in the belief that the thraldom under which they had groaned for two and twenty years would soon be at an end.

Autharis, relieved by the departure of the Franks, was able to rally his forces and to intimidate his wavering vassals; and though his decease took place the following year, he succeeded in persuading the Frankish rulers that it was not for their interest, nor for that of the barbarian powers in general, to aid in the re-establishment of Roman power in Italy; and the enterprise of Maurice was relinquished.

In their devotion to the widowed queen, the Lombards besought her to make choice of a second husband on whom they might confer the crown, and Theodelinda acted well for the public good when she selected Agilulph, the Lombard Duke of Turin.

On the death of Pelagius II the unanimous suffrages of the clergy, senate, and people were pronounced in favour of the Deacon Gregory. Gregory, while yet a layman, had discharged the important functions of pretor; and, after he received deacon's orders, during a residence of three years as nuncio or ambassador at Constantinople, had associated with the leading men of the day and known their minds. In him the Romans had a patriot Pontiff who yearned for the deliverance of Italy and for a restoration to the ancient capital of its lost importance, an aspiration in which the timid and self-seeking exarch, Romanus, failed to sympathise. That functionary would fain have satisfied his imperial master's expectations, without incurring any personal risk or anxiety. By bribes and promises he induced the Lombard governor to surrender Perugia, and he also succeeded in gaining possession of Sutri and other places which, if he had provided them with garrisons, might have served to protect Rome from insult. But the vantage-ground was soon lost; Agilulph hastened to the rescue, re-took Perugia, and Rome was indebted for her safety to the foresight and defensive preparations of her Pontiff.

It soon became evident that a continuance of the

[Margin notes: Election of Gregory the Great, A.D. 592. — A.D. 593.]

conflict with Agilulph, unless waged with greater energy, would result in additional loss of territory, and Gregory, when his appeals to the Emperor proved fruitless, began to entertain the idea of becoming a mediator of peace; but here again he A.D. 594. found himself opposed by the self-seeking exarch, to whom the continuance of indecisive hostilities brought profit.

About this time John the Faster, Patriarch of A.D. 595. Constantinople, assumed the title of oecumenical bishop, a pretension inconsistent with the established primacy of the Roman Patriarchate. In a letter to Maurice, Gregory conveyed a dignified protest against this encroachment, and in another, written in a similar strain to the Empress Constantina, he expatiates on the deplorable state of Italy. Referring back to the invasion of Alboin, he declares that for seven and twenty years the cost of defending Rome, or of purchasing forbearance from the invaders, had been supplied from the property of the church; and in another letter, addressed to the bishop of Sirmium, he denounces the ill-will of the exarch as more pernicious than the swords of the Lombards, 'Ejus in nos malitia gladios Lungobardorum vicit[1].'

So long as the war continued, he compelled the clergy and even the monks to do garrison duty and assist in the defence of the cities; while by the redemption of captives, he alleviated miseries; and when at length a truce was concluded, his in-

[1] Lib. v. epist. 20, 21.

A.D. 599. fluence was wisely and charitably used in abating animosities.

In one of Gregory's letters, he thanks Agilulph for the cessation of hostilities and asks him to discourage his dukes from seeking, as they were inclined to do, pretexts for an infraction of the truce. In another, addressed to Queen Theodelinda, he urges her to persuade 'her excellent[1] husband' not to reject association with the Christian commonwealth,—words of doubtful import, but which seem to imply that Agilulph had not then embraced Catholicism. Yet if Agilulph was still an Arian, he showed his toleration by permitting the Catholic bishops of his dominion free intercourse with Rome, and by placing no restraint on the munificent zeal of his orthodox consort.

A.D. 601. In the beginning of the seventh century much was still wanting to invest the Lombard settlements with a character of permanency. Many inland cities and nearly all the sea-ports still retained their independence, and Agilulph, who might naturally desire a less incomplete dominion, soon had presented to him a full justification for the re-commencement of hostilities. The new exarch, Callinicus, though a Roman in his aspirations, brought by his utter lack of judgment a series of disasters on the Roman cause. From Cremona, which was still held by an imperial garrison, he despatched a party of soldiers and captured, in their villa near Parma, the daughter and son-in-law of Agilulph. Agilulph, in return for

[1] 'Excellentissimum conjugem vestrum.'

this unprovoked insult, at once laid siege to Padua, where the citizens, after a gallant and prolonged defence, surrendered; and the loss of Padua was followed by that of Montselice. The miseries of this renewal of warfare are bewailed in the letters of Gregory; but Callinicus shortly received his dismissal, and Smaragdus, who had previously served as exarch, was re-instated.

More than thirty years had now gone by since the Lombard invasion began, and the fact that many of the cities still held out sufficiently proves that the charges of utter degeneracy so often made against the Romans **of Italy** ought not **to be ac**cepted without a more careful examination than they have hitherto received.

While Agilulph was engaged in the enlargement of his boundaries, the Emperor Maurice, in **the** twentieth year of his weak and inglorious reign, became the victim of a revolutionary outbreak. His abortive attempts to reform the military administration had already disgusted the army, but the immediate cause of his downfall was his refusal to ransom a large body of Roman prisoners from the Chagan of the **Avars, who put them all to the sword.** The mutiny became general, and Phocas, an obscure centurion, was invested with the command. **When** the troops reached Constantinople they found the gates open, for Maurice with his **wife** and nine children had effected his escape to the opposite shore, and the populace joined the soldiers in proclaiming **Phocas Emperor.** Phocas, after he had A.D. 602.

made his public entry, submitted himself to the ordeal of the circus, where, a dispute having arisen between the green and blue factions, his decision was in favour of the former, when a voice from the blues reminded him that Maurice was still alive. He then signed the fatal order, in pursuance of which the fugitive Emperor was arrested at Chalcedon, and compelled to witness the execution of his five sons before he was himself put to death.

It seems but natural to conclude that information as to the flight of Maurice and the elevation of Phocas would be transmitted to Rome with the least possible delay, and that the Pontiff's congratulatory letter to the new Emperor would be despatched with equal promptitude, before intelligence of the subsequent tragedy at Chalcedon could have reached him; and unless it can be shown that Gregory delayed to send his congratulations until the news of Maurice's execution had reached him, the charge made against him by Gibbon[1] of having written knowingly a courteous and even flattering letter to a ruthless murderer cannot be sustained.

A.D. 603. If Rome with her duchy, the venerable simulacrum of the 'Respublica Romana,' was at this time saved from absorption into the Lombard kingdom, her preservation was entirely due to the moral influence of the Papacy, an influence which the wise and pacific policy of Gregory the Great, during a pontificate of fourteen years, had sustained and strengthened.

A.D. 604. At Monza (Monaetia) on Easter day A.D. 604 the

---

[1] Decline and Fall, ch. xlvi.

infant son of Agilulph and Theodelinda was baptized as a member of the Catholic Church, and the letter in which Gregory offers his congratulations shows that his relations with the Lombard court were not merely tolerant, but amicable[1]. After expressing his gratitude to Agilulph for the restoration of peace, he complains that gout had of late so crippled him, as to render the further prolongation of his life precarious; and this letter was probably his last, for he died soon afterwards.

Gregory I was no independent prince; in his day the patrimony of S. Peter did not exist; his temporal position was that of a subject; yet such was his reputation for Christian zeal, so blameless his life, and so judicious the use which he made of the Church's wealth, that it seems doubtful whether any of his successors have been able to exert an influence more widely beneficial. By him, the institution of slavery was first authoritatively denounced as inconsistent with Christianity; and in him, Pitt, Wilberforce, and the leading philanthropists of modern times, had a precursor of whose existence as such they had possibly never heard.

At Monza (Monaetia), the favourite abode of Theodoric the Great, Agilulph and Theodelinda built a palace and a church. The former was adorned with paintings, commemorating the exploits of the Lombards, which being extant in the time of Paul the Deacon and seen by him, enabled him to describe the

---

[1] Epist. xii. in the xivth Book of Gregory's Letters. Gregory the Great, 590—604 A.D.

ancient dress and accoutrements of his countrymen before they conformed to Roman fashions; and in the church were kept three crowns, of which the most remarkable was the celebrated diadem whose inner circlet was said to be composed of a nail used in the crucifixion. With this, in after times, the Emperors were crowned as kings of Italy, and with this, on the 25th of May 1805, Buonaparte, wishing to be accounted a second Charlemagne, crowned himself, accompanying his act with the presumptuous boast, 'Dio mi ha dato, Guai a chi la tocca!'

CHAPTER IX.

A.D. 605-717.

Maintenance of the Lombard Kingdom by Agilulph. His death and the regency of Theodelinda. The Pantheon becomes a Christian temple. **Death of Phocas.** Heraclius I, accomplishes the humiliation of **Persia** but fails to defend his conquests against the successors of **Mahomet.** First siege of Constantinople. The Venetians elect their first Doge. Italy remains at peace under the protection of the usurper Grimoald. His death, and the joyful restoration of the exiled Bertharis. With Justinian II, the Heraclian dynasty comes to an unlamented end.

FROM the Lombard historian, Paul Deacon, we **A.D. 605**. learn that in the fourth year of Phocas, his exarch Smaragdus acquiesced in the retention by Agilulph of his recent conquests, Cremona and Mantua, and submitted to purchase a truce for the ensuing year, by the payment of twelve thousand gold *solidi*.

During the reign of Maurice, the exactions of his tax-gatherers, the sale of offices, and a total neglect of Italian interests had caused his name to be execrated and prepared the **West** Romans to welcome any change. But they soon discovered that under Phocas they would be exposed to still greater calamities.

The Persian emperor, Chosroes, at a time when his succession to the throne was disputed, had been aided by Maurice,—a circumstance which afforded him a plea for declaring war against the murderer of his ally. Phocas, hard pressed in Asia, left the exarch without resource. By the execution of the widow and daughters of Maurice he outdid his previous crimes, and, during the brief remainder of his reign, he relied on a system of terror. He sought to humiliate the Patriarch, to whose censures his excesses of cruelty had made him liable, by exalting into a supremacy the admitted primacy of the Roman See. He at the same time strove to
A.D. 608. gratify the Romans, and their Pontiff, Boniface IV, by presenting to them the noble rotunda dedicated by Marcus Agrippa, to all the gods; and it was then that the images of the heathen deities, which had been permitted to remain in their niches, were finally removed, and that the Pantheon became a Christian temple.

A.D. 609. Meanwhile, at Constantinople, the Senate held communications with Heraclius—the powerful and semi-independent governor of Africa, who before the close of the year sent his son with a considerable
A.D. 610. armament to their aid. Phocas was slain, and the young Heraclius ascended the throne of Constantine, which to the fourth generation was occupied by his descendants.

The following year, when the Huns made an irruption into Friuli, the Lombard duke fell in a brave but unsuccessful attempt to withstand their overwhelming numbers. His sons escaped; but during their flight, a Hun having snatched the youngest of them, a mere boy, from his brother's crupper, seated him on his own. The youthful prisoner, whose name was Grimoald, slipped a poniard from the belt of his captor, stabbed him in the back, took possession of his horse, and rejoined his brethren. That boy when he grew up became Duke of Beneventum, and ultimately reigned at Pavia.

The errors of Maurice, followed by the wasteful A.D. 612. misrule of Phocas, had brought the empire to the verge of ruin. At Ravenna the exarch existed on sufferance, upheld by the moral influence of the Papacy. On Heraclius devolved the task of regaining lost provinces, and of restoring prosperity to those that remained,—a work of superhuman difficulty, and one for which during the earlier years of his reign he gave no sign of needful energy or aptitude. His attempts to stay the advance of the Persians were fruitless; and Chosroes II, who had made the crimes of Phocas a plea for hostilities, continued them after his fall, adding Cappadocia with its capital, Caesarea, to his previous conquests. But this was only the beginning of losses; ere long A.D. 614. the Christian world was startled by intelligence that Chosroes had taken Jerusalem by storm, that he had carried off the wood believed to be that of the Cross, and that the Patriarch with some thousands of the inhabitants were his captives. Yet these calamities did not prevent Heraclius from taking for his second wife his sister's daughter, Martina,—a marriage of evil augury, and which after his death resulted in a disputed succession.

Before the commencement of the seventh century, Arianism, once the prevailing creed of the northern races, was everywhere on the decline. Agilulph, yielding to the arguments of the Irish Saint Columban, or to the gentle influence of his own orthodox consort, declared his adhesion to the Catholic faith; and it was at the court of Pavia that Columban, when driven from France, obtained an asylum, with means for the establishment of the monastery at Bobbio, where he ended his days.

A.D. 615. When, after a prosperous reign of five and twenty years, Agilulph died, Theodelinda, as guardian of her infant son Adaloaldus, refused to profit by the weak condition of the exarchate, and adhered to a pacific policy. During those years of free intercourse animosities were softened, and the Lombards continued to adopt more and more the habits, tastes, and creed of the Romans.

A D. 616. Yet at Ravenna discontents prevailed. The exarch Lemigius was slain in a tumult; and although his successor, Eleutherius, succeeded in putting down the insurrection, it was at the cost of much bloodshed and cruel reprisals.

Meanwhile the war between the two empires continued, and when a Persian army was encamped on the heights of Chalcedon, Heraclius, yielding to the invitations of its commander, consented to despatch an embassy, consisting of distinguished citi-

Heraclius undertakes the conquest of Persia. 191

zens, to Chosroes. But the tyrant declared that the Emperor himself should have come, threw the envoys into prison, and condemned his own general to be flayed alive! On the mind of Heraclius these atrocities and insults appear to have made a permanent impression, though the difficulties of his position compelled him to temporize. It was need- A.D. 618. ful in the first instance to secure the alliance, or at least the neutrality, of the Avars settled in Pannonia. Their Chagan, by amicable professions, induced the Emperor to meet him in the Thracian city of Heraclea, intending to seize his person, and during the confusion to make himself master of Constantinople. Heraclius with some difficulty effected his escape in disguise. The Avars then forced their way through the long wall, and, although unable to gain an entrance into the city, spoiled the wealthy suburbs.

To Heraclius the unpunished treachery of the A.D. 621. Chagan was a matter of secondary import when compared to the persistent hostilities and insulting provocations of his Eastern rival, with whom, when he had duly counted the cost, he prepared for a decisive struggle. Having supplied the deficiencies of his treasury with loans from the churches, he was able to collect an heterogeneous army consisting mainly of recruits. The only advantage which in the outset he possessed was the freedom of action given by his superior means of transport. To guard against the fatal consequences that might result from any reverse sustained near home, he embarked with

his raw levies, landed on the western coast of Asia, and established himself in a secure position on the
A.D. 622. confines of Syria and Cilicia, where he laboured with unwearied diligence in the routine of camp instruction. By sharing the toils of his soldiers, he gained their attachment; by habituating them to the use of their weapons and by the practice of evolutions, he taught them to have confidence in themselves; until he found himself at the head of disciplined legions such as the empire had not for a long series of years possessed. During the first encounters that took place the Persian cavalry lost their prestige; and, as the war proceeded, Chosroes found to his dismay that victory had deserted his banners. After four
A.D. 626. disastrous campaigns, of which the particulars would here be out of place, he sought to distract his opponent by persuading the Chagan to violate his engagements and lay siege to Constantinople; but, although the Avars were duly provided with catapultas and other means of attack, the garrison held out until the destruction of his galleys and the consequent failure of provisions compelled the faithless barbarian to withdraw.

In the Turks, then established as an independent power on the Oxus, Heraclius obtained adherents who fully compensated him for the defection of the Avars; but it was after the departure of these allies to their settlements, and independently of their aid, that he won, on the ground where Nineveh once
A.D. 627. stood, his final and decisive victory. When the power of Chosroes was irretrievably broken, his

Final and decisive victory of Heraclius. 193

satraps, by whom he had long been detested, turned against him. Siroes, his eldest son, whom he had disinherited, was proclaimed; and, with his consent, his father was thrown into a dungeon, where he died. The parricide lived but a few months, and the power of Persia never revived. A.D. 628.

While engaged in providing for the wants of the re-conquered provinces, the imperial victor was greeted with benedictions; and, the following year, when he arrived at Constantinople, bringing with him from liberated Jerusalem the wood supposed to be that of the Cross, the whole population headed by the Patriarch greeted his return with exulting hymns and heartfelt demonstrations. During the great days of Rome no bolder enterprise had been conceived, nor had any been brought to a more successful conclusion. Yet the day that Heraclius made his public entry, in a triumphal car drawn by four elephants, was followed by nine years of humiliation. The legions that had restored the prestige of the Roman name might have accomplished the recovery of Italy from the Lombards, or stayed the advancing tide of Moslem conquest. But the resources of the empire were over-strained; the spoils of Persia were found inadequate to repay what had been borrowed from the churches; the public coffers were empty, and a system of finance that could only be described as organised confiscation, was at work to perpetuate the evil.

During the continuance of the Persian war (A.D. 622-629) the status of the Lombard kingdom underwent no change. When the regency of Theodelinda was terminated by her death, and the insanity of her son made an election necessary, the Lombards showed their devotion to the memory of their Bavarian queen by conferring the crown on Arioaldus, duke of Turin, on condition that he should marry her daughter Gundeberga; and Arioaldus, while he retained the acquisitions made by Agilulph, and continued to receive the stipulated subsidy, refrained from any attempt to extend his boundaries.

With the Lombards Arianism continued to lose ground; and yet the election of the Arian Duke of Turin, and the fact that in the principal Lombard cities there were still Arian bishops, proves that a considerable minority still clung to their original creed, while the maintenance of toleration does credit to Pope Honorius, who, during a pontificate of fourteen years, was a promoter of charitable forbearance.

Arioaldus had nothing to fear from attempts on the part of the empire to disturb a domination which had now existed for three generations. A long continuance of peace had mitigated, though it could not extinguish, national antipathies. Each party had something to gain from the other. The Romans, in exchange for their civilisation, had placed before them an example of purer manners, and of that exalted appreciation of feminine virtues which is dwelt upon by Tacitus as a characteristic of the Teutonic races. It would indeed seem that with the Lombards the chivalrous spirit, of which during a dark crisis of the French Revolution Burke bewailed the extinction, already prevailed. 'A thousand swords would have leaped from their scabbards to avenge even a look that threatened Theodelinda with insult[1]'; and her daughter Gundeberga, when assailed with unfounded aspersions, had not to wait for a champion who challenged and slew her accuser. By Paul the Deacon frequent mention is made of similar duels.

During the reign of Arioaldus (A.D. 625-636) the Visigoths of Spain made themselves masters of the sea-ports and of such remnants of territory as were still held by Roman garrisons; and the ties which until then connected the country of Seneca, Lucan and Martial, of Trajan and of Theodosius the Great with the empire were finally severed. It was also during the reign of Arioaldus that a new enemy, more formidable than any that had hitherto combined for the destruction of the empire, arose.

While the Persian war was yet in its commencement, Mahomet was driven from Mecca by his persecutors. His flight from his native city (A.D. 622) served to mark the Moslem epoch, Hegira. After many failures and reverses he succeeded in uniting under his command the independent tribes of Arabia, and in making himself their absolute sovereign. With an army of enthusiastic warriors at his disposal, he became the founder of an empire whose extension knew no limits. The Caliphs, his successors, and the people whom they led from conquest to conquest, would seem to have inherited the instincts of Ishmael,

A.D. 632.

---

[1] The words of Burke with regard to Marie Antoinette.

their remote progenitor, 'whose hand was against every man'; and their system was, first to devastate, and afterwards to take possession.

A.D. 634. When their invasion of Syria began, Heraclius, though his own energies no less than his resources appear to have been in a state of exhaustion, repaired to the scene of action, and from his head-quarters at Edessa directed the unsuccessful efforts of his commanders. In less than three years after the death of the prophet, Damascus, the ancient capital, after an heroic resistance, surrendered to his successor. During the two succeeding campaigns the losses sustained by the imperial forces were enormous, and the Moslems, after a final victory obtained near the Lake of Tiberias, completed their conquest of Syria. Heraclius, foreseeing the fall of Jerusalem, secured the wood of the Cross which had been sent back there, and carried it, for the second time, to Constantinople, where his inglorious return presented a miserable contrast to his former triumph.

A.D. 637. Jerusalem, eight years after her deliverance from the Persians, surrendered to the Caliph, Omar; Antioch, the third city of the empire, underwent a similar fate; and the following year Alexandria, after a siege of fourteen months, succumbed. The destruction of these patriarchates, whose ecclesiastical independence had never been questioned, made it easier than it might otherwise have been for the Roman Pontiffs to assert their supremacy.

A.D. 638-641. During the last three years of his life, Heraclius, when not absorbed by theological disputes, was doomed to be haunted by the conviction that the toils and sacrifices whereby he had accomplished the humiliation of Persia had only prepared the way for the Saracens, and a few months after his decease his grandson, Constans II, commenced his long and inglorious reign.

Meanwhile in Italy, for whose interests Heraclius had never cared, the Lombards, on the death of Arioaldus, displayed for his widow, Gundeberga, a devotion similar to that which they had shown for her mother, Theodelinda, by conferring their crown on her second husband, Rotharis, duke of Brescia. Rotharis, encouraged by the anarchy that prevailed at Constantinople after the decease of Heraclius and the weakness of the exarch Isaacus, refused to accept the subsidy which for eight and thirty years had purchased the forbearance of his predecessors, and took permanent possession of Genoa, together with other cities on the Ligurian coast. By the Emperor, Constans II, these losses were acquiesced in, peace was restored, and the circumstances of the time favoured its continuance. The assassination of the Caliph, Omar, retarded the progress of the Moslems in the West, and the Franks were occupied with their own troubles, until the weakness of the Merovingian kings gave place to the energetic rule of Pepin Heristal. Rotharis by a renewal of the truce was precluded from further hostilities, and the power he had attained secured Italy from barbarian inroads.

A.D. 636.

A.D. 642.

For the empire there was no such respite. Constans II, as he advanced in years, showed more and more his unfitness for rule. By his misuse of power and neglect of opportunities, he allowed the Saracens to add Armenia and part of Roman Africa to their conquests, while in Southern Italy their establishment on the Sicilian coast destroyed all sense of security. In controverted questions of divinity Constans arrogated to himself infallible judgment, and by his decree the sainted Pontiff, Martin I, was dragged from the Lateran and after
A.D. 655. a series of cruelties and insults died in exile.

Constans II was the only Emperor who, since the domination of the Lombards began, consented to set his foot on the soil of Italy. Weary of residence amongst a people to whom his follies and his crimes had made him odious, he left Constantinople, intending to establish himself at Rome. But the East Romans, however little they might regret his departure, did not wish the seat of government to be removed, and detained his family. When, during the spring of 662, he landed at Tarentum, he found that the Duke of Beneventum, Grimoald, of whose exploit when a boy mention has been made, was absent, having gone with his troops to Pavia for the purpose of depriving his cousin of the Lombard kingdom and securing it for himself. Constans would fain have celebrated the commencement of his residence in Italy by the acquisition of Beneventum, and, with troops withdrawn from the imperial garrisons, invested the city, until a rumour of the duke's return caused him to desist from any further hostilities against the Lombards; but Grimoald, when he returned, punished his **attempt by** taking possession of Brundusium and Tarentum, and the empire was thus deprived of **two** harbours essential to the maintenance of its power. On Constans' arrival at Rome, he was received with imperial honours, and presented Pope Vitalian with costly offerings; but during his brief sojourn in his intended capital, he called upon the citizens for heavy contributions and deprived the Pantheon of the bronze tiles with which it was covered. He then returned to Calabria, crossed the Straits, and established himself at Syracuse, where he solaced himself, during the ensuing four years, with such amusements as that ancient but still magnificent and luxurious city might afford. But the loyalty of the Sicilians, when they found themselves stricken with ruinous imposts, grew cold; a conspiracy was formed against Constans, he was **murdered** in his bath, and succeeded by his son Constantine Pogonatus, who had been detained at Constantinople. A.D. 663.

A.D. 668.

It now becomes requisite to take up the thread of Italian history, and to describe the relations that existed between the exarchs and the Lombards from the re-establishment of the long truce by Rotharis in 642 until the restoration of Bertharis in 671. Rotharis, by the maltreatment of a consort to whom he owed so much and by the persecution of the men who had opposed his election, displayed a cruel and

revengeful disposition; yet as a legislator he seems to have possessed considerable intelligence, his code being superior to those of the barbarian states, and as a military leader the prestige of his name was a safeguard to Italy. After his death and that of his only son, who survived him but for a few months, the
A.D. 652. Lombards, still mindful of their revered Theodelinda, conferred their crown on her nephew Aribert, by birth a Bavarian prince, and in religion a Catholic. During the nine years of Aribert's peaceful reign the Lombards appear to have been in the happy condition of a people who have no history; but the affection which led him to divide the kingdom between his two
A.D. 661. sons was misdirected. Bertharis reigned at Milan, and Godebert at Pavia; but only for a few months. The disputes to which this arrangement inevitably led, ended in an appeal to arms. At the request of Godebert, Grimoald, duke of Beneventum, intervened and terminated the quarrel by placing on his own head the Lombard crown. Godebert he treacherously slew; Bertharis, having narrowly escaped a similar fate, fled to the Chagan of the Avars, but the Chagan, yielding to the threats of Grimoald, withdrew from him the rights of hospitality. His subsequent adventures, as described by Paul the Deacon, afford a glimpse of the habits of life prevalent amongst the Lombards. When driven from the court of the Chagan he came to the singular resolution of throwing himself on the generosity of his persecutor; and Grimoald, when aware of his intention, sent him a safe conduct, received him with open

arms, and assigned him a suitable pension. On neither side does there appear to have been any deficiency of loyal intentions; but the Lombard nobles were apt to frequent the house of Bertharis and to pay an indiscreet homage to the man whom they regarded as their rightful sovereign, and insinuations reached the ears of Grimoald that if Bertharis continued to live he would also reign. Jealousy combined with fear at length led the usurper to regard the death of his confiding guest as a matter of state necessity, and the end of a feast was fixed upon as the most convenient time for the commencement of an affray in which Bertharis was to have been slain; but a faithful attendant, Onolphus, who had been his companion in all his troubles, having received a warning of this plot, devised a counterplot. When, to prevent the possibility of an escape, soldiers were already stationed round the house, Bertharis was dressed as a slave and Onolphus drove him out, pursuing him with kicks and imprecations. The soldiers, never dreaming that the son of a king would allow himself to be thus handled, allowed them to pass. Horses were in readiness, and Bertharis escaped to France. A valet, who had personated him by occupying his bed, and Onolphus were arrested; but Grimoald, when they were accused before him, turned to his courtiers and said, 'By Bacchus, here are two men who have risked their lives for their prince!' and ordered that they should be handsomely provided for. Soon afterwards, meeting with Onolphus, he questioned him as to his state.

A.D. 664.

'Sire,' replied the honest Lombard, 'I owe to your generosity more than I desire, but I should prefer to share the fate of Bertharis, whatever that may be'; and the valet having expressed the same desire, they were supplied with what might be required for their journey to France.

Grimoald, notwithstanding his territorial acquisitions and his success in protecting the kingdom from the inroads of other barbarian powers, never ceased to be regarded by the Lombards as a usurper, and his decease was followed by the prompt and joyful restoration of the ex-king. Bertharis, after his escape from Pavia, had wandered from court to court, until, weary of being watched and of involving his hosts in trouble, he resolved to seek an asylum in England. He had actually embarked, and the sails were set, when a cry was heard from the shore, 'If Bertharis is aboard, let him know that he may return home; Grimoald is dead!'

A.D. 671.

At the time when, to the great joy of his countrymen, Bertharis re-ascended his father's throne, the Roman world was looking to the coming year with painful forebodings. The Caliph, Moavia, now undisputed sovereign of the vast Moslem empire, was prepared to carry out, with forces deemed irresistible, his long-cherished design. The advance of age, after a life of incessant toil, constrained him to delegate the command of those forces to his eldest son, Yezid, with a leader of experience for his mentor. The fleet, during its passage through the Dardanelles, encountered no opposition and disem-

First siege ofConstantinople.

barked the troops near the palace of Hebdomon, seven miles from the city. On the side of the Romans doubts and misgivings prevailed; on that of the Saracens, full confidence of victory. But when, in the fifth year of Constantine Pogonatus, the siege commenced, the strength of the walls and the efficiency of the engines with which they were surmounted surpassed expectation; while at sea the inferiority of the imperial fleet was more than compensated by the possession of a new and terrific agent of destruction, consisting of an inextinguishable fire that could be ejected through tubes upon the hostile galleys. A.D. 672.

From April to September the Saracens repeated their attacks with their wonted perseverance, but with heavy losses of men and ships, a considerable number of the latter being wholly or in part consumed. Moavia, who had destroyed a fleet of Constans II and established the superiority of the Saracenic navy, could not believe in its ultimate defeat; and during the five following years the conflict was resumed, but with no different result, and not only the Italians, but the barbarian powers became aware that the Moslems, whose rapid and hitherto unchecked advances had made men tremble, had at length received an effectual repulse. The powerful Chagan of the Avars was the first to send an embassy with congratulations to the Emperor, and with offers of alliance against the common enemy. Moavia, weakened by the loss of his ships, and of his bravest combatants, was not slow to A.D. 678

perceive the danger of such a combination ; and, to the surprise of the world, the man who had hitherto marched from victory to victory consented to a truce for thirty years, accompanied by the humiliating condition of an annual subsidy payable to the empire. The broken-hearted Caliph survived his failure, but only for two years.

The credit of Roman arms was re-established and security gave a new impulse to commerce. It must not however be imagined that this unforeseen and glorious result was, in any considerable degree, due to the efforts or intellectual qualities of Constantine III (Pogonatus), but rather to the horror with which all classes of citizens regarded the possibility of a sack by the merciless Saracens,—a feeling which acted as a powerful stimulant to the valour and fortitude which they are said to have displayed in aiding the garrison. Yet without the invention of the engineer Callinicus, a deserter from the service of the Caliph, and his practical instructions as to its use, the means of defence must ultimately have been exhausted.

While the conflict was in progress the fate of Italy hung in the balance. Had the Caliph come off as victor and retained his naval superiority, his galleys would ere long have been seen in the Tiber ; and neither at Rome, Ravenna, nor Pavia was there any force that could have withstood an army of Moslems flushed with success, and reinforced by countless adventurers athirst for spoil.

The happiness of Bertharis during the first seven

years after his restoration was disturbed by fearful anticipations, for Bertharis was no warrior. But when at length his anxieties were removed, he gave free vent to his instinctive benevolence, by affording help and protection to those who, like himself, had known adversity. Amongst the guests who enjoyed his hospitality was Wilfrid, the sainted bishop of York, when on his way to Rome to solicit a decree for his re-establishment in the See from which he had been unjustly driven. By Eddius, the bishop's devoted friend and biographer, who accompanied him on this journey, the king is described as 'virum humilem et quietum,—trementem sermones Dei.'

The Lombards had now for more than a century held their Italian kingdom, and from time to time extended their boundaries. Though no longer aggressive they retained all they had won; the descendants of Grimoald still ruled the Duchy of Beneventum, and the marriage of his grandson with a daughter of Bertharis secured harmonious relations between the kingdom and its great southern dependency.

Of Cunibert the son, associated colleague and A.D. 688. successor of Bertharis, it is recorded that he was a man of goodly presence, brave and generous; that he put down with energy a dangerous rebellion headed by the Lombard Duke of Brescia, but that, like his father, he was a promoter of peace; that he had for his consort Ermelinda, an Anglo-Saxon princess; that he enjoyed the love of his people, was a munificent patron of the monasteries, and that he received at Pavia with great magnificence Ceadwalla, king of Wessex[1], the father, or more probably, the brother, of his queen.

A.D. 698. During the reign of Cunibert, Venice, the first-born of Italian commonwealths, assumed a definite form of government. Two centuries and a half had gone by since the families that escaped from Aquileja, Concordia and Altinum, when Attila destroyed those cities, found a refuge in the islands and sand-banks of the Venetian shore. Having saved but little from the wreck of their fortunes, they eked out a subsistence by fishing, or by carrying on a petty commerce with the neighbouring towns. By degrees their traffic enlarged, and when their wealth became sufficient to tempt spoilers they found it necessary to combine and to place their means of defence in the hands of Paul Anapest, better known as Paoluccio, their first Doge.

A.D. 699. Cunibert, before his death, entrusted his only son, Liutpert, to the guardianship of Asprandus, a Bavarian prince; but no sooner was Liutpert proclaimed than there arose in Ragimbert, duke of Turin, a competitor for the throne. Ragimbert, having gained possession of Pavia, was recognised as king, and, after a reign of a few months, was

Reign of Aribert II, A.D. 701-712. succeeded by his son Aribert II. The following year Asprandus, supported by a considerable number of the Lombard magnates, made an unsuccessful

---

[1] Ceadwalla was on his way to Rome, where he died after receiving baptism from Sergius. Turner's History of the Anglo-Saxons.

attempt to restore his ward; but in the battle which ensued Liutpert fell wounded into the hands of the usurper, who caused him to be bled to **death in a bath**. Asprandus effected his escape to Bavaria; but his consort and the whole of his family, with the exception of his youngest son, Liutprand, were captured and treated with atrocious cruelty.

The rule of Aribert II was equitable, and his conduct evinced anxiety to maintain the blessing of peace. Yet he failed to acquire the attachment of his countrymen. To Bavaria the Lombard malcontents still looked with hope; and Asprandus, while engaged in the education of his remaining son, was watching his opportunity. Through the friendship of the Duke of Bavaria, he was at length enabled to re-enter Italy at the head of an army. After a long and sanguinary conflict the Bavarians were repulsed, and contemplated retreat; but Aribert, instead of turning the advantage to account, gave offence to his soldiers by going back **to** Pavia, and when, deserted by his own troops, he would fain have escaped, a solitary fugitive, to France, **he** was drowned **in** attempting to swim the Ticinus.

The Lombards immediately proclaimed Aspran- A.D. 712. dus, who died soon after his election, but **not until** he had the satisfaction of hearing that his son **Liut-** prand was chosen for his successor. Liutprand, during his long reign, of which **the** leading events will be described in a subsequent chapter, greatly increased the relative importance of the Lombard kingdom; and his power, though a terror to the exarchs, was in the main beneficial, for it served as a defence against barbarian inroads at a time when the Romans of Italy would have looked in vain to the empire.

While Italy, protected by the Lombard kings, had a long exemption from invasion, the prestige and the territorial boundaries of the Roman world underwent diminution. After the glorious conclusion of the war with the Caliph Moavia, Constantine Pogonatus, during his remaining seven years, turned to no account the vantage-ground that had been won, and under his son Justinian II the empire reached a stage of degradation previously unknown. An enumeration of Justinian's atrocious acts may be found in the Chronographia of Theophanes, but inasmuch as those crimes did not affect Italy beyond the limits of Ravenna, the disgusting catalogue would here be out of place.

A.D. 685-695. Justinian, before the conclusion of the first reign, so fully earned the hatred and contempt of the East Romans that they condemned him to be banished with slit nose to Cherson. Having accomplished an escape from his appointed place of exile, after an interval of ten years, and a strange series of adventures and wanderings, he returned accompanied

A.D. 705. by an army. With a jewelled nose and an insatiable thirst for vengeance he re-ascended the throne, and his second reign was even worse than the first. Meanwhile the weak and disordered condition of the empire had enabled Abdul Malek to complete the conquest of Africa, and Carthage, which since the expulsion of the Vandals had become **once more** an important centre of maritime power, succumbed **to** the Saracens. This **final loss of** a dominion where the colonists **were Romans** in blood, in language, and in religion, **was the most fatal** that the 'Sancta respublica Romana,' **already advanced in its de**cadence, could have **sustained.**

Justinian in the fifth **year of** his second reign remembered that the **citizens of Ravenna had cele**brated with joyful demonstrations his deposition and banishment. He therefore placed an armament under the command of an officer who, when he had reached the harbour and by friendly professions **had** A.D. 709. obtained permission to disembark with **his** soldiers, arrested the designated victims and carried them off to Constantinople, where **they were thrown into** prison, to await the Emperor's decision as to tortures to which they were to be subjected before they were put to death.

The Ravennati when informed of their treatment A.D. 711. flew to arms, and their revolt was followed by that **of the neighbouring cities.** But the doings of Justinian **had by this** time evoked resentments which led to **an organised rebellion.** Before the close of the year, **while attempting to escape** from Constantinople, he was **overtaken and slain, while his** innocent son, torn from the altar rails of a church, was also put to death, and thus the Heraclian dynasty came to a deplorable but unlamented end.

Philippicus, a banished general who had acted as leader of the insurgents, was then enthroned. But

P

the following year, when he had failed to defend the shores of the Bosphorus from spoliation by the Bulgarians and Saracens, he was deprived of his eyes, and replaced by Artemius, who had done good service to his country as secretary of state and who when chosen Emperor was named Anastasius.

A.D. 713.

The expectation that the Moslems, elated by their success in Africa, would ere long strike a blow at the heart of the empire, had now become general. And Anastasius spared neither toil nor money in improving the defences of the capital. But he could not remedy the state of chronic insubordination into which the imperial forces had fallen, and when he sent an armament to watch the movements of the enemy, and to check their advance, the troops, on reaching Rhodes, slew their commander, steered back to Constantinople, and, having obtained an entrance, pillaged or burned the houses. Anastasius for a while held out at Nicea, but was ultimately compelled to retire into a monastery, while one Theodosius, a tax-gatherer, was compelled against his will to put on the imperial mantle.

A.D. 716.

By this time, the preparations of the Caliph Soliman had seemed as a warning for every class to join hand in hand in resisting a subjection which all agreed in regarding with unmitigated horror. Theodosius willingly resigned the dignity that he had never coveted, and Leo, named from the country of his birth the Isaurian, was proclaimed. The abilities and courage of Leo had raised him to the highest grade in the army, and with his elevation

A.D. 717.

to the throne a new era commenced. By his reforms the decadence of the empire was arrested and the advance of the Moslem stayed, while, by the part which he subsequently took in the great controversy which agitated Christendom, the degrading moral torpor that had long pervaded the East was brought to an end.

His successful defence of Constantinople, when for the second time besieged by the successors of Mahomet, and the revolt of states against the violence with which he enforced the expulsion of images and pictures from the churches, will be treated of in the next chapter.

CHAPTER X.

ITALY UNDER THE LOMBARD KINGS. LIUTPRAND TO THE CONQUEST OF THE KINGDOM BY CHARLEMAGNE.

A.D. 717-770.

Prosperity of the Lombards under Liutprand. Leo the Isaurian Emperor. Second siege of Constantinople by the Saracens. The Iconoclastic schism. Revolt of Italy. Alliance of the Papacy with the Frankish Monarchy. Donation of the Exarchate to the See of Rome.

A.D. 717.   AT a time when Constantinople was preparing for a struggle on the issue of which depended the 'To be or not to be' of the Eastern empire, the Lombards had been for five years under the peaceful rule of their Bavarian king, Liutprand, a framer of just laws, described in the preamble to his public acts as 'Excellentissimus Rex, gentis felicissimae, Catholicae, Deoque dilectae, Lungobardorum.' Nor was this a vain formality; for happy indeed was the condition of Lombard Italy when compared with the overtaxed and misgoverned provinces of the Exarchate.

In Gregory II[1], a Roman of the old stamp, Liutprand had a cotemporary whose views as to the duty of rulers were more enlightened than those of his age. Gregory, having accompanied his

[1] Gregory II, 715-731 A.D.

predecessor to Constantinople, had acquired during a residence there an acquaintance with the actual condition of the empire. Recognising as he did the imminent danger of a Saracenic conquest, he rejoiced to see the imperial resources entrusted to a man of **ability**; and with his approbation, the effigy of the Isaurian Augustus was welcomed at Rome **with** the accustomed honours.

During the nine and thirty years that intervened since their first siege of Constantinople, the Moslems had more than recovered the humiliation of their Caliph, Moavia. No longer content with dominions that reached from the furthest limits of Persia to the Atlantic, they had (A.D. 711) crossed the **Straits**, defeated King Roderic, the thirty-third successor of Alaric, and established their dominion in Spain. Their Caliph, Soliman, had chosen his time when the empire, weakened by the loss of Africa, by a series of revolutions, and by demoralising mutinies, seemed to be on the verge of a collapse. He was now bent on a decisive trial of strength between the Crescent and the **Cross**; but he did not find the **East** Romans entirely unprepared.

The deposed emperor, Anastasius II, whose patriotism **was requited** with a monk's cowl, had shown no deficiency of foresight or of energy. No sooner, writes the Patriarch Nicephorus, was the gravity of the danger ascertained than Anastasius became wholly occupied with measures of defence. Persons unprovided with means of subsistence for three years were ordered **to leave** the city, the walls were strengthened and furnished with engines, officers appointed to their stations, and ample stores of food accumulated. The new Emperor had only to complete what had been commenced, and to multiply precautions. Not a few of the men who had borne their part in the former siege were still serviceable, and retained the secret of Greek fire, with practical skill in its manipulation, whereas, strange as it may seem, the Saracens appear to have acquired no further knowledge of this means of destruction than they possessed before. The dauntless wielders of the scimitar seem still to have dreaded it as a mysterious agent, against which no valour of theirs could avail.

Second siege of Constantinople.

A.D. 717. In August, Masalmas, the commander of Soliman's land forces, having crossed the Hellespont, commenced siege operations ; and in the beginning of September, when the Caliph himself with fifteen hundred vessels, some of which were of an unusual height, approached the port, Leo, with his fire-ships and with a favouring wind, bore down upon him. No sooner did the inextinguishable fire begin to take effect, than panic and confusion in the crowded Moslem fleet made any escape difficult, and the devouring element had food enough. In October, the Caliph, after he had witnessed the defeat of his armada, died, and his decease was followed by an early and unusually severe winter, which caused a mortality amongst the ill-sheltered horses and beasts of burthen. In the spring, when needful supplies of provisions were sent from Egypt and Africa, the Egyptian soldiers who formed the convoy deserted their charge, and, hastening on to Constantinople, acclaimed Leo their sovereign. The store-ships being left defenceless were either captured or destroyed, and, in the camp of the besiegers, sickness caused by the inclement winter was aggravated by scarcity of food. When an abandonment of the siege could no longer be postponed, the troops that still held together were harassed in their retreat by the Bulgarians, and not more than a fifth part of the original number reached Damascus.

The dangers and sacrifices incurred in the defence of the imperial city, when for the second time beleaguered by the Moslems, cannot be compared with those of the previous siege; yet the skilful use that Leo made of his advantages, and the successful result of a conflict which for fourteen months had been anxiously watched, secured to him a worldwide renown. The political anarchy that had long prevailed was brought to an end, and sanguine hopes for the future were entertained. Yet Leo could not fail to perceive that without a complete change in the military and fiscal arrangements there could be no permanent revival of prosperity, nor security for peace. It was not indeed probable that the Moslems would **continue** to waste their strength in an enterprise for which neither their habits nor means of warfare were suited; but, in the field, their armies of enthusiastic warriors had never been broken; the provinces still lay at their mercy, and by destroying the sources of revenue, they might render the imperial government powerless.

Leo was the originator of a new military system

which, during five centuries, served to protect the Eastern empire from subversion. For the maintenance of an efficient army, a more regular collection of the taxes became necessary; and in an age when loans were unknown the difficulties of carrying out financial reforms must needs have been great. Leo, nevertheless, accomplished his undertaking, and Italy might have shared in the benefit if he had not, in the tenth year of a successful reign, sought to exercise the powers of a dictator in questions of ecclesiastical discipline and reform.

A.D. 726.

Iconoclastic schism. That before the end of the sixth century the use of images in churches had grown into a flagrant abuse appears from two letters of Gregory the Great[1]. Gregory, while in general terms he praises the anxiety of the bishops to prevent the worship of things made by men's hands, reproves their too hasty zeal in causing images to be ejected from the churches and broken in a way that had given offence to the congregations. Yet while he orders the retention of images and paintings, as a means of conveying instruction to the people who could not read, he adds the injunction 'Adorari vero imagines omnibus modis veta.'

As to the right of the Emperor to dictate in matters of usage and practice no less than in questions of doctrine, Leo had no misgivings. He seems indeed to have considered that the bishops and clergy were as much bound as the officers of his army to obey his orders. Yet his first decree

[1] Lib. ix. epist. 105; and Lib. xi. epist. 13.

could scarcely be considered wanting in moderation, inasmuch as it only required that the pictures or statues should be placed at such a height that the people could not kiss them; and virtually the dispute hinged on the question as to the right of the temporal power to interfere at all. John of Damascus, the ablest writer of his day, utterly denied that right, on the ground that the gospel was not preached by emperors or kings, but by the apostles; that to the temporal rulers the defence and temporal welfare of the state was confided, while the guidance and government of the church belonged exclusively to its bishops and pastors.

Leo nevertheless persisted, and when opposed became a persecutor. His convictions seem to have been sincere, but the violence wherewith he sought to impose them on his subjects cannot be defended. Impatience of his new system of taxation had already alienated the inhabitants of the Greek islands, who then enjoyed a considerable portion of the commercial prosperity afterwards monopolised by Venice; and when Leo began to enforce his decrees, the smouldering discontent of the islanders found vent in an open rebellion, rashly undertaken, and easily suppressed. At the time when the A.D. 727. schism assumed a definite form, Gregory II, whose patriotism no less than his other merits endeared him to the Romans, was in the thirteenth year of his pontificate. While the unwilling East submitted to irresistible force, the less dependent West revolted. Rome became the centre of opposition, and the

Pontiff, when he placed himself in direct hostility to his temporal sovereign, could rely on the almost unanimous support of his countrymen. In two thundering monitories he informed Leo that the successor of S. Peter had authority to rebuke and to punish the kings of the earth; that the Papacy constituted the link whereby the connection of Italy with the empire had been maintained; and that, if pressed too far, he might be driven to accept the alliance and to rely on the protection of the Lombard king; a menace which he would have been most unwilling to execute.

Though three-fourths at least of inland Italy had become subject to the Lombards, the maritime towns of which they had obtained possession were comparatively few. Naples, Bari, Taranto, with their adjacent districts, the ports of the Roman duchy, and on the opposite coast Rimini, Pesaro, Fano, Sinigaglia and Ancona, still formed part of the 'Respublica Romana'; but however anxious to remain so, they were not prepared to accept the Emperor's dictation or to obey the orders of his exarch, in matters relating to the doctrine or discipline of the Church.

Gregory, when he found his monitories of no avail, took the lead in a general resistance to the capitation tax, and Leo was believed to have authorised in revenge a conspiracy against his life, on the discovery of which the imperial agents, or suspected agents, became the victims of popular indignation. Orders were then sent to the exarch, Paulus, for the Pope's forcible deposition; but the Romans, aided by the Lombards of Spoleto and Tuscany, were able to prevent the entrance of the **Emperor's** troops into the duchy. The cities of the Pentapolis [1] joined the insurrection, and even at Ravenna the exarch was outnumbered, and lost his life in a tumult.

The leaders of the rebellion, elated by success, desired that the deposition of Leo should be declared, and that they might be allowed to follow an Emperor, chosen and proclaimed in Italy, to Constantinople. Nor was such a project altogether extravagant; for at Constantinople, no less than in the Italian cities, the bulk of the population was disaffected, having seen with horror Leo's soldiers force their way into the churches and destroy the time-hallowed objects of their veneration. But the Pope refused to sanction an enterprise which, by lighting up a civil war in Christendom, would have encouraged the Moslems or facilitated the more complete subjugation of Italy by the Lombards.

Even to the peace-loving Liutprand the confusion A.D. 729. that prevailed and the weakness of the exarch presented a temptation too strong to be withstood. After a short siege he obtained possession of Ravenna and, together with other spoil, carried off to Pavia an equestrian statue in bronze, supposed to represent Antoninus Pius, which in the time of Muratori still adorned the market-place [2], but was

[1] Rimini, Pesaro, Fano, Umana, and Ancona, on the Flaminian way.
[2] 'Bella statua di bronzo, stimato Antonino Pio, la quale serve d' ornamento alla lor piazza ed é da loro chiamata il Regisole.'

destroyed when the city was taken and sacked by the French republicans in 1796.

The Venetians, though in their dislike of the obnoxious decrees they were at one with Rome, dreaded the possibility of the severance of Italy from the empire; and before the close of the year were able by an unexpected attack to expel the Lombards and restore Ravenna to its rightful sovereign.

About the same time Liutprand, having occasion to put down the rebellion of his troublesome vassal, the Duke of Spoleto, took up a position which from its nearness caused uneasiness at Rome. Gregory at once decided to try the effect of a personal interview, and addressed him as a son of the Church. Touched by this show of confidence, the Lombard king threw himself at the Pontiff's feet, accompanied him to the shrine of S. Peter, and hung up his Regalia, *ex voto*. But notwithstanding these ostensible approaches to a less hostile feeling, in the hearts of the Romans an undercurrent of national antipathy ran deep.

A.D. 731. The death of Gregory II deprived Rome of a Pontiff by whom, in times of difficulty, the independence of the city and duchy had been ably maintained. His successor, Gregory III[1], though a Syrian by birth, was like his predecessor a Roman in heart, and became the originator of a policy which resulted in the establishment of a new empire of the West, with Rome for its ecclesiastical centre.

[1] Gregory III, 731–741 A.D.

About this time the victory obtained over the A.D. 732. Moslems at Poitiers placed Charles (Martel), duke of Austrasia, Mayor of the Palace, and virtual ruler of the Frankish monarchy, in a conspicuous position, as the defender of Western Christendom. The Caliphs, having consolidated their power in Spain, had crossed the Pyrenees and extended their ravages into the heart of France, when Eudes, duke of Aquitaine, whose territory had been the first to suffer, obtained the generous aid of his former enemy, Charles (Martel). These two paladins, after an obstinate and prolonged conflict, completely routed the Emir Abd-el-Rhaman, who did not survive his overthrow.

While Charles Martel and the Pontiff were occupied, the one in the defence of France and the other in an anxious contest with the Iconoclast Emperor, the alliance of the Lombard king was desired and cultivated by both, and as a testimony of respect for Liutprand, Martel sent his son Pepin to Pavia, in A.D. 735. order that he might receive from him an honorary adoption as his son[1].

While the Saracens were devastating with im- A.D. 733. punity the Eastern provinces of the empire, and carrying off the inhabitants for slaves, the forces of the empire were engaged in a different direction. Leo felt that unless Ravenna could be secured, and the hostile spirit of its inhabitants subdued, Central

---

[1] Paul the Deacon relates how, in token of this adoption, Liutprand cut the youthful Pepin's hair! 'Quomodo Rex Liutprandus Pippino, Caroli filio, capillum totondit!' Lib. iv. c. 53.

Italy would be lost. He therefore equipped a powerful armament which, after it had entered the Adriatic, was dispersed by a succession of tempests. When, after much delay, the troops were able to land, they found the Ravennati prepared, and their commander, who had been commissioned to bring the Pope for trial to Constantinople, escaped with difficulty to his ships.

During the remainder of Leo's reign, while in matters relating to the Image controversy his exarch was powerless, in the appointment of the judges, collectors of taxes, and other public functionaries the routine was undisturbed, and neither at Rome nor elsewhere was there any denial of allegiance.

The Moslems, notwithstanding their defeat at Poitiers, retained possession of Narbonne and Languedoc. When their aggressions were resumed Liutprand assisted Martel in the protection of Arles and Provence; and his position as an established and tacitly recognised Christian ruler, may be judged by the circumstance that the Devonshire missionary and martyr, S. Boniface, when on his way to Rome to confer with the Pope on the conversion of Germany, resided for a while at his court, was received with great honour, and escorted on his journey.

A.D. 738-739.

Yet, great as were the advances of the Lombards in civilisation and knowledge, between them and the Romans no real, or at least no permanent friendship could exist, and as soon as their aid in resisting the Iconoclast could be dispensed with dissensions broke out. Trasmondo, duke of Spoleto, in his rebellion against Liutprand could rely upon his Roman neighbours for sympathy and protection; and when Trasmondo was deposed, they assisted in the accomplishment of his temporary restoration. After such a proof of implacable aversion, a continuance of the generous forbearance so lately exhibited by Liutprand could no longer be expected, and hostilities became imminent.

Such was the perilous crisis of affairs when A.D. 741. Gregory III, during the last year of his pontificate, despairing of any help from Constantinople, sent two embassies to Charles Martel, conjuring him not to prefer the friendship of the Lombards to that of S. Peter; an exhortation to which he added a more mundane inducement when, in the name of the Senate and people, he offered him the sovereignty of Rome with the title of Patrician. The death of Martel took place on the 18th of June, soon after he received Gregory's overture, and the terms in which he replied have not come down. That he accepted the protectorate of the Roman See may be inferred from the language used by his descendant, Louis le Débonnaire, when he enjoined his sons to watch over and defend the Church of S. Peter as his great-grandfather, Charles (Martel), his grandfather Pepin, and his father Charles the Great had done. But though Martel may have consented to watch over and protect the Roman Church, there is nothing to show that he intended to act against his friend and ally, Liutprand, or that any change at that time took place in the relations between Rome and the empire.

In November the death of Gregory III induced Liutprand to delay any attack on the duchy, and the newly elected Pontiff, Zacharias I[1], having formed a correct estimate of his placable disposition, com-

A.D. 742. menced negotiations, the result of which was perfectly successful. Zacharias obtained restitution of such places as had been occupied by Lombard garrisons, together with a truce for twenty years,—a transaction indicative of the position attained by the Pontiff as temporal ruler of Rome. Republican forms were preserved, but it was the Pope who negotiated treaties and discharged the functions of the executive.

The decease of Leo the Isaurian, which took place some months before that of Gregory, brought no cessation of the ruinous discord that for fifteen years had prevailed. Constantine Copronymus, whose views coincided with those of his father, relied as his father had done on the efficacy of persecution. While in the first year of his reign he was engaged in resisting the Moslems a report of his death reached Constantinople, and his more popular brother-in-law Artabasdus was at once elected in his place. Constantine's attempts to regain the throne were at first unsuccessful, and Artabasdus during a reign of about two years re-established the images; but when Constantine,

A.D. 743. who inherited the energy of his race, was able to collect adequate forces, he laid siege to Constanti-

---

[1] Zacharias, 741-752.

nople, reduced the city by famine, and, when he obtained an entrance, disgraced his victory by treating his dethroned brother-in-law and the sons of his only sister with atrocious barbarity.

During these years of civil war, Zacharias abstained from any act or declaration whereby he might have compromised his position as a peacemaker, or betrayed a want of loyalty to the legitimate head of what was still called the 'Sancta Respublica.' When a Lombard army was assembled for the purpose of wresting from the feeble exarch the territories committed to his charge, it was by the personal entreaties and by the presents of the Pontiff that Liutprand was induced to desist, and even to give up the towns that his troops had occupied. Zacharias on his return to Rome was greeted with heartfelt joy, as a triumphant peace-maker, and the decrees of a council held soon afterward are dated 'Anno Liutprandi Regis trigesimo secundo.' This was the first, and it would seem the only public recognition of the existence of a Lombard king that was ever made at Rome.

Liutprand died the following year, and with that A.D. 744. event Paul Warnefrid (the Deacon), after pronouncing a just eulogy[1] on the best and greatest of the Lombard kings, terminates his national history; a circumstance much to be regretted, as

---

[1] 'Vir multae sapientiae, consilio sagax. Pius admodum, et pacis amator. Bello potens. Delinquentibus clemens. Castus. Pudicus. Orator pervigil. Eleemosynis largus. Literarum quidem ignarus, sed Philosophis aequandus.' Lib. v. c. 58.

Paul's life being prolonged for forty years, he might as a contemporary writer have supplied the lamentable deficiency of reliable information which exists during almost the whole of that interval.

A.D. 745. From Rachis, duke of Friuli, the successor of Liutprand, Zacharias obtained a renewal of the truce, and during the four uneventful years that
A.D. 749. ensued there was peace; until Rachis, moved by some unknown provocation, laid siege to Perugia, and when persuaded by the Pope to desist, sought a respite from kingly cares in the cloister of Monte Cassino, having for his successor his brother Astolphus, whose ambitious projects accelerated the inevitable extinction of an independent Lombard kingdom.

A.D. 751. In 751 an embassy arrived at Rome from Pepin the Short, who, with no higher title than Mayor of the Palace, had succeeded his father Charles Martel as virtual ruler of the whole Frankish monarchy, to demand the authoritative opinion of the Pontiff as to whether the Franks might justly withdraw the merely nominal allegiance which they still rendered to the imbecile Merovingians and confer their crown upon himself. The reply of Pope Zacharias implied that the person who had inherited and who permanently exercised kingly power might, without offence, be invested with its
A.D. 752. emblems. Pepin was then crowned by S. Boniface, and Chilperic, the last Merovingian king, lived out the remainder of his days in a monastery, and a precedent was established, to which future pontiffs

might refer, when they claimed the right of giving or withholding temporal sovereignties.

The Image controversy had by this time done much to weaken **the ties which,** since the time of Constantine **the Great, had been kept up** between the church and the empire. The energetic Copronymus, during his long reign (A.D. 741–A.D. 775) persisted in his violence as an iconoclast, and in A.D. 754 he obtained the sanction of a council consisting of no less than three hundred and thirty-eight bishops, including the submissive patriarch of Constantinople; but those of Rome, Antioch, Alexandria, and Jerusalem, refused to send representatives. A.D. 754.

After the death of Pope Zacharias, the ambition of Astolphus rendered the preservation of **peace** between the Lombards and the Roman duchy impracticable. As a step towards the complete subjugation of Italy, Astolphus made himself master of Ravenna, and dated his decrees from the imperial **palace.** When from thence he extended his invasion to the duchy, **the** remonstrances of the newly-elected Pope, Stephen II[1], or the presents of which his envoys were the bearers, induced him to conclude a truce which in less than four months he violated. When Stephen entreated the Emperor Constantine Copronymus to make good his promises by sending an army sufficient for the defence of Rome and the liberation of Italy, the reply that his envoys received A.D. 753. precluded all further hope of protection from the East; **and** then it was that Stephen, in accordance

---

[1] Stephen II, 752–757.

with the policy initiated but not carried out by his predecessors, despatched a confidential agent to Pepin, who responded to his appeal with assurances of effectual succour, together with an invitation to visit him at Paris.

At this time a *Silentiarius*, or confidential minister, arrived from Constantinople with a mandate to the Pope requiring him to urge upon the king of the Lombards the restitution of the exarchate. In obedience to the command of his temporal sovereign, Stephen accompanied the *Silentiarius* to the Lombard capital; but his unwelcome intervention proved fruitless, and when he left Pavia, intending to avail himself of Pepin's invitation, it was only by hard riding that he evaded the obstacles placed in his way by Astolphus, and was able to reach the French confines in safety.

A.D. 754. His first reception by the king took place in one of the royal villas, where they remained for some days occupied in an exchange of their mutual views and wishes, the upshot of which was an understanding that the exarchate, when taken from the Lombards, should not be restored to the empire, but granted by Pepin to S. Peter, or in other words to the Roman Church. They then proceeded to Paris, where[1] Stephen solemnly consecrated Pepin and his two sons, Charles and Carloman, as kings of France and patricians of the Romans. Now the title Patrician was sometimes merely honorary, but it was also used to denote a governor.

[1] In the church of S. Denis.

By his agreement to accept the exarchate, Stephen undoubtedly committed an act of treason against the Emperor, whose subject he still was, and whose right to the territory in question he had recently supported.

Astolphus, when pressed by the superior forces of Pepin, consented to all his demands, but during the following year he again violated his engagements, and, aided by the Lombards of Beneventum, invested Rome. In the name of S. Peter, whom he assumed the right to personify, Stephen once more addressed himself to Pepin, to his sons, and to the great Catholic nation of the Franks, and, placing before them the alternative of eternal life or everlasting condemnation, he adjured them to secure Heaven as the sure reward of prompt and effectual action[1]. In answer to this appeal, so characteristic of the age, Pepin with a numerous army hastened to the rescue and compelled Astolphus to abandon the siege.

A.D. 755.

It was in vain that Constantine Copronymus sent a mandate to Pepin, enjoining him to re-conquer the exarchate for the empire. His envoy discovered that the Franks had already crossed the mountains for a different object; and when he insisted on his master's right, and declared his willingness to defray the cost of the war, Pepin replied with an avowal of

---

[1] 'Cette lettre est importante pour connaitre le génie de ce siècle là, et jusqu'où les hommes les plus graves scavoient pousser la fiction quand ils la croyoient utile.' Fleury, Histoire Ecclésiastique, T. xliii. 755.

his resolution to confer the exarchate on S. Peter, and added that all the gold in the world would not induce him to abandon his purpose.

Astolphus on his approach made a hasty retreat from before Rome, and finding that he was no longer safe at Pavia, submitted to give up the exarchate, and also Comacchio, until then a Lombard possession. Pepin, according to Anastasius, caused the keys of all the cities included in his magnificent grant to be placed, together with a deed of donation, on the altar of S. Peter; but since of this document no fragment has been preserved, its tenor and contents can only be conjectured. A territorial gift or grant implied, as a general rule, reservation of superiority or sovereignty on the part of the donor. Father Pagi maintains, and other ecclesiastical writers have concluded, that from this time forth the Popes were sovereigns, not only of the exarchate but of Rome itself, but without any convincing argument. When Pepin wrested the exarchate from Astolphus, it was his by right of conquest. But that he divested himself of his rights as lord paramount, or that the constitution of Rome and the duchy underwent at that time any change, there is no evidence.

A.D. 756. After a reign of eight years the energetic but rash and faithless Astolphus was killed by a fall from his
A.D. 755. horse while hunting; and Desiderius, duke of Istria, of whose previous life nothing is known, became the favoured candidate for the Lombard crown. In the ex-king, Rachis, he had for a while a competitor.

Rachis, aweary of monastic seclusion, assembled his partisans and took the field, but yielding to the Pope's advice declined the risks of a battle, and retired once more to Monte Cassino. The kingdom which, for the second time, he found himself constrained to relinquish was already threatened with a disruption. Several of the most powerful feudatories, influenced by their sense of Pepin's irresistible power, had already transferred to him their allegiance. In checking the progress of this defection, Desiderius appears to have acted with no A.D. 757. small amount of energy. Having first overpowered and imprisoned the duke of Spoleto, he proceeded to re-establish his regal predominance at Beneventum, deposed the rebel duke and conferred that magnificent fief on his own son-in-law, Arichis. In the commencement of his reign he received from Stephen II a conditional encouragement, the condition being that he should restore to S. Peter and to the republic certain cities taken by Astolphus, and held in pledge by the Lombards. Stephen died the same year and was succeeded by his brother Paul I[1]. The new Pope omitted nothing that might strengthen and perpetuate the good understanding, established by his brother between the powerful king of the Franks and the Papacy. When Desiderius hesitated or refused to fulfil his engagement, Paul's appeals to Pepin were urgent. But the fears that he frequently expressed to his great patron, of an attack on Rome and Ravenna by Constantine

[1] Paul I, 757-768.

Copronymus, appear to have been imaginary, or invented with a view to widen the breach between Pepin and the empire.

A.D. 767. The decease of Paul I was followed by a year of disorder at Rome, caused by an attempt made by the governor of Nepi to obtain the Papacy for his brother, though still a layman. The governor's forces obtained an entrance into the city, and for a while were unresisted. Desiderius, when applied to by the clergy, did not hesitate to give his aid, and by Lombards brought from the neighbouring duchy of Spoleto the scandal was brought to a close. The antipope was dethroned. Stephen III[1], when duly elected, sent to inform Pepin of his elevation and to engage his support. But before the embassy had traversed France, Pepin died, in the eighteenth year of his successful reign over the vast Frankish monarchy. With the consent of the chief vassals arrangements had been made for the division of the component states between Pepin's son, Charles, afterwards known as Charlemagne, and his brother Carloman.

Death of Pepin the Short.

A.D. 768.

The Lombards, during these years of their national decadence, had no historian of their own, and it is possible that the prejudices of Roman and ecclesiastical annalists may have led them to put the worst construction on the doings of Desiderius. But that after a trial of fourteen years as king, a low estimate of his character and position did not prevail amongst his contemporaries may be inferred

[1] Stephen III, 768–772 A.D.

from the anxiety shown by Berthrada, Pepin's widow, A.D. 770. to contract marriages between his family and her own. When on the thorny subject of the territorial division Charlemagne and Carloman were at variance, their mother proved herself a successful peace-maker, and when harmony was restored Stephen III wrote to congratulate the brothers on the happy result; but subjoined a solemn warning, that unless they joined in obtaining for the holy see plenary justice from the Lombards, they would have to give account.

Berthrada, in a personal interview with Desiderius, obtained his willing consent to the proposed intermarriages, though, owing to the Pope's opposition, that of Charlemagne to Desiderius' daughter Desiderata was the only one of them that she was able to carry out.

That intelligence of Charlemagne's engagement to a Lombard princess should have been received by the reigning Pontiff, Stephen III, with grief and dismay was only natural, inasmuch as it threatened extinction to the fondly cherished hopes of himself and of his predecessors. By an alliance between the Frankish and Lombard kings, the complete subjection of Italy to the latter would have been facilitated, and the advances lately made in the acquisition of temporal power by the Papacy would have been rudely checked. But that Stephen III should have given way to his feelings in the language ascribed to him, would seem incredible.

In the forty-fifth letter of the Codex Carolinus, he

is made to caution Charlemagne and his brother against any connection with the 'perfidious and fetid' race of the Lombards,—a race unfit to be so much as named amongst nations. He then proceeds to remind both the princes that they are already, in obedience to their father's wish, united in marriage to ladies of great beauty—of their own nation, and that it was unlawful for them to repudiate their wives.

Now if Charlemagne and his brother were already married with their father's approval, it seems to the last degree improbable that their mother, Berthrada, should not have known the fact, or that knowing it she should have acted as she did.

The learned Muratori does not hesitate to assert that of the many chroniclers of those times, there is not one who corroborates the statement as to the marriage of Charlemagne and his brother contained in this epistle, and he also expresses in terms sufficiently clear his disbelief in the authenticity of the letter itself, ascribing it to 'some inventive genius of the day,' of whom there may have existed many at Rome, eager to disparage, 'per fas et nefas,' the 'gens nec dicenda' of the Lombards.

That Charlemagne, before his marriage with Desiderata, was the father of two sons by a lady named Himiltruda, there is no question. The elder of them, known in after years as Pepin the Hunchback, became involved in a conspiracy against his father's life, was shaved and condemned to pass the remainder of his days in monastic seclusion, while his companions in treason were either hanged or beheaded.

As to the grounds on which Desiderata was repudiated, and Charlemagne's marriage with Ildegarda, of Swabia, which took place immediately afterwards, A.D. 771 was justified, neither Eginhard nor any other contemporary affords information.

CHAPTER XI.

ITALY UNDER CHARLEMAGNE.

A.D. 771-814.

Charlemagne, king of the Franks and patrician of the Romans, acquires the Lombard kingdom. His second son, Pepin, declared king of Italy. Betrothal of his daughter to the infant son of Irene, regent of the empire. Death of Pepin and of his elder brother. Proposed marriage of Charlemagne and Irene. He recognises Bernard, Pepin's natural son, as king of Italy. Decease of Charlemagne, leaving his only remaining son, Louis the Débonnaire, to succeed him.

A.D. 771. THE decease of Carloman in the prime of life enabled Charlemagne as sole patrician to treat confidentially with the Pope, and in Adrian I[1], the successor of Stephen III, he had an informant and a counsellor on whose intelligence and judgment he could rely.

Carloman left two infant sons, the fruit of a morganatic marriage. Though, with the Franks, legitimacy of birth was not invariably insisted on, the exceptions were generally in favour of some tried and popular warrior. It cannot therefore seem strange that these infants should have been passed over, or that if remembered their claim should have been promptly set aside, when contrasted with that of a prince who had already attained his twenty-

[1] Adrian I, 772-795 A.D.

seventh year, who had won **his spurs in his father's** wars, who was a man of goodly presence, **with a** stature and strength exceeding that **of his contemporaries**; and Charlemagne, **when, in accordance** with the **wishes of the feudatories,** he succeeded to his late brother's dominions, **became the** leading potentate of the West.

With Desiderius the only hope of retaining an independent position lay in a division of the Frankish power, and when the mother of Carloman's children **desired to place** them under his protection, he accepted the charge, and, as the most likely means of winning adherents to their cause, **desired** to obtain for them recognition and consecration by Pope Adrian. Having failed to do so he tried compulsion, and occupied part of Pepin's donation with his troops, but offered to withdraw them if the Pope would grant him an interview. When Adrian required that the cities he had occupied should be given up **as a** preliminary, he refused, **and** having assembled **an army, laid waste** the exarchate, and approached the Roman confines. Adrian being well supported by the Senate and people, put the city in a state of defence, threatened the Lombards with excommunication, and sent messengers by sea to **apprise** Charlemagne.

Charlemagne it appears made large offers of gold with a view to a peaceful settlement, and when those offers were refused, we are told by Eginhard, that 'having considered with great care the differences between the Lombards and Romans he resolved to go to war in defence of the latter.' When with irresistible forces he descended into Italy, Desiderius had no better resource than to shut himself up in Pavia. Charlemagne invested the city in person, and kept Christmas under the walls, but finding that it could only be reduced by famine, he turned the siege into a blockade, and spent Easter at Rome, where he was received with the honours formerly accorded to the imperial representative, and confirmed to his confidential adviser the Pope his father Pepin's donations.

Meanwhile the cities of Ultrapadane Lombardy gave in their submission, and when Pavia at length capitulated, Desiderius was permitted to spend the residue of his life in French monasteries. His son Adelgisus who had held out at Verona then effected his escape to Constantinople, but for the children of Carloman, who had been placed under his care, he made no provision, and of the fate that betided them nothing is known.

A.D. 774. When Charlemagne, king of the Franks, lord of Southern Germany and patrician of Rome, became without a battle and almost without effusion of blood king of the Lombards, the event had been so far anticipated as to seem like little more than a change of dynasty. Between Lombards and Franks antipathy of race could not be said to exist, for both derived their blood, their language, and their habits of life from the same Teutonic origin. Yet after a time the Lombards of Northern and Central Italy began to regret the independence of their elective monarchy, and were encouraged by their **countrymen** in the South, who persisted in their refusal to give in their submission. Arichis II, the ruler of the great Lombard fief of Beneventum, had married a daughter of Desiderius, and Arichis, after the fall of his father-in-law, deemed that the right and the duty of maintaining a position which **for more than two centuries** had been enjoyed by his countrymen, devolved upon himself. He therefore declined to acknowledge **the great** Frank as his liege lord, **assumed** the independent title of prince, **and began to coin** money with his own image and superscription.

Although the disturbed condition of **Germany** compelled Charlemagne to temporise, this assumption by no means accorded with his **views or** intentions; and still less with those of Pope Adrian, for at **Rome** dislike of the Lombards and **a latent fear** of their re-establishment was the prevalent feeling. It was A.D. 776. not long before Adrian conveyed to the patrician, of **whom** in all matters relating to Italy he was the vigilant and trusted adviser, information of a conspiracy got up against him by the **Duke of Friuli**; **and though,** by Charlemagne's prompt intervention, the rebellion was nipped in the bud, the malcontents only awaited an opportunity for the re-establishment of their self-government.

At this time the hostile preparations **and** actual aggressions of the Moslems compelled Charlemagne to cross the Pyrenees, and he had succeeded in dislodging them from Catalonia, when a renewal of the struggle **in Germany by the** Saxon hero, Witikind, compelled him to withdraw his forces; and as they were passing the defiles of Roncesvalles they fell into an ambuscade laid for them by the faithless Gascons. Before they had time to recover from their surprise, their rear-guard was cut to pieces, the paladin Roland being amongst the slain.

A.D. 781.   In the spring of A.D. 781 Charlemagne, during a temporary cessation of his war with the Saxons, found time to visit Rome a second time, taking with him his two younger sons, Carloman and Louis. The former, being re-baptized, had his name changed to Pepin, and received from his godfather, Pope Adrian, consecration as King of Italy, while Louis with like solemnities was declared King of Aquitaine.

Though Adrian, when he took upon himself to consecrate a king of Italy, committed an open violation of his allegiance to the empire, it does not appear that his conduct drew any remonstrance from Irene, who as guardian of her son Constantine VI bore rule at Constantinople. But in order to show the change that had taken place in the relations of Italy with the East it is necessary to advert to the course of events there, since the death of Constantine V (Copronymus) in A.D. 775. Constantine V during a reign of thirty-four years carried out his father's administrative improvements, and thereby promoted the welfare of his subjects. Though he could not, like his father, lay claim to any decisive victory over the Moslems, he had effectually stayed their advance, and he had, moreover, evinced philanthropic sentiments by his discouragement of the slave trade.

Yet these merits did but insufficiently atone for the tyrannical violence with which he sought to establish his own absolutism in Church and State. After he had obtained the sanction of the Eastern clergy assembled at Constantinople in A.D. 754, there was no excess of barbarity from which, in his attempts to stamp out all liberty of conscience, he refrained. To bow before a statue or a picture, or to pray before a relic, were crimes for which scourging in the market and deprivation of the eyes or of the tongue were the ordinary penalties; and the army being at the Emperor's devotion his word became law, not at Constantinople only, but throughout the Eastern cities, where monasteries were suppressed, their property confiscated, and where persecutions still more barbarous were enforced.

During the short reign of Constantine's successor, Leo IV (A.D. 775–A.D. 780), there was no abatement of intolerance, but on Leo's death the guardianship of his infant son devolved on his widow, the orthodox Irene, who during the nine following years governed as regent. On the attainment of power by Irene the persecution of image-worshippers, a persecution which had tended to strengthen their cause, came to an end. But not so the controversy, for throughout the East the parties were evenly balanced, and it was only in the eighth year of Irene's regency that the Second Council of Nicaea ventured to pronounce the adoration of images and pictures as a sign of reverence to be an orthodox practice, though not

A.D. 780.

to be confounded with the worship due to the Deity only.

A.D. 781. It was during the stay of Charlemagne and Ildegarda at Rome in the year A.D. 781 that an embassy arrived from Irene, demanding for her infant son Constantine their daughter Rotrude, and with the Pontiff's approval the betrothal took place. Instructors were appointed to teach Rotrude Greek. The engagement continued for several years, and it was probably on account of this family connection that Irene and her advisers abstained from remonstrances against the consecration of Charlemagne's son as king of Italy.

A.D. 783. By Queen Ildegarda, who died the following year, Charlemagne had three sons; Charles, who it was hoped might have lived to be his successor; Pepin, whom the Pope had consecrated as king of Italy; and Louis, the survivor of the three, who in after years became only too well known by his unfitness for empire.

A.D. 785-786. When the final submission of the Saxons and the conversion of Witikind, whether due to the superior discipline of the Franks, or to the missionary labours of Boniface, afforded a peaceful interval, Charlemagne visited Rome for the third time, and his arrival there did not take place too soon. After due consideration of the facts and warnings communicated by Pope Adrian, he resolved to tolerate no longer the independence of Beneventum. It was in vain the Prince, Arichis, attempted to pacify him with friendly protestations; he refused to suspend his march until his demands were complied with. Yet he had no wish to drive the Southern Lombards to combine with those of the North; and it was therefore finally agreed that Arichis should retain his territories, but with the same relations of vassalage to the king of Italy that he had formerly borne to his own king; that he should defray the cost of the war; pay an annual tribute; and that his younger son, Grimoald, should go to Aix-la-Chapelle as a hostage.

Before the end of the year, the bitterness of this humiliation and sorrow for the untimely death of his elder son, Romoald, carried Arichis to his grave, to the great grief of his countrymen,—for to him they were indebted not only for a just and enlightened government, but also for making their capital famous for the cultivation of letters. Arichis by a kind and liberal reception had attracted from Greece, or wherever else they were to be found, men of learning and capable instructors; and had induced them to settle at Beneventum; and it was there that Paul Warnefrid (the Deacon) after the fall of Desiderius found a grateful asylum and composed his history. A.D. 787.

The Beneventans, when left without a ruler, petitioned Charlemagne to liberate his hostage Grimoald; and Charlemagne, notwithstanding Pope Adrian's remonstrances, consented,—a politic decision, which enabled him to forestall and prevent a troublesome combination. Grimoald, who during his residence at Aix-la-Chapelle had formed an exalted idea of the power and sagacity of Charlemagne, consented to all his demands, and became for a while his faithful vassal. Adelgisus, the fugitive son of Desiderius, had at this time obtained the support of the regent, Irene, who, when for some unknown reason the engagement of her son Constantine to Charlemagne's daughter Rotrude was broken off, supplied the pretender to the Lombard throne with an armament equipped in Sicily, with which he landed in Calabria, but only to encounter a decisive overthrow from his sister's son, Grimoald.

A.D. 788.

As to the position held by Charlemagne in the city and duchy of Rome, the impartial Muratori arrives at the conviction that as Patrician he possessed and exercised sovereignty in the same way as it had previously been exercised by the exarchs, in the name and on the behalf of the Emperor. Pepin, king of Italy, though allowed to act independently in the prosecution of hostilities and in the defence of his kingdom, appears to have been entrusted with little or no part in its civil administration, which remained in the hands of the ministers appointed by his father.

A.D. 789.

The Image controversy had by this time done its work in the alienation of Rome and Italy from the Eastern empire. It was only by force of arms that the authority of the exarch could be re-established, and any such intervention had long ceased to be feared. It remained for the Roman Pontiffs to negotiate freely, and to enter into reciprocal engagements with the greatest of the Western potentates, whose confidence they enjoyed, and to whom they might look with sanguine expectation, as the founder of a great Christian empire, with Rome for its spiritual centre, where an ecclesiastical organisation might be established, co-extensive with that of the civil power.

When the Emperor Constantine V attained his twentieth year, his mother Irene was compelled to resign the regency, but before seven years had passed the incapacity of Constantine enabled her to regain the power that she loved. As reigning Empress she then attained a position which no other woman had held. Yet her memory is stained by a crime such as no other woman could have committed, when, in order to prevent a possibility of his restoration, it was by her *fiat* that Constantine was deprived of his eyes (A. D. 797). Throughout the West this elevation of Irene led to the desire for the establishment of a new empire under Charlemagne. A.D. 790.

During a pontificate of three and twenty years Adrian I had freely employed the wealth of the Church in works of beneficence, in a much needed restoration of the city walls, and in other objects of public utility. By the Romans his decease was felt as a calamity, and by Charlemagne it is said to have been bewailed with tears. A.D. 795.

His successor Leo III[1], like Adrian, a Roman, obtained from the Senate, clergy, and people an

---
[1] Leo III, 795–816 A.D.

unanimous election and was consecrated the next day; for since Zacharias, no Pope had awaited the imperial fiat. But when Leo sent Charlemagne the keys of S. Peter's shrine, with the banner of the 'Urbs Romana,' and a request that he would name a representative to receive from the citizens an oath of submission, he overshot the mark, and sacrificed his popularity. For with the Romans of Italy, no less than with the Lombards, a feeling had become rife that as long as they had a Frank for their ruler, Franks would be promoted to places of trust; and even in Rome discontent was on the increase. Yet the malcontents were aware that against the power of the Franks, combined with the influence of the Papacy, their efforts would be hopeless, and as Leo III had openly avowed him-

A D. 799. self the zealous adherent of Charlemagne, they desired to replace him with a Pope of their own party. Having first loaded Leo with accusations as unfounded as they were degrading, they proceeded to acts of violence. While taking part in a procession, the unoffending Pontiff was dragged from his palfrey, and though an attempt to deprive him of his eyes and tongue failed, he was thrown into a place of confinement, from whence, when liberated by his adherents, he was enabled by Count Winigis, a Frank who had been invested with the neighbouring duchy of Spoleto, to reach Germany.

By Charlemagne, whose head-quarters were then at Paderborn, he was received with honours; but before any decision as to the recent outrage could be arrived at, the advice of **Charlemagne's** trusted counsellor, Alcuin, was required. Alcuin in his reply recommended caution and forbearance. The tenor of his letter showed that **he considered** the outbreak **at** Rome as indicative of widely spread **disaffection.** In guarded, yet sufficiently intelligible terms, he expressed apprehension that the Roman malcontents, if coerced, might combine with **the Lombards.** 'Componatur pax,' wrote the wary Yorkshireman, 'cum populo **nefando si** fieri potest.'

The counsels of Alcuin prevailed. Leo remained at Paderborn until the excitement had abated and every precaution for his safety had been taken. He then returned to Rome, and a mixed commission of nobles and prelates was empowered **to try the** leaders of the insurrection, **who,** though declared guilty, had their sentences postponed.

In his choice **of** the men to whom he entrusted the civil administration of his son Pepin's kingdom, Charlemagne **had shown no small** amount of intelligence. **The first** of these was Angelbert, who had been a pupil **of Alcuin, and who had afterwards** associated with the leading men of his time until **he** withdrew from the court **to the monastery of** Centola, where he **devoted his time to study until** called upon by his sovereign to undertake the toils and anxieties of public life. While Pepin under his father's direction was engaged **in the** acquisition of military experience, Angelbert, as Primicerius, became for several years virtually **regent.**

The case of his successor, Adalard, Abbot of Corbie, was not dissimilar. Adalard, no less than Charlemagne himself, was a descendant of Charles Martel. Like Angelbert he had sought the leisure required for mental culture in the seclusion of a cloister, a habit which in those times was not unfrequently indulged in by men of distinguished position. To these two ministers the Italian kingdom, while under the nominal rule of Pepin, was indebted for such an intelligent and impartial administration as did much to allay jealousies and inspire contentment.

Charlemagne was already in all but name Emperor of the West. His military resources were equal, if not superior, to those by which of old the world had been subjugated. In Germany his sovereignty was no longer disputed. For seven and twenty years he had, as king of the Lombards, been lord of Northern and Central Italy; whilst as Patrician of the Romans and Defender of the Church he possessed a moral influence which formed the keystone of his power.

Though the occupant of the Eastern throne was still *de jure* supreme head of the Roman world, the actual occupant was Irene, then in the third year of her reign as Empress, and the question arose as to whether the Romans of Italy should so far abandon Roman precedents as to recognise a female sovereign.

A.D. 800.

In a council convened at Rome during the preceding year the expediency of conferring on the

Patrician fuller powers, with the less ambiguous title of Emperor, had been openly discussed; and it was under these circumstances that Charlemagne, in accordance with the Pope's urgent exhortations, hastened to Italy. With forces withdrawn from Germany, where they were no longer required, he first made sure of Ravenna, and then proceeded by Ancona to Rome. From Ancona, he despatched Pepin to Beneventum, where Grimoald, when the freshness of his gratitude to his liege-lord wore off, omitted by degrees every act or observance that savoured of fealty, and his attitude was one that could no longer be tolerated.

On Charlemagne's arrival at Romento, twelve miles from the city, he was met by the Pope, who dined with him there, and returned; and when on the 24th of November he made his public entry, he **24 Nov.** was received with more than regal honours. By his command, after an interval of seven days, an assemblage of the **nobles and clergy was** convened to complete the trial of the leaders in the late outrage, and the sentence of death was pronounced. But Leo, after a solemn denial of the charges they had brought **against** him, interceded **in** favour of his accusers, and they **were ultimately subjected to** no severer penalty than banishment to France.

On the day of the **Nativity the** Basilica of the **25 Dec., A.D. 800.** Vatican was the scene of a memorable solemnity. In the presence of a dense congregation the Pontiff advanced towards Charlemagne, bearing a golden crown, and placed it on his head; an act by which few, if any, of the spectators could have been taken by surprise, for, as if prepared to act their part, clergy and laymen, senators and plebeians joined in the thrice repeated acclaim 'To Charles the chosen of the Most High,—the religious and pacific Augustus,—Long life and victory.'

Three hundred and twenty years had passed since the Senate, clergy and people of Rome, weary of having Emperors chosen and liable to be deposed and put to death by a Ricimer, consented to name Odoacer their protector and to acknowledge the Eastern Augustus, Zeno, as sole Emperor. They now re-asserted their right.

Charlemagne, after he had assigned to his son Pepin the task of bringing the Beneventan Lombards into subjection, remained at Rome until Easter, fully occupied with pressing affairs, ecclesiastical as well as civil; and before his departure directed a palace to be built, which he never returned to occupy.

Meanwhile the Duke of Beneventum persisted in his refusal to acknowledge dependence on the kingdom of Italy, and when asked to do homage to Pepin, is said to have replied,

> 'Liber et ingenuus sum natus, utroque parente,
> Semper ero liber, credo, tuente Deo.'

Whereupon a war began which, though prolonged and sanguinary, had no decisive result. Grimoald, confiding in the devoted attachment of the Beneventans and in the strength of Salerno, his principal sea-port, maintained his independence[1]. Having no descendants, his elected successor was his chief minister, Grimoald Storesaiz; and this second Grimoald, though placed between two great powers, was able in like manner to preserve his independence. Until after the decease of Pepin, he obtained through the influence of Adalard a concession from Charlemagne of sovereign rights, on payment of an annual subsidy.

Irene had now occupied the Eastern throne for about five years, and on finding that her popularity had begun to wane she sought to strengthen herself by a treaty of alliance between the two empires, and, according to Theophanes, her overtures for peace were accompanied by one for her marriage with Charlemagne[2], a project which he states to have been approved by Pope Leo, as favourable to a reunion of the Roman world[3]. But to the Senate and people of Constantinople the idea of having a Frank for their Emperor was odious, and the apprehension of such an arrangement, whilst it hastened the fall of Irene, facilitated the elevation of the patrician Nicephorus. Irene, to whom the servile magnates had bowed the knee as to a second Semiramis, was then banished to Lesbos and con-

A.D. 802.

[1] 'Pertulit adversas Francorum saepe phalangas,
    Salvavit patriam sed, Benevente, tuam.'
                                    Quoted by Muratori.
[2] Theophanes, Chronographia, p. 737. Niebuhr.
[3] That the overture for the marriage of Charlemagne was actually made is clearly stated by Theophanes. Eginhard's omission to mention it is not surprising, as the proposal, owing to Irene's dethronement, went no further.

demned to spend the remainder of her days in poverty and exile.

Charlemagne, after his return to Aix-la-Chapelle, appears to have paid but little personal attention to the affairs of Italy. Urged by ambition, or perhaps by the necessities of the case, he became engaged in the conquest of Bohemia, in resisting the advances of the Slaves, and in punishing the Danes or Northmen, whose inroads had begun to be troublesome.

Aix-la-Chapelle meanwhile became the resort of all who wished to obtain from the great arbiter of the West protection or counsel. In him the newly-converted Hungarians, when driven from their settlements by Slaves, obtained an able and willing restorer; in him the Corsicans, when ruined by the predatory descents of the Saracens, found a defender; and through his influence with the Pope, Eardolphus, king of Northumberland, when dethroned by a combination of prelates headed by the Archbishop of York, obtained restitution.

Pepin, when of an age to act on his own impulses, attacked the Venetians, and, according to Eginhard, forced his way into their city. Andrea Dandolo, in his account of his invasion, and of the devastations inflicted by the Franks on his countrymen, declares that they never entered Rialto, as Venice was then called. The authority of Dandolo, who compiled his dry and spiritless annals some five centuries later, cannot be regarded as of much weight, and the question is one of small importance since, on the death of Pepin, hostilities came to an end. Bernard, the only male offspring left by Pepin, was of illegitimate birth; but Charlemagne regarded the boy Bernard with an affection and regard equal to that which he might have been expected to entertain for a legitimate grandson, and with the consent of a diet caused him to be proclaimed king of Italy, having first placed the administration of affairs in the hands of the same ministers that had been entrusted with power during the lifetime of Pepin.

A.D. 810.

A.D. 812.

The death of Pepin, followed within a year by that of his elder brother Charles, frustrated all the arrangements made by Charlemagne and approved by the great vassals (A. D. 806) for a division of his states. Louis had already shown incapacity for government by his maladministration of Aquitaine. Yet he now stood in the position of heir to a vast and ill-cemented empire. Charlemagne, aware of the weakness of his remaining son, resolved, as the most likely means of maintaining peace and preventing a disruption, to declare him his colleague. In the presence of an assemblage consisting of the chief feudatories and prelates, he addressed to Louis a series of grave admonitions, and then commanded him to take the imperial crown and to place it on his head.

It is to be observed that, on this occasion, no ecclesiastical dignitary was asked to take part in the ceremonial, and that the Pope's name was not mentioned,—an omission which, it would seem, was made by Charlemagne with a view to conciliate the men to whose services he was indebted for his conquests, who viewed with jealousy the concessions made by their great leader to the Roman See, and the preference that he had shown for churchmen as his political advisers.

Jan. 28, A.D. 814.
In less than six months after this, his last public act, Charlemagne died.

CHAPTER XII.

FROM THE ACCESSION OF LOUIS THE DÉBONNAIRE TO THE DISMEMBERMENT OF CHARLEMAGNE'S EMPIRE.

A.D. 814-888.

Weakness of Louis. Suspicions entertained against king Bernard, and banishment of Adalard. Aspirations of the amalgamated Italians and Lombards. Louis declares Lothaire his colleague. Discontent of Lothaire's brothers. Rash enterprise and cruel treatment of Bernard. Marriage of Louis with Juditha of Bavaria. Hostilities of sons against their father, and of brother against brother. Temporary dethronement of Louis and Juditha. The Saracens infest the coast. Rome indebted to Gregory IV for preservation. Louis in the midst of war endeavours to promote the arts of peace. His encouragement of organ-building. Death finds him engaged in persevering efforts to secure territories for his son by Juditha. Lothaire Emperor. His defeat at Fontenay, followed by the partition treaty of Verdun. He names his eldest son, Louis, king of Italy, but leaves him without support. The Saracens sack the Vatican. Leo IV builds and fortifies the Leonine city. His reception of Prince Alfred. Resignation and death of Lothaire. Louis II Emperor. Failure of his attempt to dislodge the Saracens from Bari, but ultimate success when supported by the Emperor Basil. Conspiracy of the prince of Beneventum, whose prisoner the Emperor becomes. His liberation. Successful return to Pavia and death, leaving an only child Ermengarda. Charles the Bald, the son of Louis and Juditha, crowned as Emperor. Leaves Italy to be governed by Count Boson, the Empress Richilda's brother. On Boson's marriage with Ermengarda, he is created Duke of Provence. The death of Charles the Bald. Imperial interregnum. Pope John VIII, being opposed to the German branch, has resort to France. His reception at Arles by Boson, for whom he attempts, but in vain, to obtain the crown of Italy. Charles the Fat, Emperor. Boson and Ermengarda retain the kingdom of Arles. The Saracens acquire a permanent footing on the Garigliano. Charles the Fat becomes nominal head of a vast empire, which he is unable to defend. Deposition and death of Charlemagne's last male descendant.

LOUIS, surnamed the Débonnaire, is said to have been endowed with a robust frame, and with qualities that might have adorned a private station. But though he began his reign with all the advantages of his father's prestige, his administration of the petty kingdom of Aquitaine had not served to inspire observers with confidence in his judgment.

A.D. 814. Before a year had passed that timid and vacillating judgment gave proof of its liability to be misled. The king of Italy, being suspected of designs inconsistent with the imperial authority, was summoned to Aix-la-Chapelle. On his prompt obedience to the summons, Bernard was acquitted of all blame, and sent back with presents to Pavia. But the question was not allowed to rest there. Adalard either because he considered that his appointment ended with the life of Charlemagne, or because he felt himself to be distrusted, retired to his Abbey at Corbie, yet was sentenced to banishment, and his brother Walla found it prudent to adopt the habit and tonsure of a monk.

When three more years had passed, Louis, with the consent of his barons, named Lothaire his colleague. He at the same time invested his two younger sons with the kingdoms of Aquitaine and Bavaria. But Pepin and Louis were by no means grateful for an arrangement which placed them in subjection to their brother, and their cousin, the King of Italy, had equal reason to complain. King Bernard's case was somewhat peculiar. Being the son of Louis the Débonnaire's elder brother, he would, but for the circumstance of his birth, have been reigning at Aix-la-Chapelle.

At the same time the now amalgamated Lombards and Italians had reason to distrust the imperial government which seemed to grudge their prosperity, having condemned the ministers whom they regarded as its authors.

Bernard, deprived of those faithful mentors, and A.D. 817. trusting to fallacious assurances of support, resolved to strike a blow, if not for empire, for independence; enlisted troops, and occupied the mountain passes. But when he took the field, the insufficiency of his forces to cope with those arrayed against him became apparent, and, without considering that in his uncle's consort, Ermengarda, he had a dangerous enemy, he resolved to throw himself on his uncle's generosity. But though provided with a safe conduct, he and his companions on their way through France were arrested, and deprived of their eyes, A.D. 818. an outrage which he did not long survive.

Neither the piety nor the benevolent disposition that gained for Louis the name of the Débonnaire saved him from acquiescence in a crime, which even

S

in those days of remorseless cruelty was beginning to be regarded with horror. His empress Ermengarda died the same year, and the courtiers, fearing that Louis would renounce the world and withdraw into a monastery, obtained for him a second consort in
A.D. 819. Juditha, a beautiful daughter of the Bavarian house of Guelph.

A.D. 820. When Louis invested Lothaire with the vacant kingdom of Italy, he made large additions to the territories previously conferred on his two younger sons, but with a proviso which forbade them to marry, to declare war, or to conclude peace without the consent of their elder brother.

A.D. 823. The empress Juditha having given birth to a son, who was named Charles after his grandfather Charlemagne, desired that he should be endowed with dominions equal to those that had been allotted to her husband's younger sons by his previous marriage, and with Louis the gratification of her wish became the leading object of his life. But it was one that could only be effected by abstracting from Pepin and Louis territories with which they had been invested, and which they considered their own. The disturbances and dangers caused by family discontents were aggravated by a general aversion for the Duke of Settimania, a minister whom Louis had allowed to exercise a monopoly of public appointments and who, when a general insurrection took place, made no attempt to uphold his master's interests, but fled to Spain. Juditha, accused of criminal intercourse with the fugitive minister, was compelled to take the veil. But the endeavours to induce Louis to become a monk failed, since by so doing he would have left his wife and son Charles to the mercy of their enemies. Encouraged by the support of the German Franks, he held out until a reaction ensued. Juditha obtained from the Pope[1] absolution from her vows made under duress. But the temporary restoration of Louis was followed by a series of rebellions of sons against their father, and by hostilities of brother against brother, which for an interval of ten years continued to impoverish and depopulate France and Germany. Events of seeming importance but unproductive of any permanent result, promises and treaties, only made to be violated, followed in rapid succession. Amid these vicissitudes the one object never lost sight of by Louis and Juditha, and which they ultimately obtained, was a kingdom for their little Charles, while that pursued with equal tenacity by Lothaire, by Pepin of Aquitaine, and by Louis the Germanic[2], was to promote, each one for himself, and without scruple as to the means, his own aggrandizement.

A.D. 831.

Contemporary writers attribute the long continuance of these evils to the intrigues and selfish ambition of Lothaire, who, in order that he might reign as sole Emperor, would have driven his father to

[1] Gregory IV.
[2] For the sake of clearness the name afterwards given to Louis, as the founder of the great German monarchy, is given him here.

renounce the world—an aim which he had well-nigh accomplished, when thwarted by the jealous opposition of his brothers. But while those writers concur in praising the parental kindness and long-suffering of Louis the Emperor, they do not attempt to deny or to palliate the want of judgment and of decision which frustrated all his endeavours in the cause of peace.

A.D. 840. Of Louis it may be said that the tendencies of the age were opposed to a development of his virtues. His attempts to rescue from neglect the schools established by Charlemagne, and to benefit his rude countrymen by introducing amongst them the arts and enjoyments of civilised life might in peaceful times have borne good fruit; and one instance may be quoted in which his efforts were successful. That organs had long since been invented and used in the East is proved by the fact that an organ was one of the presents sent by Constantine Copronymus to Pepin the Short. But in the West, where only a few had been obtained at great cost from Constantinople, these wonderful instruments were still regarded with profound astonishment, until Louis established at Aix-la-Chapelle a Venetian monk who had acquired the secret of their construction, from whose workshop they were widely disseminated, and the monk received, as the reward for his services, a French abbey.

Italy, though during the reign of Louis exempt from civil warfare waged within her borders, became exposed to a new danger. The Caliphs of

Spain and Africa, since they obtained a footing in Sicily (A.D. 828), had extended their occupation to the greater part of the island, and established themselves at Palermo, from whence their corsairs infested with impunity the adjacent shores. The precautions taken by Charlemagne for the defence of the maritime inlets had been neglected, and but for the timely exertions of Gregory IV, a predatory armament might have approached Rome with impunity. Gregory being aware that applications to King Lothaire would be fruitless, rebuilt and fortified Ostia, and by personal inspection ascertained that the bulwarks were so well provided with engines as to make an ascent of the Tiber perilous. A.D. 832.

A.D. 833.

In A. D. 839, an embassy arrived from Constantinople with offers for a defensive alliance against the Saracens. The proposal was favourably received, but led to no result, for at this time the Eastern empire, like that of the West, was deficient in naval power; and when the Emperor Theophilus, with a fleet fitted out by the Venetians, ventured to attack the Caliph Saba off Taranto, he encountered a signal overthrow. The Caliph followed up his victory by further aggressions and by the sack of Ancona. A.D. 839.

On the decease of Pepin in the prime of life, Louis and Juditha resolved to add his kingdom of Aquitaine to the dominions of their beloved Charles. But the people proclaimed the elder of their late king's sons as Pepin II of Aquitaine. Before the confusion caused by this dispute had abated,

A.D. 840. intelligence came that Louis the Germanic had assembled an army for the purpose of contesting certain territorial arrangements in favour of his half-brother Charles, and of securing for himself the whole of Germany. The care-worn Emperor took the field once more in defence of his paternal authority, but when he reached Mayence his health, which had long been failing, completely gave way. When asked on his death-bed to extend forgiveness to his rebellious son he consented, but with a proviso that Louis should be informed, how by his misconduct he had caused his father to die of grief.

Reign of Lothaire, A.D. 840-855.

Lothaire, on the death of his father, sent messengers to the existing authorities throughout the Frankish states to assure them of his desire to promote their interests. He then hastened from Pavia to Aix-la-Chapelle, intent on a re-establishment of such an imperial predominance as his own conduct towards his father had largely contributed to destroy. He purchased with lavish promises the adhesion of his nephew Pepin II of Aquitaine, and to his half-brother Charles he repeated promises

A.D. 841. already made. He then marched against Louis the Germanic, who had taken arms in opposition to his authority and compelled him to fall back, but only to complete preparations for war.

Of the time thus gained Lothaire did not scruple to make use in wresting from his brother Charles, whose interests he had so lately promised to protect, a portion of his territories. Charles nevertheless retained in Neustria and Burgundy a powerful body of adherents, with which he joined **his brother** Louis the Germanic.

On the 25th of June the **decisive conflict, which** precipitated the inevitable disruption of **Charle-**magne's empire, took place at Fontenay in the county of Auxerre, about one hundred and **sixty miles from** Paris.

The unwieldy numbers brought into **the field by Lothaire** and by the young **king of Aquitaine** were confronted **by the far less** numerous but more dis-ciplined levies of **Louis the Germanic, supported by** those of his half-brother Charles, **who must in future** be distinguished as Charles the Bald. The **valour** and energy displayed by Lothaire during the **vicissi-**tudes of the battle are admitted, though **in the end** they produced no better result than an increase **of** carnage. His overthrow was decisive; **yet** he con-tinued to keep the field until finding himself hard pressed, he paid a hasty visit to Aix-la-Chapelle, and **from** thence taking with him the imperial moveables, **retreated to** Lyons, leaving his capital to be occu- A.D. 843. pied by his **brothers. He** then consented **to** treat, and after repeated delays **the** partition treaty was concluded at **Verdun. Charles the** Bald, whose mother Juditha lived to see her wishes fulfilled, had almost the whole of France. **Louis the Germanic,** the founder of the Germanic monarchy, added to his Bavarian kingdom extensive territories in Saxony and Hungary, with all the provinces on the right bank of the Rhine. Lothaire was allowed to retain Aix-la-Chapelle **with the country between the** Rhine and the Meuse, Provence, Savoy, Switzerland, the Grisons, together with his Italian kingdom, and the sovereignty of the eternal city.

The joyful anticipations of permanent peace indulged in by the suffering populations were by no means realised. For, with the Carlovingian princes, neither the ties of kindred nor their mutual assurances of reconciliation and forgiveness prevailed over the greed for territorial increments, or prevented, when the opportunity offered, some fresh appeal to arms.

Meanwhile the Romans of the city and duchy became jealous of interference on the part of a foreign power which still claimed their allegiance, though it had altogether ceased to afford protection. A.D. 844. On the decease of Gregory IV, they caused his successor, Sergius II[1], to be consecrated without awaiting the imperial fiat,—an omission for which Lothaire did not fail to show resentment. Having decided to hand over the government of Italy to his eldest son Louis, he sent him to Rome accompanied by an army, and no sooner had his mercenaries entered the duchy than they began to rob and maltreat the inhabitants. Sergius on their approach shut the gates, and though he had caused a palace to be prepared for Louis, did not permit him to enter until he had given assurances that he came as a friend. Louis then received consecration as king of Italy, but when the Roman nobles were asked to swear allegiance to him, Sergius, as immediate head of the

[1] Sergius II, 844-847.

states, replied on their behalf that the Romans having never been subject to the Lombards could only be asked to swear fidelity to the Emperor.

It was not long before the young king had **reason** to feel that the charge with which he had been entrusted **was no** sinecure, and that an enemy was at the gate whose system it was to make devastation a prelude to conquest. While the waste of human life, caused by the sanguinary wars of the Carlovingian princes, encouraged the sea-kings of the North to ascend the Seine, and while Paris for lack of defenders lay at their mercy, the Beneventan Lombards, by inviting **the** Saracens to **take part in their** quarrels, had given them a footing in Calabria, and **a** strong hold at Bari from whence, having the **command** at sea, they could carry on with impunity their predatory and destructive descents.

Before Louis had time to become fully established A.D. 846. at Pavia, their war galleys having overcome the defences of the Tiber, they sacked the Vatican, and, ere their return, burned Fondi, carrying **off the** inhabitants for slaves. The good Pontiff, Sergius, did not long survive this calamity, and in the election of his successor, Leo IV[1], the Romans made a good choice. A.D. 847.

At the time of his elevation the Moslems were engaged in the siege of Gaeta, when the almost total destruction of their fleet by a tempest afforded a respite.

The following year King Louis was able to visit Beneventum, and by dividing Southern Lombardy

---

[1] Leo IV, 847-855 A.D.

between the rival claimants, put an end to their ruinous disputes. But the enemy had no sooner repaired their losses at Gaeta, than they inflicted on the Tuscan city of Luni a destruction so complete, that it was never rebuilt, and the bishopric was transferred to Sarzana.

On the Pontiff the warning of Luni was not lost. Leo spared neither pains nor cost in strengthening the defences of the port and city, and the semi-independent communities of Naples, Amalfi, and Gaeta, encouraged by the firmness of his attitude, placed at his disposal such war galleys as they were able to arm.

Meanwhile Lothaire's imperial palace at Aix-la-Chapelle was pillaged and set on fire by the Normans, the noble cities of Treves and Cologne having previously been abandoned to their fate. Louis had thus a practical warning that he must not look to his father for assistance. Nevertheless, when urged as to the necessity of expelling the enemy from Bari, he made a vigorous but unsuccessful attempt to force his way into the place. After which he found himself compelled to postpone his enterprise, being in no condition to undertake a regular siege.

A.D. 851.

A.D. 852.

During this interval of doubt and dismay Rome and Italy were indebted to the Papacy for preservation from the worst calamities. Leo IV did not hesitate to employ freely the wealth of the Church in the defence of his country. When some thousands of Corsicans, whose island had fallen in the grasp of the Caliphs, and who had narrowly escaped the doom of slavery, sought refuge in Rome, he located them with their families in such a manner that they had no wish to return, and became useful subjects of the state. But the greatest of his works was the Leonine city, so called because its construction had been planned by his predecessor Leo III, and carried to its completion by himself. The Vatican ceased to be an isolated Basilica; surrounded by a newly-built ward of the city, it was protected by solid walls and gates; and it appears that our Alfred, while still a youth, having been sent by his father Ethelwolf to Rome, was a witness of the great change that had been effected, and received from the good Pontiff adoption as a son.

With the Romans of the city and duchy, the neglect of their protection by Lothaire had given rise to a feeling that their connection with the Franks had become a disadvantage, and that virtual liberty might be secured by the acknowledgment of a nominal allegiance to the Augustus enthroned at Constantinople. By the energy of Leo IV this tendency was kept under, and a dangerous interval tided over, until Louis was able to oppose effectually the advances of the Saracens, and to avert from Italy a fate similar to that which had already befallen Spain. A.D. 853.

Leo IV had for his successor, not the Papessa Joan, as affirmed by a ridiculous legend of the thirteenth century, but the shortlived Pontiff Benedict III, on whose decease Louis successfully used his influence in promoting the election of Nicholas I, a Pontiff on whose loyal co-operation he could rely. A.D. 854. A.D. 858.

Death of Lothaire, A.D. 855.

Lothaire, when approaching the end of his days, obtained the consent of his barons to a further subdivision of the states, which by the treaty of Verdun he had been permitted to retain. For Louis he did nothing more than confirm to him the kingdom of Italy. To his second son, Lothaire, he allowed the provinces between the Rhine and the Meuse, which being erected into a kingdom were called after their first king Lotharingia (Lorraine). To his third son, Charles, he gave the kingdom of Provence. Before his decease he betook himself to a monastery near Treves, and having assumed the habit of a monk died soon afterwards.

Reign of Louis II as Emperor and King of Italy, A.D. 855-875.

While the condition in which Louis found himself left by his father incapacitated him for any immediate trial of strength with the Saracens, the Lombard princes of Beneventum and Salerno joined in a brave but unsuccessful effort to rid their country of its invaders, and their defeat aggravated the evil. At Beneventum, during the self-sustained independence of their predecessors, instructors from Greece had received a cordial welcome, and Greek lore had been appreciated. But there, as at Pavia, the ground that had been gained was now lost, and during these dark times, it was only in the East that literary pursuits continued to be had in honour. That they

Photius.

were so may be inferred from the case of Photius, a man of undoubted learning, but who appears to have possessed no other title to the respect in which he was held by his countrymen.

When by the tyrannical act of Michel III, the patri-

arch Ignatius was deposed and banished, **Photius, a distinguished member of the aristocracy, was named** his successor, and in six consecutive days obtained Dec. 25, the requisite orders. It was in vain then that Pontiff 857.
Nicholas I interposed **with a view to obtain the re-** A.D. 860.
storation of the unjustly deprived patriarch [1]. There was no artifice to which Photius did not stoop in order to retain a possession; and when hard pressed **he did** not hesitate to launch excommunication against the Pope **or to** encourage the eastern bishops to declare the Latin Church heretical. Such was the commencement of the Greek schism which still **exists.**

Photius, with all his faults, is admitted to have been a great scholar. **His 'bibliotheca' is said to** contain comments on no less than two **hundred and** eighty-five works, many of which would have been entirely lost but for the extracts which **he has** preserved, and his criticisms are allowed to evince sound judgment combined with purity **of taste.** The composition of such a work by one patrician and its presentation to another sufficiently shows that, in these dark times, the taste for literary pursuits was by no means extinct at Constantinople.

While France and Germany, weakened by the selfish quarrels **of** the Carlovingian princes, were exposed to the predatory inroads of Danes and Northmen, Louis, on the death of Charles, king of Provence, without male issue, obtained, as his share of the inheritance, the greater part of that kingdom,—an augmentation **of his** resources, which

---

[1] Nicholas I, 858–867 A. D.

induced him to listen to the cry and undertake the
A.D. 866. rescue of the Beneventans. Having assembled an army he proceeded to the scene of action, and on reaching Monte Cassino, accompanied by the Empress Angilberga, was welcomed as the deliverer of Southern Italy. The abbot, having surrounded the great monastery with solid walls, had saved it from the destruction that had betided the neighbouring abbeys. But the expected deliverance of Beneventum was delayed. In his disaffected vassal, the prince-bishop of Capua, Louis had a personal enemy, whose hostility in case of a reverse might have been troublesome. The reduction of Capua occupied three months, and the Sultan of Bari had time to improve his defences. With a strong fortress for his base, and the sea open for provision and recruits, his position was
A.D. 867. one of great strength, and Louis, after a severe repulse, found it necessary for the second time to retreat from before Bari and to await the arrival of reinforcements expected from his brother Lothaire.

When he resumed the siege, the accession of Basil I (the Macedonian) to the Eastern throne made a complete change in the relations of the Eastern empire with Rome and Italy. The Emperor Basil desiring to obtain for his son a marriage with Ermengarda, the only child of Louis, became for a while his zealous ally.

A.D. 869. When by the decease of his brother, Lothaire, Louis became entitled to Lorraine, his uncles, Louis the Germanic and Charles the Fat, taking advantage of his absence, usurped and divided the inheritance; but Louis did not permit this flagrant wrong to divert him from his undertaking. When, after a siege or blockade of three years, he took Bari by storm, and a general massacre of the Saracens ensued, the life of their vanquished Sultan was spared, and he obtained a promise that he should be consigned to the keeping of Adelchis, the A.D. 871. reigning prince of Beneventum.

As to the degree in which the co-operation of the Eastern Augustus contributed to the successful result at Bari much obscurity exists, though it is said that Louis having refused to carry out the engagement with regard to the marriage of his daughter, Basil retaliated by the withdrawal of his fleet. But Basil might perhaps fear lest the successful action and prolonged residence of the Frank in Southern Italy might confer upon him an influence subversive of his own; and in a letter at that time addressed to Louis he denies his right to call himself Emperor of the Romans,—a denial in which the people of Constantinople would have been ready to join. For by them the popular fiction of their descent from the vast immigration that accompanied Constantine to his new capital was still cherished, and the exclusive right of their Emperor to the title of Roman believed in. Louis in a temperate reply justified his use of that title as conferred upon his ancestor Charlemagne by the Romans and sanctioned by the Pontiff.

Though in expelling the infidels from a position of

menace which they had held for nineteen years, and that at a time when their power was becoming more and more formidable, Louis conferred on Southern Italy a signal deliverance, it was one which the people, in their dislike to Frankish intervention, and of the burdens which it entailed, were prone to undervalue. The Lombard princes, who had been the auxiliaries of Louis, thought he had not sufficiently appreciated their aid, and their wives disliked the haughty manners of the Empress Angilberga. Prince Adelchis had become weary of a guest to whom he unwillingly paid an annual subsidy and longed in secret to transfer his allegiance to the Eastern Caesars, under whom he might hope to enjoy a greater amount of independence. That his barons harboured a like desire was no secret. Adelchis had moreover reason to suspect that he was distrusted by Angilberga, and that sooner or later she would not fail to accomplish his ruin. In his prisoner, the ex-Sultan of Bari, he had a crafty and interested adviser, who sought to deter Louis from attempting to complete his triumph by the capture of Palermo from his own countrymen, and between them a scheme was concocted whereby they hoped to accomplish a final elimination of the Franks from Southern Italy.

Pressed by the difficulty of obtaining provisions, Louis had permitted the bulk of his army to seek in distant cantonments the means of subsistence, when he discovered that his communications were cut off and the palace in which he resided surrounded by Beneventan troops. Though bravely defended by his guards, he found it necessary to surrender, and by a strange vicissitude found himself a fellow-prisoner with his lately vanquished enemy, the Sultan. He remained so for three weeks, when intelligence came that an army, assembled by the Moslem rulers of Spain and Africa to avenge the slaughter of their co-religionists at Bari, had effected its landing near Salerno.

Adelchis being aware that his outrageous treatment of the Emperor had been denounced at Rome, and would assuredly bring down upon him the vengeance of the French and German princes, consented to set Louis at liberty, having exacted from him a promise, ratified by oaths and imprecations, that he would, as soon as the common enemy was repulsed, depart in peace, and never more approach the Beneventan confines.

The crisis was one that admitted of no delay. A.D. 872. The Moslems had invested Salerno and Capua, and were preparing to advance against Beneventum. Hesitation might have placed Louis himself in their power, by the prompt union of his forces with those of Adelchis the invaders were overmatched and compelled to re-embark. Louis having obtained from A.D. 873. the Pope absolution from his promises was once more a free agent, yet he did not venture to provoke the universal enmity of the people by punishing Adelchis, who, under cover of the Pontiff's convenient intercessions in his favour, obtained an unasked pardon. Wisely, though unwillingly, Louis consented to avoid the risks of besieging him in Beneventum. The descendants of the Greek colonists, who constituted no small part of the population, especially in the ancient municipalities, regarded the Franks as barbarians and longed for their departure, while the Lombard lords of the soil, whose fathers had withstood the power of Charlemagne, were not unnaturally averse to a prolonged occupation of their territory by his descendant.

Louis nevertheless did not condescend to make a hasty retreat, but continued to hold a magnificent court at Capua, and having his head-quarters there, was sufficiently within reach to deter the Saracens from a renewed siege of Salerno. When, after an absence of five years, he returned to Pavia, his health was beginning to fail, and he sought such rest and retirement as political affairs allowed at Olonne, his favourite abode near that city, until, during the summer of 875, he died at Brescia, leaving to his only child, Ermengarda, the envied but perilous distinction of being accounted the richest heiress in Christendom.

On the decease of Louis II without male issue, the Lombard Italian kingdom became with his uncles, Charles the Bald of France and Louis the Germanic, the subject of a sanguinary contest. Charles was first in the field, and secured the support of the barons. His brother, being advanced in years, sent forces under his younger son Charles, afterwards known as Charles the Fat, and subsequently under his elder son Carloman, but with no good result.

Louis, the founder of the German kingdom, did not long survive his disappointment, and on Christmas day, Charles, the beloved son of Louis the Débonnaire by his second consort, was crowned by John VIII with Charlemagne's imperial crown. A.D. 875

The new Emperor obtained from the Lombard Italian feudatories his election as their protector and their king, but from him they had no protection. While engaged in a fruitless attempt to deprive the sons of his deceased brother of their inheritance, he left France exposed to the depredations of the Normans, and Italy, where he created his empress Richilda's nephew Count Boson his viceroy, to the renewed inroads of the Saracens. Adelchis, prince of Beneventum, sought to purchase the forbearance of the Caliph, by releasing his prisoner the ex-Sultan of Bari; and the inhabitants dreading the return of that worthy, renounced all further allegiance to the successors of Charlemagne, and placed themselves under the protection of the Emperor Basil. Naples, consulting the interests of her commerce, entered into an understanding with the too powerful infidels, and it was with difficulty that Rome was withheld from rebellion against an absent and powerless sovereign.

Urged by the entreaties of the Pontiff, the Emperor at length consented to visit Italy. But while engaged in festivities at Pavia, intelligence came that his nephew, Carloman, was advancing against him at the head of an army; and during a hasty return to France he contracted a fever, of which he died, having borne the imperial title a year and ten months.

The deceased Emperor and his consort Richilda, when on their way to visit Italy for the last time, celebrated with great pomp at Vercelli in Piedmont the marriage of Boson with his imperial bride Ermengarda ; and it was on this occasion that Charles invested his brother-in-law with the duchy of Provence.

The decease of Charles the Bald was followed by an imperial interregnum of four years. But that no prince should be called Emperor, had become a matter of secondary importance ; for though still an object of ambition, that title had ceased to confer substantial power.

A.D. 877. Carloman, on the death of his uncle, sent promises of concessions to the Pope with a demand for consecration as Emperor. But John VIII had resolved to prevent, if possible, the too powerful Germanic branch from obtaining predominance, and his reply was evasive.

Carloman, who had contracted during the winter a malady from which he never recovered, when aware of the Pope's hostility, determined to try the effect of intimidation, and delegated to the dukes of Spoleto and Tuscany the task of compulsion. The insulting conduct of these leaders, and their devastation of the Roman territory, drew from the Pontiff anathemas and personal invectives, couched in no measured terms, but failed to bend Carloman's resolution. John VIII then desired, by a personal application, to enlist the support of Louis, king of France, son and successor in that kingdom of the late Emperor, and, on finding the road by land closed against him, embarked. When he reached Arles, he had a magnificent reception from Duke Boson, who escorted him to Troyes, where the court was residing. But when he had observed the **king's** weakness and the **distracted** condition of the country, he renounced all hope of obtaining help from thence, and resolved to support Boson as successor in Italy to the dying Carloman. Having summoned an assembly of the electors at Pavia, he hoped to obtain from them an absolute nomination to the crown of Italy; but the dukes, marquises, and counts, suspecting his intentions in favour of Boson, refused to obey his summons.

During the hopeless illness of Carloman, his brothers Louis and Charles had agreed, in accordance with the wishes of the electors, that Louis should have the German kingdom, and Charles that of Italy; and when Carloman's decease took place, the Pope had already come to the conclusion that by the one or the other of them, the kingdom must be possessed; he therefore began to cultivate their goodwill, assuring them that he did not approve of the act of Boson, who, profiting by the weakness of France, had erected his duchy into an independent kingdom, named after its capital, which the intelligence, energy, and wealth of his consort Ermengarda enabled her, after the death of her husband, to hand down to her son. Charles the Fat, already elected king of Italy, having engaged

A.D. 879

A.D. 880.

himself to act with generosity towards the Church and with vigour against the Saracens, then received at the Pope's hands the imperial crown.

A.D. 881.

Reign of Charles the Fat.

The interregnum came to an end, and the new Emperor, being the survivor of his family, inherited eventually most of the realms that once constituted the empire of Charlemagne, now a merely nominal dominion. When the Roman duchy was suffering from Saracenic incursions, the imperial aid was invoked but in vain. The electors of Pavia soon discovered that in their king, who had sworn to protect them, they had no protector; and in the midst of these distresses the Pope died.

A.D. 882.

Of John VIII it has been said, that in his anxiety to avert from his country impending calamities, he allowed himself to be occupied more than was meet with temporal affairs. Yet it cannot be denied that during his pontificate of eleven years, he displayed on behalf of Italian interests, foresight and sagacity. When on the death of the patriarch, Ignatius, at the desire of the Emperor Basil he acquiesced in the restoration of the exiled Photius, it is fair to take into consideration the fact that it was only to Basil that Rome and Italy could look for protection from the worst calamities. After the decease of the vigilant Pontiff, the Saracens acquired a permanent settlement at the mouth of the Garigliano, from whence they were able to extend their devastations, and from whence they pillaged and broke up the noble Benedictine establishment at Monte Cassino.

When Paris had undergone a long siege or block-

ade by the Normans, Charles assembled an army.
But it was by means of a disgraceful convention that A.D. 886.
he obtained relief for the beleaguered city; and in his
haste to quit the country which he left infested by
the northern invaders, he contracted an illness which
impaired his mental no less than his bodily faculties.

The following year, when his imbecility became A.D. 887.
complete, the principal feudatories invited Arnolph,
the natural son of his elder brother Carloman, to
assume the reins of government,—an arrangement
in which the unfortunate Emperor appears to have
acquiesced, asking nothing for himself but a small
appanage where he might end his days in peace.
But those days were numbered, and the new year
was only in its commencement when this great
grandson of Charlemagne terminated his inglorious A.D. 888.
career.

Berenger, duke of Friuli, who claimed descent
from one of Charlemagne's daughters, then obtained
the Italian kingdom, but was unable to maintain his
independence against the overwhelming power of
Arnolph, whose suzerainty he acknowledged.

Berenger's subsequent career was one of strange
contrasts. Having survived no less than five
phantom emperors, he obtained coronation as one
of them. After his assassination (A.D. 924), there
was an interval of feudal anarchy for eight and thirty
years, and no Emperor was named until the great
Saxon Otho took possession of the Italian kingdom,
was crowned with the iron crown, and the following
year at Rome with an imperial diadem. A.D. 961-2.

Such was the commencement of the holy Roman empire of the Germanic nation, which, though subject to vacancies and to variations of weakness and power, continued to exist until resigned by the Emperor Francis in the sixth year of the present century.

INDEX.

A.

Adrian, during a Pontificate of twenty-three years employs the wealth of the Church as a patriot, 245.

Aetius, after the dethronement and execution of the elected Emperor, Johannes, in whose service he had been engaged, obtains condonation and promotion, 44; he compels Theodoric, King of the Visigoths, to sue for peace, ib.; the story of his intrigues against the proconsul Bonifacius, and their connection with the loss of Roman Africa, 45-46; deprived of his command by Placidia, he stands on the defensive, and inflicts on Bonifacius a fatal wound, 47; the terror of his Hunnish supporters enables him to obtain a second condonation and uncontrolled power, ib.; in the great conflict of Chalons, with the support of his previous opponent, Theodoric the Visigoth, he repulses Attila, but allows him an unmolested retreat, 57; the following year, having left the mountain passes unguarded, he permits Attila to overcome the prolonged resistance of Aquileja, and to devastate Northern Italy, 58; his assassination by the courtiers of Valentinian III, 60.

Africa lost to the Vandals, 46; regained by Belisarius 111; final loss of to the Moslems, 209.

Agilulph, Duke of Turin, becomes King of the Lombards, 180; his power being superior to that of the Exarch, Rome is indebted for her safety to Gregory the Great, 184; his conversion by Theodelinda; their palace and church at Monza, 185; the historical crown, 186; Agilulph's death, 190.

Alaric, a scion of the great Visigothic family of the Balti, employed as an auxiliary by Theodoric the Great, 6; account of his marvellous career, 7-32; his death and burial, 33.

Alaric II, eighth King of the Visigoths, assists Theodoric the Great against Odoacer, 88; his surrender of Egidius to Clovis, 90; slain in battle by Clovis, 94.

Alboin, the Lombard king, after a siege of three years takes Pavia, 170; his death, and the permanency of his conquest, 172.

Amalasunta, the only surviving child of Theodoric the Great, becomes by the early decease of her husband, Eutaric, guardian of their son Atalaric; gives offence to the Ostrogoths by attempting to bring him up like an educated Roman, 100-102; the magnates conspire against her, and their leaders are executed; the death of her son terminates her regency; after

an unsuccessful attempt to retain power, she is strangled, 114.
Anastasius recognizes Theodoric as King of Italy, 91.
Anthemius, Emperor of the West, 72; disappointment of the hopes to which his nomination gave rise; his destruction by Ricimer, 77.
Antonina, the wife of Belisarius, 105; does good service in collecting provisions, 125.
Arcadius, the elder son of Theodosius, succeeds in his eighteenth year to the Eastern empire, 2.
Arianism, general decline of before the seventh century, 190-194.
Aribert, King of the Lombards, divides his kingdom between his two sons, 200.
Arioaldus, King of the Lombards, his maintenance of all their possessions, 194.
Aspar, a leader of barbarian descent in the service of Placidia, 43; his failure when employed against Genseric, 46; his absolute command of the imperial forces prevented by the elevation of Marcian, 53; on the death of Marcian he nominates Leo, a dependant of his own, 68; who ultimately condemns both him and his son to death, 76.
Astolphus succeeds Rachis as King of the Lombards; his ambitious projects and faithlessness accelerate the fall of the Lombard kingdom, 226; his death, succeeded by Desiderius, 230.
Ataulphus, the brother-in-law and successor of Alaric, 26; his marriage to Placidia, 36; Roman predilections and death, 37.
Attalus, the puppet emperor, 29; made and unmade by Alaric, 30; his reappearance in a different character, 36.
Attila, Autocrat of the Huns, overpowers the East Roman generals and imposes hard terms on the Emperor Theodosius II, 51; his just contempt for Theodosius, 52; directs his first attack against the Western Empire, and assumes to be the accepted suitor and champion of the Roman princess Honoria, 54; his repulse in the great conflict of Chalons, 56; destructive invasion of Northern Italy, 57; reception of Leo I, acquiescence in that Pontiff's demands, and death, 58-60.
Augustine, St., death of during the siege of Hippo, 46.
Autharis, King of the Lombards, romantic history of his marriage with Theodelinda of Bavaria, 177; successful defence of his kingdom, and death, 179.
Avitus, his proclamation at Arles; his past services as praetor of Gaul are forgotten; having given offence to Ricimer, he consents to accept a bishopric. 66-67.

B.

Bari, the acquisition of, gives the Moslems a fortified base of operation, 265; retaken by Louis II, 271.
Basil I, in the hope of obtaining for his son Ermengarda the only child of Louis II, becomes his ally, 270.
Basiliscus, brother-in-law of the Eastern emperor Anthemius, defeated by Genseric, and suspected of being actuated by a desire to gain favour with Aspar, 74.
Belisarius, suppresses the Nika insurrection, 105; reconquers Africa from the Vandals, 106;

successful conduct of the Gothic war, 115-140; condonation of his disobedience by Justinian, 141; sent back to Italy, 148; his efforts for the relief of beleaguered Rome end in disappointment, 152; occupies the dismantled city and defends it against Totila, 155; his subsequent misfortunes and recall, 157.

Bertharis, King of the Lombards, driven into exile by his cousin Grimoald, Duke of Beneventum, 200; his life of wandering and adventure, 201; when already embarked for England, he hears of the death of Grimoald; his joyful restoration and peaceful reign; his reception of Wilfrid, Bishop of York, and of Eddius, the bishop's biographer, 205; succeeded by his son Curibert.

Boniface, St., the Devonshire missionary and martyr, the guest of the Lombard king, Liutprand, 222.

C.

Carthage, sacked by Genseric, 49; regained by Belisarius; finally conquered by the Saracens, 209.

Cassiodorus of Calabria, as minister to Odoacer, negotiates an advantageous treaty with Genseric, 85.

Cassiodorus, Aurelius, Secretary and friend of Theodoric the Great in 514 A.D.; sole Consul, 93; his retirement, and return to Pavia as adviser of Amalasunta, 100-101.

Chosroes I crosses the Euphrates and takes Antioch by storm, 135.

Chosroes II, declares war against Phocas, 188; and takes Jerusalem, 189.

Clovis, defeats Siagrius, the last Roman governor of Northern Gaul, 90; important consequences of his nominal conversion, 92; endeavours of his brother-in-law, Theodoric, to mitigate his ferocity; he defeats on the plain of Vouillé Alaric II, King of the Visigoths, whom he kills with his own hand, 94.

Claudian, the venal laureate of Stilicho, 15.

Columban, the Irish saint, a guest of King Agilulph, 190.

Constans II, Emperor, 197; long and inglorious reign, 198-199.

Constantine, the Usurper, elected at York, 17; crosses the channel, restores order in Gaul, 18; establishes himself at Arles, 34; his surrender to Constantius, and execution, 35.

Constantine III (Pogonatus), Emperor, the defender of Constantinople during the first siege by the Moslems, 203.

Constantinople, first siege, A.D. 672-678, 203; second siege, A.D. 717, 215.

Constantius, Count, a veteran Roman officer, succeeds Stilicho in the command, 33; his services to Honorius, 35; marriage to Placidia, proposed exaltation to the Western Empire, and death, 39.

D.

Damascus, after an heroic resistance, surrenders to the Moslems, 196.

Deogratias and Paolinus, Bishops of Carthage and Nola, their redemption of Roman captives from slavery, 64-65.

Desiderius, the last King of the Lombards, restrains the disaffection of his vassals, and confers Beneventum on his own son-in-law Arichis, 231; marriage of his daughter with Charlemagne, and her repudiation, 235; accepts the charge of protecting Carloman's children, 237; condemned by Charlemagne to spend his days in a French monastery, 238.

E.

Ecdicius, the Roman governor of Clermont, repulses Euric, King of the Visigoths, 78.
Edecon, ambassador of Attila to Theodosius II, 51.
Egidius, unaffected by the prepotency usurped by Ricimer, maintains an independent position at Soisson, 67.
Eudes, Duke of Aquitaine, in conjunction with Charles Martel, accomplishes the deliverance of Western Christendom by the overthrow of Moslems at Poitiers, 221.
Eudocia, the daughter of a Greek sophist and consort of Theodosius II, 41.
Eudoxia, the consort of Arcadius, joins Gainas in effecting the downfall of Eutropius, 11.
Euric, seventh king of the Visigoths, his great power and the extent of his dominions, 89.
Eutropius, the eunuch-minister of the Emperor Arcadius, 6; his fall from power and condemnation, 11.

F.

Faenza, defeat of the imperial generals by Totila, 144.

G.

Gainas, by command of Stilicho, causes Rufinus to be cut to pieces, 8; assists in the destruction of Eutropius, 11; attempts to make himself an anti-Roman dictator, is defeated and slain, ib.
Gaul, neglect of by Stilicho, and cruel fate of the colonists, 16.
Gelimer, usurper of the Vandal throne, defies Justinian, 103; puts Ilderic, the rightful king, to death, 107; as the prisoner of Belisarius, prostrates himself before Justinian, 112.
Genseric, obtains a footing in Roman Africa, 46; sacks Carthage, 50: and Rome, 63; destroys the Armada assembled for the reconquest of Africa, 75; respects the power of Odoacer, 86; his death, ib.
Greek schism, origin of, 269.
Gregory the Great, before he took orders had served as Pretor, 180; his residence at Constantinople, ib.; his patriotism in providing for the defence of Rome, 181-182; the validity of Gibbon's charge against him questioned, 184; his denouncement of slavery, as incompatible with Christianity, 185; death, ib.
Gregory II, Pontiff, 212; takes the lead in resisting the decree against images, 218; maintains the independence of the city and duchy, 220; death, ib.
Gregory III, a Roman in heart, 220; the originator of a policy which led to a new empire of the West, with Rome for its centre, ib.; his embassy to Charles Martel, 223.
Gregory IV, provides for the defence of Rome by the fortification of Ostia, 261.
Grimoald, King of the Lombards, his escape from the Huns, 189; usurpation of the crown, 200; his unacceptable but useful reign, and death, 202.

H.

Hegira, the Moslem epoch, 195.
Heraclian, Count, the executioner of Stilicho, 23; his subsequent rebellion and execution, 36.
Heraclius, 188; undertakes and effects the conquest of Persia, 190-193; death, 197.
Hippo Regius, besieged by Genseric, 47.
Honorius, the younger son of Theodosius the Great, inherits a magnificent empire with Rome for its capital, 3.
Hunneric, the son and successor of Genseric no sea-king, 86.

I.

Ildegarda of Swabia, the wife of Charlemagne, dies, 242.
Image controversy begins, 216.
Iron Crown of the Lombards, 186.

J.

Jerusalem, taken by the Persians, 189; liberated by Heraclius, 193; taken by the Saracens, 196.
Justin I, provokes Theodoric the Great by his intolerance, 97; sanctions the marriage of Justinian, 101.
Justin II, nephew and successor to Justinian, 166.
Justinian, employs Tribonian to draw up his Pandects, 101; eventful reign of thirty-eight years, 101-167.

K.

Knight-errantry of the Lombards, 195.

L.

Lampadius, his remonstrance against the dictation of Stilicho, 20.

Leo I (the Great), influence social and political, of the Pontiff, 58; his interview with Attila, 59.
Leo III, Pontiff, unfounded accusation and cruel treatment of, 246.
Leo, Emperor, nominated by Aspar, 68; incurs the stain of consenting to the death of his benefactor, 76.
Leo I, the Isaurian, the defence of Constantinople during the second siege, 211; decease, 224; succeeded by his son Constantine Copronymus, ib.
Leo IV, Pontiff makes needful preparation for the defence of Rome and Italy against the Moslems, 266-267; his reception and adoption of Alfred, ib.
Liutprand, the Bavarian King of the Lombards, begins his long and prosperous reign, 207; his honorary adoption of Pepin the Short, 221.
Longinus, the first imperial exarch, 167.
Lothaire, Emperor, 262; his efforts to restore the imperial authority defeated at Fontenay, 263; by a partition-treaty he is allowed to retain Aix-la-Chapelle and other territories, together with his kingdom of Italy, 264; which he handed over to his eldest son Louis, ib.; having assumed the habit of a monk, he ends his days in a monastery, 268.
Louis, named by his father Lothaire, King of Italy, 264; succeeds him as Louis II, Emperor, 268.
Louis I (the Débonnaire), weak and cruel treatment of King Bernard, 257; invests Lothaire, his eldest son, with the kingdom of Italy, 258; selfish conflict of his sons, 259; his death, 264.

M.

Mahomet, his expulsion from Mecca, 195; his caliphs conquer Syria and Jerusalem, 196.

Majorian, Emperor of the West, his great services and patriotic efforts, 68-69; circumvented and put to death by Ricimer, 71.

Marcellinus, Roman Governor of Dalmatia, holds out against Ricimer, 71.

Marcian, Emperor, his Platonic marriage with Pulcheria; refusal to bend before Attila, 53; good effect of his policy, 59.

Martel, Charles, Mayor of the Palace, and the Duke of Aquitaine defeats the Moslems at Poitiers, 221; accepts the sovereignty of Rome, 223; his death, ib.

Maurice, Emperor, misrule and cruel execution, 183.

Maximus, Petronius, elevation and fall, 62-63.

Middle Ages, commencement of, 83 note.

Milan, having revolted against the Goths, is surrounded by Uraius, the nephew of Vitiges, and sacked, 132.

N.

Naples, besieged and taken by Belisarius, 118.

Narses, takes the part of Johannes at Rimini, 131; his successful conclusion of the Gothic war, 165.

Nepos, Julius, Emperor, 78; his nominal reign of five years at Salona, ib.

O.

Odoacer, overthrows Orestes, 80; peaceful admission into Rome, 81; as a military protector, and with the rank of Patrician, his power is employed beneficially, and without giving umbrage to the Pontiff Simplicius, 85; final overthrow by Theodoric the Ostrogoth, and assassination at a banquet, 88.

Olybrius, proclaimed by Ricimer as successor to Anthemius, his short and uneventful reign, 77.

Olympiodorus, his description of Rome at the time of Alaric's entry, 32; and of the marriage of King Ataulphus with Placidia, 36.

Olympius, the minister of Honorius and the betrayer of Stilicho, his incompetency and fall, 21-22.

Orestes, ambassador of Attila to the court of Constantinople, 52; the betrayer of Nepos, 78; overthrow by Odoacer, 80.

P.

Pandects of Justinian, 101.

Pantheon, the, becomes a Christian temple, 168.

Paolinus and Deogratias, self-sacrifice of these Bishops and its reward, 65; redemption of slaves, ib.

Patrician, meaning of the title, 228.

Paul the Deacon, the Lombard historian, 176, 186; terminates his history, 225.

Pepin the Short, succeeds his father Martel as Mayor of the Palace, and is crowned King of the Frankish monarchy, 226; having obtained Ravenna and the Exarchate by conquest from the Lombard King Astolphus, grants them to the Papacy, 230.

Pepin, Charlemagne's second son, whose original name was Carloman, is re-baptized and receives from Pope Adrian consecration as King of Italy,

240; his indecisive conflicts with the Lombard Duke of Beneventum, 250; death, leaving an illegitimate son Bernard, acknowledged by Charlemagne as King of Italy, 253.

Persian Empire, extinction of by Heraclius, 193.

Phocas, proclaimed Emperor, 183; signs the death-warrant of the dethroned Emperor Maurice and his family, 188; his death, and the succession of Heraclius, ib.

Photius, a member of the East Roman aristocracy and a layman, named Patriarch; in reply to the Pope's remonstrance he declared the Latin Church heretical, 269; his 'Bibliotheca,' ib.

Placidia, Daughter of Theodosius the Great by a second marriage, the captive of Alaric, 33; becomes the consort of Ataulphus, 36; after the death of her child and of her husband, re-married to the Roman General Constantius, 39; mother of Valentinian III, and Regent of the West, ib.

Pollentia, battle of, 13.

Procopius, accompanies Belisarius as his secretary, 106.

Pulcheria, daughter of the Emperor Arcadius, and guardian of her brother Theodosius II, 41; causes to be promulgated in his name the Theodosian Code, 48; invested with supreme power, 52; her Platonic marriage with Marcian, 53.

R.

Radagaisus, the failure of his invasion, and the destruction of his army by Stilicho facilitated by the holding out of Florence, 16.

Ravenna, affords to Honorius and his court a refuge from Attila, 12; the residence of Odoacer, 85; and of the Exarchs, 167; by Pepin the Short it is taken from Astolphus and granted to the Papacy, 230.

Ricimer, a barbarian magnate, obtains, after the fall of Aetius, the command of the Western forces, 66; with great abilities defeats every attempt to employ the resources of the Western Empire for its benefit, 76; condemns Rome to be sacked, and adds to the list of imperial victims his own father-in-law, Anthemius, 77; his death, ib.

Rome, splendour and population of, 32; sack of by Alaric, ib.; by Genseric, 63; by Ricimer, 77.

Rotharis, King of the Lombards, 199; his code of laws, 200.

Rufinus, Prefect of the East and guardian of Arcadius, 4; failure of his design to obtain the young emperor for his son-in-law, 6; his suspicious intercourse with Alaric, King of the Visigoths, 7; his unlamented death, effected by Gainas under the direction of Stilicho, 8.

S.

Sarus the Goth, employed by Stilicho against the usurper Constantine, and fails, 18; surprises and puts to the sword Stilicho's body-guard of Huns, 22.

Senate, beneficial revivals of its influence in times of anarchy and confusion, 4.

Siagrius, the last Roman Governor in Northern Gaul, looked up to by the colonists as their king; when no longer able to resist Clovis, throws himself on the protection of the Visigothic king, Alaric II, who gives him up to be slain, 90.

Sidonius Apollinaris, the poet-orator, and Bishop of Clermont, 78.

Silverius, Pope, his cruel treatment by Belisarius, 124.

Stilicho, position, on the death of Theodosius the Great; commander of the imperial forces and husband of the late emperor's niece, 4; accused by Zosimus of gross corruption, 5; his destruction of Rufinus, 8; defeats and surrounds Alaric, but permits him to escape, ib.; puts down the rebellion of the Roman governor of Africa, 9: marriage of his infant daughter, Maria, to the boy-emperor, 10; in the battle of Pollentia the children of Alaric fall into his power, 14; his defeat of Alaric at Verona, ib.; the resistance of the Florentines enables him to crush Radagaisus, 15; for the second time Consul, 17; on the death of Maria, he supplies Honorius with a wife, in her sister Thermanzia, 18; he overawes the Senate, 19; the circumstances that preceded his fall, 22–24.

Syria, conquest of by the Mahometans, 196.

T.

Telemachus, the monk, by his self-sacrifice hastens the abolition of death struggles on the stage, 14.

Theodatus, breaks faith with Amalasunta and consents to her murder, 113.

Theodora, her marriage to the Emperor Justinian, 101; death, 157.

Theodoric, son of Alaric, fourth King of the Visigoths, 54; persuaded by Avitus to support Aetius, 55; slain at Chalons, and avenged by his son Thorismond, 56.

Theodoric, the Ostrogoth, invades Italy, 87; having overcome and slain Odoacer, reigns at Ravenna, 89; his amicable relations with Rome and the Pontiff, 92; ill-requited toleration, 97; becomes, after a prosperous reign of thirty years, a tyrant and a persecutor, ib.; repentance and death, 99.

Theodosius, the Great, his partition of the empire between his sons by no means intended to interfere with the unity of the Roman world, 2.

Theodosian Code, published by Pulcheria in the name of her brother Theodosius II, 48.

Thorismond, King of the Visigoths, restores the conflict at Chalons, 56; called back by Aetius, 57.

Tiberius II, succeeds to power, 173; his reign of four years, succeeded by Maurice, 175.

Totila, chosen by the Gothic chiefs as their leader and king, 142; defeats the Roman generals at Faenza, 144; takes Naples, 146; obtains an entry into Rome and abandons it, having broken up the defences, 153; is defeated in his attempt to re-enter the dismantled city, 155; re-enters, 159; invades Sicily, 161; failure of his attempt to create a navy, 162; his defeat in the battle of Tagina and death, 164.

V.

Valentinian III, marriage with his cousin, 48; concurs in

the assassination of Aetius, 60;
his own assassination leaves
the Western throne without
an hereditary claimant, ib.
Venice, first settlers, 57; first
Doge, 206.
Vitiges, chosen by the Goths for
their leader and king, 118;
garrisons Rome and returns
to Ravenna, ib.; Belisarius
having expelled the garrison,
he returns and undertakes the
siege, 120; his disastrous failure,
129; is carried off from Ravenna
by Belisarius, 141; becomes
the dependant of Justinian,
142; and resides at Constantinople, ib.

W.

Wallia, adopts the Romanizing
policy of his predecessor,
Ataulphus, 38; his death, succeeded by Theodoric, ib.
Wilfrid, Bishop of York, a guest
of the Lombard King Bertharis,
205.

Z.

Zacharias, Pope, his return to
Rome as a triumphant peacemaker, 225.
Zeno (the Isaurian) accepts the
title of sole Emperor, and recognizes Odoacer as patrician of
Italy, 82.

www.ingramcontent.com/pod-product-compliance
Lightning Source LLC
Chambersburg PA
CBHW032052230426
43672CB00009B/1566